HANDICAPPED IN WALT DISNEY WORLD ® :
A GUIDE FOR EVERYONE

"We all live under the same sky, but we don't all have the same horizon." ——-Konrad Adenauer

AN UNOFFICIAL GUIDE TO WALT DISNEY WORLD

HANDICAPPED IN WALT DISNEY WORLD ®:
A GUIDE FOR EVERYONE

by
Peter Smith

SouthPark Publishing Group, Inc.

Dallas, Texas

Copyright©1993 by Peter Smith
First Edition
All rights reserved. No part of this book may be reproduced or transmitted in any form or by any means, electronic or mechanical, including photocopying, recording, or by any information storage or retrieval system without written permission from SouthPark Publishing Group, Inc., except for the use of brief quotations in a review.

Published by:
SouthPark Publishing Group, Inc.
4041 W. Wheatland Road
Suite 156-359
Dallas, Texas 75237-9991
(214) 296-5657

Printed and bound in the United States of America

Library of Congress Cataloging in Publication Data

Smith, Peter, 1951 Sept. 8-
  Handicapped in Walt Disney World® : A Guide for Everyone / by Peter Smith
    p. cm.
  Includes bibliographical references and index
  ISBN 1-881971-49-X: $10.95
  1. Walt Disney World (Fla.) — Guidebooks. 2. Physically handicapped — Florida — Orlando Region — Recreation — Guidebooks.
  I. Title
  GV1853.3.F62W3466 1993
  791'.06'875924 — dc20   93-3069
                                          CIP

TABLE OF CONTENTS

Chapter 1:   Introduction............................. 14
    Who Is Disabled And Why Are They Handicapped?..... 17
    What Is Walt Disney World?........................ 19
    Map of Florida.................................... 20
    Map of Orlando Area............................... 21
    Map of Walt Disney World.......................... 22
    The Magic Kingdom, The EPCOT Center, And The
        Disney-MGM Studios............................ 23
    How Much Time Does It Take To Visit Each Area?.....24

Chapter 2:   Planning Your Trip to Walt Disney World...26
    Introduction — Why You Need To Plan 27
    First Things First — When To Visit Walt Disney World ..28
        Climate 29
    What To Bring With You............................ 30
    Saving Money By Planning Ahead.................... 31
    Other Tips.. 32
        Reservations.................................. 32
        Pet Care...................................... 33
        Money — How To Pay For Things................ 33
        Admission Prices.............................. 34
        More Information.............................. 34
    Advice For Disabled People......................... 35
    Traveling With Children............................ 38
    Advice For Senior Citizens......................... 39
    Travel — Planes, Automobiles, Trains, And Buses...... 40
        Air Travel — General Information For Disabled Travelers..41
        Air Travel Information For Everyone................ 47
        Automobiles, Vans, and Recreational Vehicles........... 48
        Bus Travel.................................... 52
        Train Travel 53
    Accommodations 54
        Lodging In Walt Disney World.................. 56
        Lodging Outside Walt Disney World............. 68

Chapter 3:   The Magic Kingdom....................... 78
    Introduction To The Magic Kingdom 79
        So What is the Magic Kingdom And Why Go There?...... 79
        How big is the Magic Kingdom?................. 80

Map of the Magic Kingdom............................81
    Getting to the Magic Kingdom......................82
    What to take with you.............................82
    Admission tickets and passport....................83
    Wheelchair rental................................ 83
    Locker rentals....................................83
    Restrooms.. 84
    Monorail or Ferry?............................... 84
    Monorail... 84
    Ferry.. 85
    Ramps.. 85
    Information.......................................85
Main Street, U.S.A....................................86
    Orientation...................................... 86
    Walt Disney World Railroad — An Overview Of The
    Magic Kingdom...................................87
    The Walt Disney Story............................87
    Main Street Cinema.............................. 88
    Penny Arcade.................................... 88
Adventureland....................................... 89
    Swiss Family Treehouse.......................... 89
    Jungle Cruise................................... 89
    Pirates of the Caribbean......................... 90
    Tropical Serenade............................... 91
Frontierland..92
    Diamond Horseshoe Jamboree..................... 92
    Country Bear Jamboree...........................93
    Frontierland Shootin' Arcade......................93
    Splash Mountain................................ 94
    Big Thunder Mountain Railroad................... 95
    Walt Disney World Railroad...................... 96
    Tom Sawyer Island.............................. 97
Liberty Square....................................... 98
    Liberty Square Riverboat..........................98
    Mink Fink Keelboats............................. 99
    The Hall of Presidents...........................100
    The Haunted Mansion...........................100
Fantasyland...102
    Magic Journeys................................. 102
    Peter Pan's Flight.............................. 102
    It's a Small World.............................. 103
    Skyway to Tomorrowland....................... 104

  Fantasy Faire 104
  Dumbo, the Flying Elephant 104
  Cinderella's Golden Carousel.. 105
  20,000 Leagues Under The Sea 106
  Mad Tea Party. 106
  Mr. Toad's Wild Ride 107
  Snow White's Adventures. 108
 Mickey's Starland 108
  Grandma Duck's Petting Farm 109
  Mickey's House. 109
 Tomorrowland. 110
  Grand Prix Raceway 111
  Space Mountain. 112
  SkyWay 115
  Starjets. 115
  WEDway PeopleMover. 116
  Carousel of Progress 117
  Tomorrowland Theater. 118
  Dreamflight. 118
  Circlevision 360 American Journeys 119
  Mission to Mars. 121
 Live Shows, Parades And Fireworks In The Magic Kingdom 122
 Places To Eat In The Magic Kingdom. 127
 Shopping In The Magic Kingdom. 139

Chapter 4: The EPCOT Center 150
 Introduction To The EPCOT Center 151
  What Is The EPCOT Center 151
  Getting To The EPCOT Center. 152
  Admission to the EPCOT Center 153
  Wheelchair Rentals. 153
  Locker Rentals 154
  Information — Earth Station 154
  Orientation. 155
 Map Of The EPCOT Center 156
 Future World 157
  Spaceship Earth. 157
  Communicore 161
  Universe of Energy 164
  Wonders of Life. 166
  Horizons. 171
  World of Motion. 173

Journey into Imagination	175
The Land	177
The Living Seas	180
The World Showcase	183
Mexico	185
Norway	187
China	188
Germany	191
Italy	192
The American Adventure	194
Japan	197
Morocco	198
France	200
United Kingdom	203
Canada	208
Fireworks And Live Shows In The EPCOT Center	211
Dining In The EPCOT Center: A World Of Choices	214

Chapter 5: Disney-MGM Studios 236
Introduction And Other Things You Should Know	237
What Is Disney-MGM Studios And How Big Is It	237
Getting To The Disney-MGM Studios	238
Map Of Disney-MGM Studios	239
Wheelchair Rental	240
Locker Rentals	240
Movie Theme Park	240
Hollywood Boulevard	240
The Great Movie Ride	243
Superstar Television	245
Monster Sound Show	247
Indiana Jones Epic Stunt Spectacular	248
Star Tours	250
Jim Henson's Muppet*Vision 3-D	252
Honey, I Shrunk The Kids Movie Set Adventure Playground	253
Teenage Mutant Ninja Turtles	254
New York Street Back Lot	254
Studio Animation Tour	255
Backstage Studio Tour	257
Inside The Magic Special Effects And Production Tour	259
Dining At The Disney-MGM Studios	261

Chapter 6: The Rest Of The World 268
    Introduction 269
    Pleasure Island 269
        Restaurants On Pleasure Island 271
        Shops On Pleasure Island. 272
    Typhoon Lagoon 273
        The Humunga Kowabunga 275
        Shark Reef 275
        Other Water Attractions. 275
    River Country. 276
    Discovery Island. 278
    Walt Disney World Village. 279
    Crossroads Of Lake Buena Vista Shopping Center. 280

Appendix 282

Bibliography

Index

ABOUT THE AUTHOR

Peter Smith is a paraplegic and has used a wheelchair since 1978. In September of that year, while hiking in Switzerland, he fell and damaged his spinal cord. The accident ended his career as a field geologist — traveling to and studying remote areas of the world. He adapted and spent the next 11 years as an exploration geologist in the oil and gas industry. However, he never recovered from his love for travel and adventure.

Born in 1951, in Kenosha, Wisconsin, Peter has a B.Sc. Degree from the University of Wisconsin-Madison. Trained to observe, interpret, and describe, he is now a writer and author. Combining travel experience with that of his disability, he offers unique insight to millions of disabled people, their friends, and families.

Peter currently lives with his wife near Dallas, Texas.

ACKNOWLEDGMENT

The author admits being stubbornly independent and feels this helps in dealing with his disabilities. However, there comes a time when it is important to give credit where credit is due. First, he would not be here without the kindness and courage of Mme. Jeane Wiest, who found him on that mountainside in Switzerland. Many doctors, nurses, and therapists played a role (and some continue) in his rehabilitation. None however, were more important than Dr. Urs Marti, the Swiss Doctor whose gentleness and honesty gave the author his initial hope and motivation. Along the way, the author has known many people with disabilities equal to and more severe than his own. He will be forever in awe of people's ability to survive, adapt, and triumph. The examples of their courage has carried him through many dark hours.

He can not give enough thanks to his parents, Andy and Norma Smith, for educating and caring for him in his times of need. His sister, Georgia Owens, provided inspiration for the book and support during its research and writing. Larry and Martha have been supportive since the beginning.

Susan, the editor at SouthPark Publishing Group, Inc., deserves immeasurable credit for her long, patient hours of working with me on the manuscript. Bill Reed of Palmworks Studios created the cover art and provided the design and layout for the book.

Finally, no one deserves more credit than my wife. Her continual love, support, criticism, and courage, makes everything possible.

WARNING — DISCLAIMER

This book is an unofficial guide for disabled people, their friends, and families. Its purpose and function is the dissemination of information and knowledge, so everyone has an equal opportunity to visit and enjoy Walt Disney World. The author and the SouthPark Publishing Group, Inc. are not medical or health care professionals. We recognize that everyone has different abilities — you, the reader must evaluate your situation and be responsible for your actions. Anyone using this book, for any purpose, does so at their own risk. Anyone requiring expert advice of a technical nature should consult a competent medical professional.

The author and publisher made every effort to be accurate and honest in description and definition. There can be mistakes in content or typography; prices, times, and telephone numbers, etc. change. The publisher encourages criticism and will make the appropriate corrections in subsequent editions.

For the purpose of clarity, illustration, and comment, the author fairly used the quotation of excerpts from Walt Disney World, *The Disabled Guests Guidebook*. The free booklet is available by calling (407) 824-4321, or from any of the wheelchair rental shops in Walt Disney World.

The author and publisher respect and follow convention in using the registered trademarks of Walt Disney Company, Inc. These include, but are not limited to the following names, shows, and attractions: Adventureland, AudioAnimatronics, Caption EO, Disneyland, EPCOT, Fantasyland, Magic Kingdom, New Orleans Square, PeopleMover, Space Mountain, Walt Disney, and Walt Disney World.

Handicapped in Walt Disney World is an unofficial guide. The author and publisher are independent, and no part of this book has been approved, reviewed, or otherwise sanctioned by the Walt Disney Company, Inc.

Please mail any commentary to:
SouthPark Publishing Group, Inc.
4041 W. Wheatland Road, Suite 156-359
Dallas, TX 75237-9991

CHAPTER

INTRODUCTION

"It is not because things are difficult that we do not dare; it is because we do not dare that they are difficult"——Lucius A. Seneca

Tom and Ellen are a fictitious couple, but their story is familiar and all too common. Anyone can become disabled in the blink of an eye. Read any newspaper; it happens every day. There are 43 million Americans[1] who, like Tom, are disabled. If you consider all the countries of the world, there are over 500 million disabled people.[2]

Tom and Ellen are an average couple from a medium-sized town in a midwestern state. They met in high school. Ellen was a bright student and on the swim team. Tom played football and baseball. They talked about getting married and raising a family, but agreed on waiting until they finished college. Ellen teaches elementary school and Tom writes computer programs. They are a typical, All-American couple. The only thing making them different from anyone else, is Tom, sitting in his wheelchair.

In the summer of their junior year in college, one of the realities of life dealt them a cruel blow. The human body can be fragile. Tom had a job on a construction project. He was in a ditch when a large timber fell, striking Tom in the back and bending him over. An ambulance rushed him to an emergency room. He had few outward injuries but couldn't feel anything below his waist. The doctors took X-rays and discovered two dislocated lumbar vertebrae. The falling timber had broken Tom's back and bruised his spinal cord. He was paralyzed. There was nothing the doctors could do. They told him he would never walk again. There is no way of repairing a damaged spinal cord.

After the intensive care ward, Tom's doctors transferred him to the Rehabilitation Institute of Chicago. The doctors, nurses, physical and occupational therapists taught him to take care of himself and use a wheelchair. They told him he

---

[1] Evan J. Kemp, Jr., Chairman of the U.S. Equal Opportunity Commission, from the *Dallas Morning News*, June 22, 1992, p. 7D.

[2] Mr. Michel Gillibert, French Minister for the Handicapped, from his Address to the General Assembly of the United Nations, October 13, 1992. From SATH *(Society for the Advancement of Travel for the Handicapped)*, Vol. 13, No. 4, 1992.

could do almost anything he wanted; it all depended on his motivation. The process was painful, but after three months, Tom went home. Ellen loves Tom and stayed with him through the ordeal, even when he would get frustrated, scream at Ellen, and tell her to leave.

It was a full year before Tom returned to school. He changed his major to computer science. He needed a job where his disability was not a handicap. He figured he could sit at a desk and wrestle with a computer as well as anyone. He was right.

Ellen and Tom went ahead with their wedding plans. They wanted a honeymoon in a special place, somewhere they had never been before. Neither had traveled much and they worried about finding a place where they could do things together. They already had a taste of some of the problems faced by people using wheelchairs. How would they travel; where would they stay; what could they do when they arrived? A friend suggested Walt Disney World in Florida.

Ellen and Tom planned their marriage and honeymoon for the winter. They knew how miserable a midwestern winter was for someone using a wheelchair. The sunshine and warmth of Florida sounded appealing. They had heard of Disney World and wanted to go there since they were children. Ellen asked their friend, "Yes, it sounds nice, but isn't it just for kids?" "Oh no!" their friend said, "There's the Magic Kingdom, and that's mainly for kids, but there's also the EPCOT Center and the Disney-MGM Studios, dozens of restaurants, shops, parades, fireworks, and music everywhere. It's such a happy place — I mean there's a million things you could do." Intrigued by the possibilities, Ellen called a few travel agents.

The travel agents were eager to help and explained how Tom and Ellen could fly to Florida and find a hotel or motel with "handicap-accessible" rooms. They could even rent a car with hand controls if Tom wanted to drive. The travel agent assured Ellen that disabled people travel all the time. Then Ellen asked about Disney World and what they could do while visiting.

Ellen learned that Walt Disney World is huge. There are three major theme parks, two large swimming parks, a wildlife park, a nighttime entertainment complex, and a nature preserve. It sounded fascinating, but none of the travel agents answered Ellen's main question. What could Tom do? He had to use a wheelchair; he couldn't stand and walk and Ellen couldn't pick him up. Was there any point in visiting Walt Disney World if Tom found many of the attractions inaccessible? Tom and Ellen's honeymoon was important and expensive. They wanted more information before making a commitment.

They went to the library and found a few books about Disney World. The books were full of information but contained little mention of disabled people. Even though Tom was strong, healthy and active in his wheelchair, could he ride a roller coaster? What about the other rides? Could he get on them? Would it be uncomfortable getting around in a wheelchair? Would Disney welcome them or treat them like second-class citizens? Tom and Ellen went to Disney World anyway. They had fun, but wished they had more information before leaving. It would have saved them money, time, frustration, and some disappointment.

We dedicate this book to Tom and Ellen and people like them. We maintain that everyone, including the 43 million Americans and 500 million disabled people in the world, can visit and enjoy Walt Disney World.

WHO IS DISABLED AND WHY ARE THEY HANDICAPPED?

Defining who is disabled is difficult; even the Government has trouble. People can have physical, sensory, and mental disabilities, in any combination and in varying degrees. Of the Americans with "activity limitations," 89.2% have physical disabilities that can impair their mobility; the remaining 10.8% have mental, visual, or hearing impairments.[3] We

---

[3] La Plante, M. P. (1988) *Data on disability from the National Health Interview Survey*, 1983-1985. An InfoUse report. Washington, DC: National Institute for Disability and Rehabilitation Research.

think conditions in Walt Disney World will handicap physically disabled people more than others. If a person can't get to, in, or on something, it makes no difference if they can see, hear, or comprehend. Therefore, we devote most of our attention to people with physical disabilities impairing their mobility.

A physical disability often limits or eliminates a person's ability to stand, walk, and climb. Many afflictions are responsible. Spinal cord injury and paralysis, as with Tom in the previous story, are examples. In a report titled *1993 Heart and Stroke Facts,* the American Heart Association says seventy million Americans live with a cardiovascular condition, including high blood pressure and coronary heart disease. They also state that strokes are the number one cause of serious disability in the United States, and approximately 3 million stroke victims are living today.[4]

Orthopedic impairments (bones and muscle), arthritis, intervertebral disk problems, asthma, and conditions like muscular dystrophy, multiple sclerosis, and cerebral palsy can interfere with a person's ability to stand, walk, or climb. Almost everyone knows someone with a disability. This explains the staggering number (43 million) of disabled Americans. These people want to live and travel as much as anyone. Many work, some are retired, and many have the financial resources and time for travel. Walt Disney World can serve them well. Often, the only thing preventing physically disabled people from traveling is a fear of the unknown and a lack of information. We help people overcome the handicaps in Disney World.

We address three categories of physically disabled people with mobility impairments. Disabled people know which category fits their situation. First, there are people who can stand and walk, but with difficulty. Second, for many disabled people, standing and walking is impossible. They use wheelchairs, but due to the strength and coordination of their upper bodies, they routinely transfer in and out of their wheelchairs. Third, the most severely physically dis-

---

[4]Reported in *The Dallas Morning News,* Monday, January 18, 1993, p. 4A.

abled use motorized wheelchairs and are unable, by themselves, to move into another seat or vehicle. How, you might ask, are they "Handicapped in Walt Disney World?"

People have disabilities; handicaps are imposed on them. In terms of presenting handicaps to disabled people, Disney World is perhaps better than many places. However, many attractions are inaccessible. We describe the handicaps in detail in the following chapter. Visiting any of the three major theme parks in Walt Disney World involves a substantial amount of walking. This causes sore feet, blisters, and heat exhaustion among non-disabled people. There are miles of paths to walk, thousands of people rushing around, multiple rides to get on and off, and dozens of theaters, shops, and restaurants. All physically disabled people experiencing mobility impairments will be handicapped in Disney World. We offer critical information and guidelines for everyone.

People experiencing difficulty walking can rent wheelchairs and eliminate most of their handicaps. People using wheelchairs and unable to stand and walk, can still get around and get on and off many of the rides — if they can make a transfer. Even the most severely disabled, those using wheelchairs and unable to transfer, can still participate in many activities. The remainder of the book shows everyone how they can visit and enjoy Walt Disney World.

WHAT IS WALT DISNEY WORLD?

Almost everyone has heard of Walt Disney World, but not everyone knows it is one of the most popular attractions worldwide. Approximately 15 million people visit every year. This incredible vacation playground covers 43 square miles of central Florida, as much area as a large city. It contains three theme parks — the Magic Kingdom, the EPCOT Center, and the Disney-MGM Studios. There are two water theme parks, Typhoon Lagoon and River Country. Pleasure Island offers entertainment with six nightclubs and a ten-screen movie theater. There are dozens of restaurants and shops, several golf courses, hotels, four lakes, a shopping

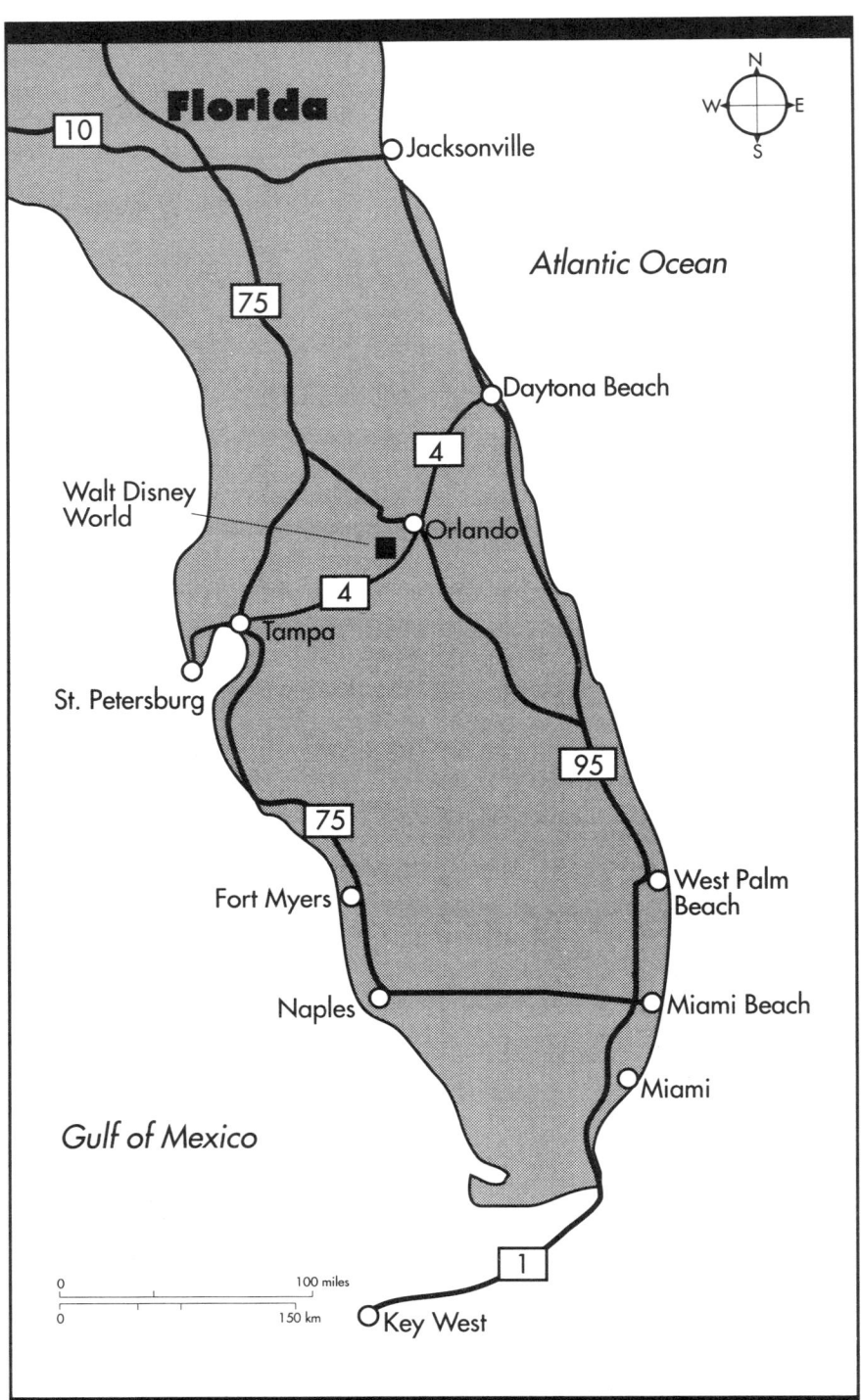

INTRODUCTION 21

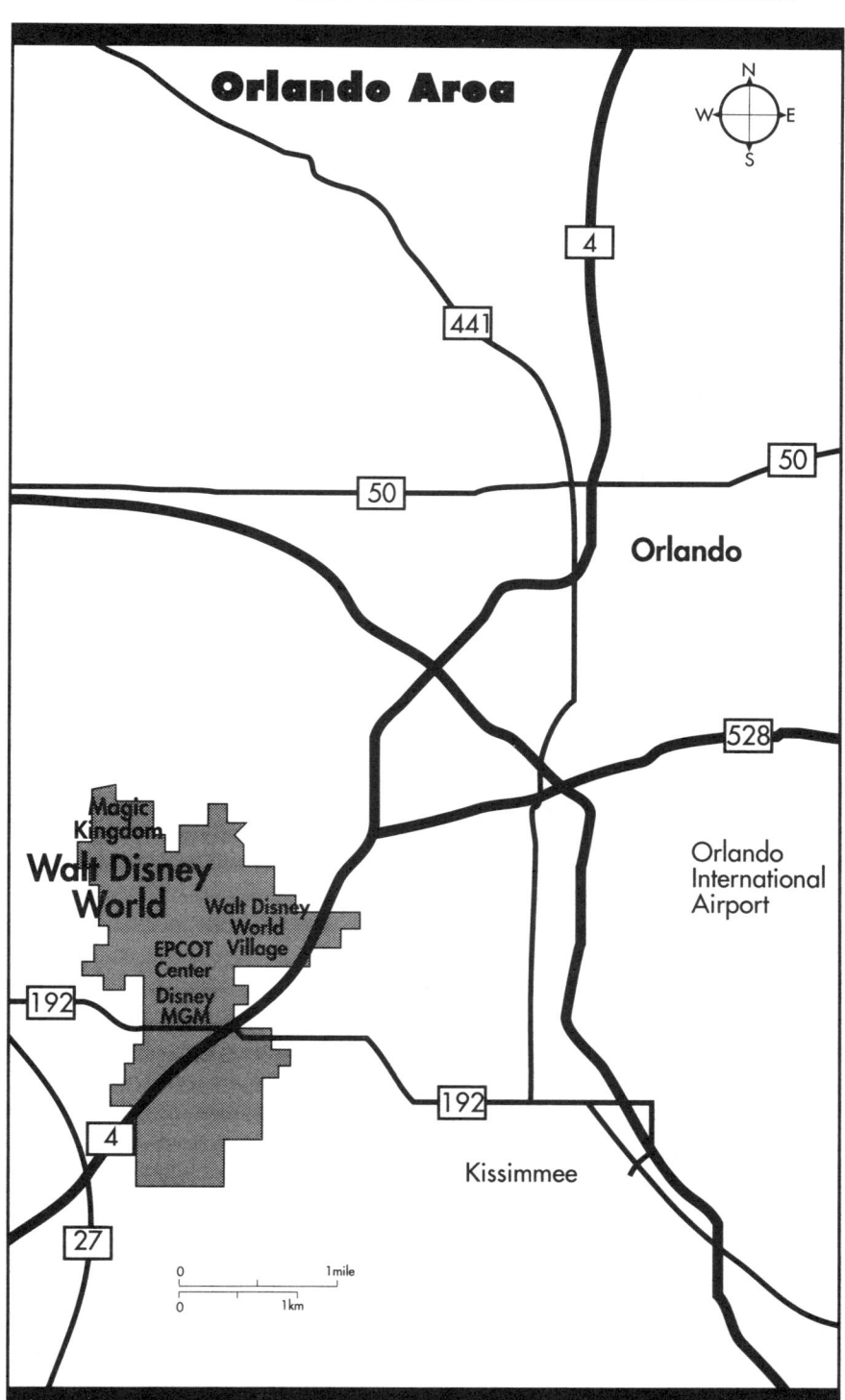

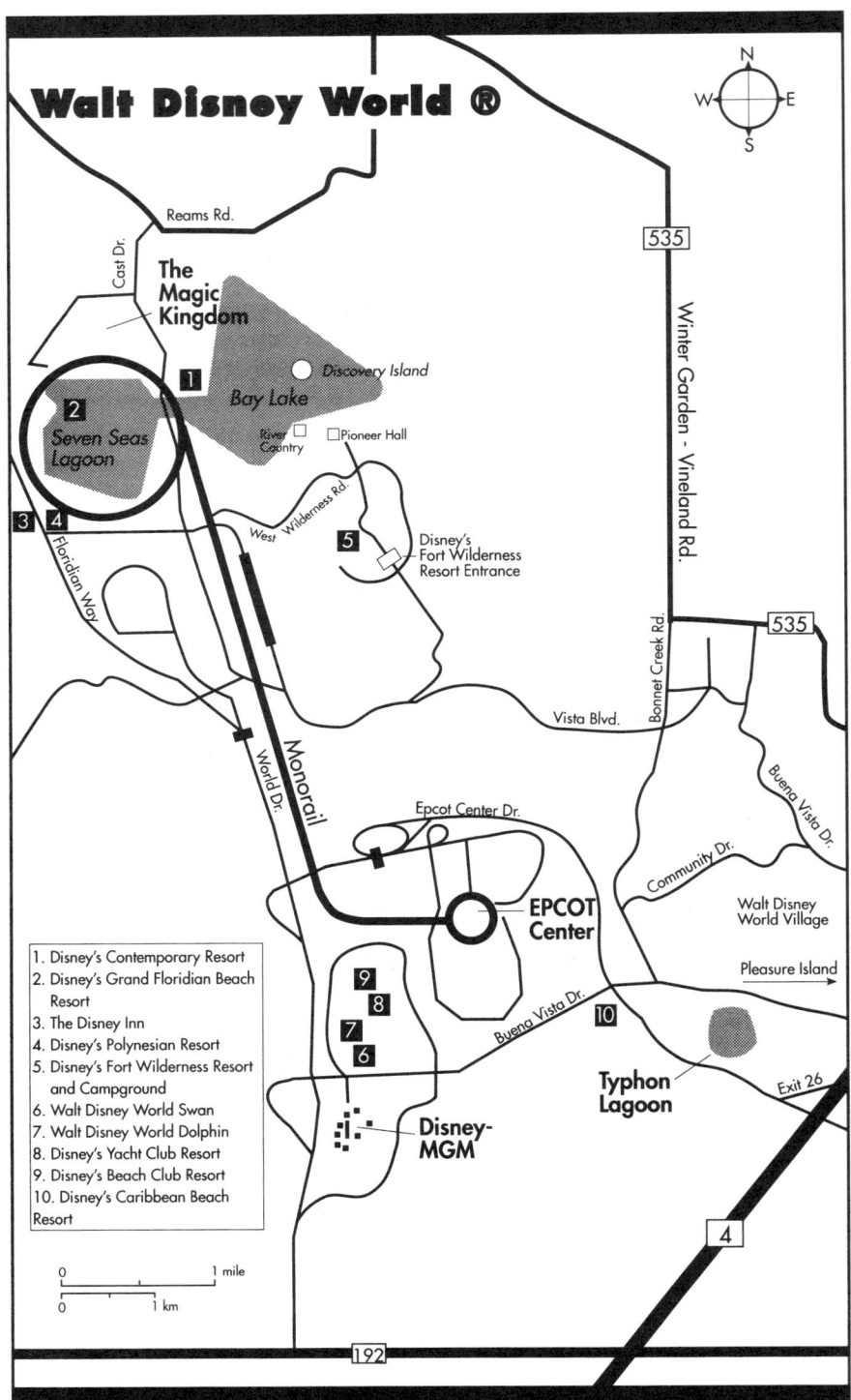

complex, a convention center, and a transportation network of four-lane highways, a monorail system, and canals.

The primary attractions in Walt Disney World are the Magic Kingdom, the EPCOT Center, and the Disney-MGM Studios. They also contain the fewest handicaps for disabled people, so we describe these areas first and in the greatest detail.

THE MAGIC KINGDOM, THE EPCOT CENTER, AND THE DISNEY-MGM STUDIOS

Each of the three major theme parks in Walt Disney World is unique, but there are more similarities than differences. The "Disney touch" is visible everywhere. All of them use animated characters and combine Disney's imaginative and fantastic special effects. Each theme park is equally neat and clean. Finally, the Disney cast members (employees) are always friendly and courteous.

Children usually prefer the Magic Kingdom. The EPCOT Center appeals to teenagers and adults, while the Disney-MGM Studios has a little of something for everyone. The Magic Kingdom plays off the popular Disney children's movies and cartoons. The Disney-MGM Studios utilize more adult-oriented films in their themes. Both the EPCOT Center and the Disney-MGM Studios cater to people's interests in education and entertainment.

Physically disabled people have more problems with access in the Magic Kingdom than in the EPCOT Center or at the Disney-MGM Studios. Approximately half of the rides in the Magic Kingdom require people to get out of their wheelchairs. The EPCOT Center has a few rides that fall into the inaccessible category, while the Disney-MGM studio has only one. Some of the rides in all three areas are too rough for physically disabled people with limited strength in their arms and hands.

The Disney employees interact with physically disabled people in a friendly and thoughtful manner. When they see someone sitting in a wheelchair, they often approach and ask them to use another entrance, moving them out of the sun and heat, and providing a shorter waiting time.

In all cases, as polite as the Disney employees are, they can't and won't actually pick up a physically disabled person and help them on a ride or into an attraction. At the most, they might lend an arm for support. Even this, is rare. It is not because they are unkind or thoughtless. It is management policy.

There are a few handicaps physically disabled people can't avoid. One is the handicap created by the crowd of other visitors. Moving through a mass of people is difficult for anyone, especially for those using wheelchairs. Waiting in line is no fun for anyone. Again, it is even more unpleasant for disabled people.

HOW MUCH TIME DOES IT TAKE TO VISIT EACH AREA?

We think physically disabled people need a minimum of three days just for seeing all of the EPCOT Center. Most people can probably do the Magic Kingdom in two days. The Disney-MGM Studios is smaller, requires less walking, or rolling, and you can see it's major attractions in one day.

Walt Disney World may seem like a fantasy world for some people. The physical challenge it presents to disabled people is real. If you consider making a trip to Walt Disney World, we suggest you plan and prepare yourself ahead of time. Get yourself in the best physical condition possible.

Ask yourself the questions, "How much time do we have?" "How crowded will the park be?" Ask, "What can we see and what is most important to us?" In other words, prioritize your options. Finally, continue reading this book; there is more.

CHAPTER

PLANNING YOUR TRIP

"Patience and time do more than strength or passion"
——Jean de La Fontaine

INTRODUCTION — WHY YOU NEED TO PLAN

A trip to Walt Disney World is an adventure for anyone. For disabled people, it might seem like an attempt on Mt. Everest. That's the way we want people to think of a trip to Walt Disney World — as a fun expedition. Regardless of how people travel, how far they come, and how long they stay, a visit to Walt Disney World involves a significant investment of time, money, and energy. The best advice we can offer anyone, disabled or not, is PLAN BEFORE YOU GO.

Adventurers must make many decisions. They must decide **when** to go, **how** to get there, **where** to stay, **what** to bring, and **how** to get around after arriving. They need a **game plan**. They should familiarize themselves with the attractions in Walt Disney World, and decide which attractions they can and want to visit. This involves a measure of each individual's interests and abilities versus a knowledge of each attraction. This book is the only guide we are aware of, that provides the information disabled people need.

Everyone can relate to the frustration of rushing to the store, returning home, and discovering they forgot something. Amplify the situation. Picture yourself planning a dinner party for some favorite friends. Your menu includes an exotic dish. It requires a 20-mile trip across a large city to buy some specialty foods. You make the trip and return home. While preparing dinner, just before the guests arrive, you discover a missing, critical ingredient. You made a costly mistake you could easily have avoided. You regret not reading your cookbook more carefully, and making a list before going shopping. The same thing applies when you're traveling. The cookbook is this book, fun is on the menu, and we provide the recipe for a successful visit to Walt Disney World.

Disabled people need careful planning because of the handicaps they face. If they make a mistake, the consequences can be disastrous. Everyone has their travel horror stories. One of the author's favorites, is when an airline lost his wheelchair on a flight to Rome, Italy. He sat for hours, in a lounge chair in the lobby of Leonardo da Vinci International Airport, while the airline employees searched. When it arrived, it was missing a key part. Try finding an American wheelchair part in Italy on a Sunday. He managed by holding his chair together with his belt. Italian-American relations were at their lowest point since World War II. Since then, Italian airline or not, he double-checks the tagging of his chair and hides spare parts in his carry-on luggage. We don't know who said, "Hope for the best and prepare for the worst," but it applies to disabled travelers.

Planning doesn't have to be drudgery. It can be enjoyable, and it will enhance the pleasure of your trip. Read about where you're going. Learn all you can about the area. Learn about the climate. Think about your situation. Ask yourself questions. What kind of clothes will I need? What medications do I need? What if I need medical help; where can I find it? How much money will I need? What accessories will I want, like cameras, sunglasses, hats and packs, purses, or belt pouches? In this case, before visiting Walt Disney World, read about the Magic Kingdom, the EPCOT Center, and the Disney-MGM Studios. Compare what you learn with your own and your companion's interests and abilities. This book provides critical information, so read it before leaving.

FIRST THINGS FIRST — WHEN TO VISIT WALT DISNEY WORLD

Assuming you can travel whenever you wish, we advise avoiding the peak season and the most crowded holidays. Basically, there are two peak seasons. The first peak season is known as the "Summer Season" or "Family Season." It presents the most crowded conditions because millions of school children are on their summer break, and their parents bring them to Walt Disney World. The summer season lasts from the middle of June through the end of August. This is also the warmest time of the year. Combining crowded conditions with extreme heat is asking for frustration.

The second so-called peak season runs from a few days before Christmas to a few days after Easter. Visitor numbers are at their highest from Christmas Day through New Year's Day. Thanksgiving, Washington's birthday, the college spring break, and the two weeks surrounding Easter are also busy. What does busy mean? Try imagining over 90,000 people visiting the Magic Kingdom in a single day.

The best times for visiting, in terms of having the smallest crowds and the nicest weather, are from the beginning of September until Christmas (excluding the week of Thanksgiving), and from about January 3rd through the month of May. We would avoid spring break and Easter week.

The least crowded days at Walt Disney World are Thursday, Friday, Saturday, and Sunday. The first part of the week attracts more visitors because they arrive on the weekend, and rush to see the attractions full of energy and enthusiasm on Monday, Tuesday, and Wednesday. By the end of the week, they're burned out and headed home. Chart your own course, visit on off days, at odd times, and during the quieter months.

Climate

The following is a graph showing the average daily high and low temperatures (in degrees Fahrenheit) for Orlando, Florida. The temperatures rarely exceed 90 or drop below 50.

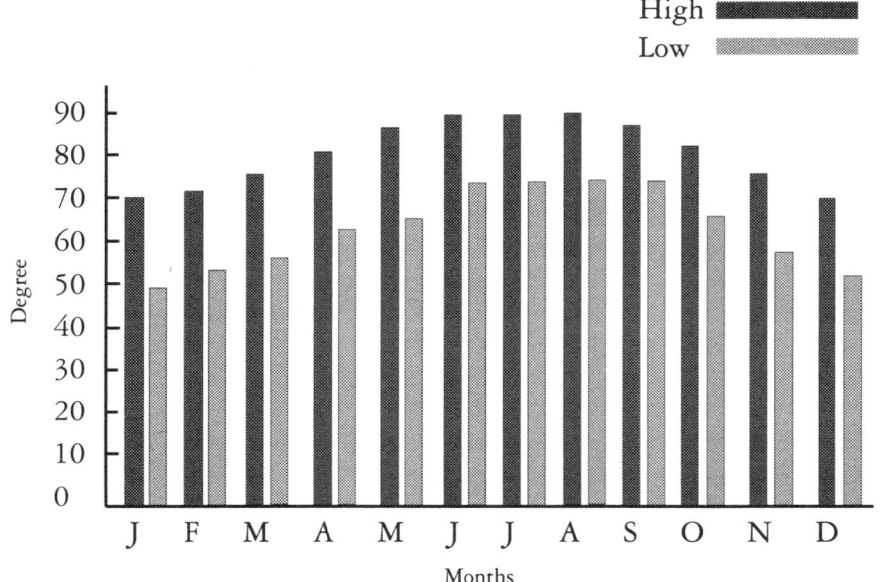

WHAT TO BRING WITH YOU

Most people visiting Walt Disney World dress casually. In terms of clothing, the key word is comfort. In central Florida, the winters are mild and the summers hot and humid. People visiting in the winter, should bring light jackets and sweaters. In the summer, cotton fabric provides the most comfort. Many people wear shorts or casual slacks and skirts. Cotton shirts or blouses and T-shirts are appropriate. Even in the summer, carrying a light jacket or cotton sweater is smart, because nearly every building is air-conditioned. Be prepared with clothing that is easy to put on and take off.

The author finds loose clothing is preferable. He uses his wheelchair every day, all day. A tight shirt, sweater, or jacket restricts his arm movements and makes pushing his wheelchair difficult. He does not have armrests on his wheelchair, and a long jacket interferes with the wheels. He prefers waist-length garments. A nylon, wind-breaker-type jacket is ideal. It offers just the right degree of warmth; it is easy to take on and off, and it provides some protection from the rain.

Some kind of hat can be valuable. It shades the sun while keeping your head dry in a rain shower. A baseball-type hat or a floppy cap works well. The sunshine in Florida can be brutal for pale northerners, so some kind of sunscreen lotion is in order. Sunglasses are important any time of year. Since many of the attractions are in darkened rooms or theaters, a strap for your sunglasses is helpful. You will be taking the sunglasses on and off, and don't want to lose them. A compact umbrella is a handy accessory. The author can not use an umbrella while pushing his wheelchair, but a companion can use an umbrella to shelter both. Rain ponchos are an option for people using wheelchairs, but they have a tendency to interfere with the wheels.

Comfortable shoes are vital for people who can walk. The author prefers sturdy shoes to protect his feet, and the easier they are to get on and take off, the better. People pushing their own wheelchairs usually wear some kind of gloves. The author likes the leather gloves weight-lifters wear. They leave the tips of his fingers exposed, and he can leave them on and still manipulate a camera or find his wallet.

Many people attach a small pack to the back of their wheelchairs by looping the straps over the handles. This is a functional way of carrying things, and the added weight is not noticeable. The author dislikes this method because he often rolls around on his own and has difficulty reaching behind himself to access the bag. He also dislikes the idea of having his valuables behind him where he can't keep an eye on them. If someone using a wheelchair has a companion, the pack on the chair works well.

Another handy carry-all is a belt pouch. These fit around your waist and hold nearly everything you need. If you don't mind looking like a kangaroo, they are an excellent idea. Pockets in pants don't work for someone sitting in a wheelchair. It is difficult reaching a pocket when you can't move your lower body. The author wears a small leather pouch on his belt, and carries his wallet and spare keys in it.

The author prefers the hard, plastic-type of suitcases, especially when flying. The baggage handlers in airports can really be rough. The hard suitcases protect delicate items like cameras and electric appliances. When flying, the author usually has some kind of carry-on luggage. A briefcase, again the hard-bodied kind, works well. When flying, it is important to carry with you the items you can not live without. This includes your medicines, valuables, and even things like a toothbrush and a partial change of clothes. The airlines have been known to send checked baggage to strange destinations, and you can wait a long time before seeing it again.

SAVING MONEY BY PLANNING AHEAD

There are many ways of saving money with some advance planning. You can save money on travel costs by shopping around. Calculate the cost of driving, the time it requires, the cost of lodging en-route, and meals. Compare this with the cost of flying and renting a car. Sometimes flying is actually less expensive.

Saving money on lodging is also a matter of doing some research. You can probably save, or waste, more money on lodging than with any other aspect of your trip to Walt Disney World. Visiting in the off-season and staying in a budget motel can save hundreds of dollars. Of course you want to be comfortable. In his younger, poorer, and able-bodied days, the author never gave this much thought. Now in his wimpy old age, he values comfort more than a little additional cost. Sure he can make-do with less than ideal motel rooms, but an accessible bathroom is a blessing, if not a necessity. We recommend that other disabled people choose comfort over cost if possible. The idea is to enjoy, rather than endure, your visit to Walt Disney World. However, the stubbornly cost-conscious can order the *National Directory of Budget Motels*, for $5.95 from Pilot Books, 103 Cooper St., Babylon, NY 11702; (516) 422-2225.

The other way of saving money is in choosing how and where you eat. The many cafeterias and fast-food restaurants are usually less expensive than full-service restaurants. There are many all-you-can-eat buffets. If you are not opposed to eating large meals, you can get away with eating only once or twice a day. You can find some lodging with kitchen facilities and cook your own meals — but then it's not really a vacation, is it? As with anything, there are pros and cons to everything. The author dislikes cafeteria, buffet, or fast-food restaurants. He finds negotiating through crowds and choosing and carrying food, while pushing his wheelchair, is usually not worth the lower cost. Finally, remember that eating outside Disney World is less expensive than eating inside.

OTHER TIPS
Reservations

It is always a smart move to make your travel and lodging reservations as far in advance as possible. In the case of the busy months or special holidays at Disney World, this can mean months in advance. You can make many reservations in Walt Disney World through their Central Reservations Office. The telephone number is (407) 934-7639. People speaking French or Spanish can call (407) 824-7900. They are open from 8:30 a.m. to 10:00 p.m., seven days per week. It is best if you call after 6:00 p.m. and on weekends.

Pet Care

Disney allows guide dogs for blind people in all areas of Walt Disney World. Otherwise, they do not allow pets in the Magic Kingdom, the EPCOT Center, the Disney-MGM Studios, or any of the Disney resorts. Visitors bringing pets can leave them in four Pet Care Kennels. Each is air conditioned, and your pets should be cool and happy. The Pet Care Kennels are close to the Transportation and Ticket Center at the Magic Kingdom, at the entrance to the Disney-MGM Studios, on the left side of the Entrance Plaza in the EPCOT Center, and at the entrance to the Fort Wilderness Campground. Finally, never leave your pets in your cars. The Florida sunshine can turn the cars into ovens. Besides, it is against the law to leave a pet in an automobile.

Money — How To Pay For Things

Disney accepts American Express, MasterCard, and Visa credit cards, traveler's checks, personal checks, and cash for all admission tickets. Personal checks are only accepted if accompanied by a valid driver's license, and imprinted with the person's name and address. The signer must have a credit card and the checks must be drawn on a U.S. bank. Your secret Swiss bank account won't do. The fast-food restaurants try to be fast and only accept cash. The full-service restaurants accept credit cards, traveler's checks, and cash. The Sun Bank has branches on Main Street in the Magic Kingdom, near the entrance to the EPCOT Center, and in the Disney Village Marketplace. They will give cash advances on MasterCard and Visa credit cards, cash traveler's checks, help with transfers of money from a person's personal bank account, and change most foreign currency. Traveler's checks are a good idea because they are refundable if lost. Everybody loses a wallet or purse at some time. Make sure you sign all the checks and keep the receipts some place other than where you hold the checks themselves. The best advice is carrying a small amount of cash, credit cards for convenience, and a few traveler's checks for a back-up. Hope for the best and plan for the worst.

Admission Prices

The price of admission to each of the three Walt Disney World theme parks is the same, but visitors have four options. The exact prices might vary from those we quote.

- **One day ticket:** This is only for use in the park in which you purchase it. Adult tickets are $35.00 and children three through nine years old pay $28.

- **Four-day passport:** You can use this in any of the three theme parks, and it allows the unlimited use of any part of the Walt Disney World transportation system. Adults pay $117 and children (3-9 years) pay $93.

- **Five-day super pass:** This is valid in the three theme parks for five days, allows unlimited use of the transportation system, and includes admission to Typhoon Lagoon, River Country, Discovery Island, and Pleasure Island. It is good for seven days from when you first use it. Adults pay $153 and children (3-9 years) pay $123.

- **Annual Passport:** The Passports allow unlimited use of the three theme parks, transportation system, and free parking for one year. The cost for adults is about $200 and children (3-9 years) pay $175. Renewal rates are about $25 less. Admission to Typhoon Lagoon, River Country, Discovery Island, and Pleasure Island is extra.

NOTE: In our experience, seeing all of the Magic Kingdom, the EPCOT Center, and the Disney-MGM Studios in five days is difficult, especially for disabled people. We recommend planning for as much time as possible. It would not hurt to pinch pennies in some other area, and, as odd as it might seem, buy an annual pass. By the time you add the cost of parking ($4 per day at each theme park), an annual pass costs little more than the five-day, so called, super pass. If you have an annual pass and have the time, you can relax and enjoy Walt Disney World without the pressure of trying to see everything in a few days. After all, a vacation is supposed to be relaxing.

More Information

You can obtain more information and some colorful brochures by writing:

Walt Disney World Guest Information
P.O. Box 10040
Lake Buena Vista, FL 32830-0040
or you can call (407) 824-4321.

Interested people can subscribe to *Disney News*. For $14.95 they receive eight quarterly (two years) issues. To order, write:
Disney News
P.O. Box 3310
Anaheim, CA 92803-3310.

ADVICE FOR DISABLED PEOPLE

First of all, Disney does an admirable job accommodating disabled people, but there is one important point to consider. Disney employees are not allowed to lift anyone on or off a ride.

We discuss this in more detail later in our book. We offer some solutions to this problem, so read on and plan ahead. There are designated and reserved parking areas for disabled visitors. Everyone refers to this as handicapped parking. These areas are near the entrances to the Magic Kingdom, EPCOT Center, and Disney-MGM Studios. Ask for instructions at the Auto Plazas when driving to each theme park. All of the Monorail stations are accessible to people using wheelchairs except the one in the Contemporary Resort. Vans with wheelchair lifts are available for moving people around Disney World. Visitors needing one can order it at the Entrance Plaza in the EPCOT Center, City Hall in the Magic Kingdom, and at Guest Services in the Disney-MGM Studios.

Wheelchair rental: Many people have difficulty walking for a variety of reasons; however, they do not normally use a wheelchair. We don't blame them; walking is always preferable. If people have trouble walking, we strongly recommend they rent a wheelchair. We suspect that many people dislike riding in a wheelchair because it makes them feel handicapped; nobody likes that. At least people using wheelchairs at any of the three Disney theme parks are not alone. Every day, hundreds of people rent wheelchairs or bring their own. If using a wheelchair makes the difference between enjoying your visit or being miserable, the choice should be obvious.

Disney rents the wheelchairs on a first-come, first-served basis. When we checked, the cost was $5 per day with a $1 deposit. Visitors to the Magic Kingdom needing a wheelchair, should try the Transportation and Ticket Center. This is near the handicapped parking area. If they fail at renting a wheelchair there, they have another chance at the entrance to the Magic Kingdom at Strollers — Wheelchairs, just past the turnstiles and to the right. For whatever reason, visitors can replace their rental wheelchairs at Space Port in Tomorrowland, Tinkerbell Toy Shop in Fantasyland, and the Frontierland Trading Post in Frontierland.

Wheelchairs and some three-wheeled, electric convenience carts are available in the EPCOT Center at three places. The carts cost $25 per day plus a $20 refundable deposit. The primary location is inside the Entrance Plaza and to the left. The other rental spots are at the Gift Stop on the right side of the ticket booths, and at the International Gateway, near the French pavilion. In the Disney-MGM Studios, Oscar's Super Service rents wheelchairs. Disney's booklet titled, *The Disabled Guests Guide Book*, is available at each of the wheelchair rental locations.

Restrooms: Most restrooms in the three Disney theme parks have stalls wide enough to accept people using wheelchairs, and have grab bars. They are conveniently located all around the Magic Kingdom, the EPCOT Center, and the Disney-MGM Studios. Our maps for the three theme parks show the restroom locations.

Medical Needs and First Aid: Disney provides registered nurses at First Aid Stations in each of the three theme parks and in the following locations: in the Magic Kingdom, near the Crystal Palace Restaurant in Main Street U.S.A.; in the EPCOT Center in the Odyssey Complex, between the World of Motion and the Mexico pavilion; and at the Disney-MGM Studios in the Guest Services Building.

Everyone should bring copies of needed medical prescriptions and the names and numbers of their home-town physicians. People staying in any of the Disney Resorts have the option of using a service called HousMed. They can call 648-9234 and a physician will come to their hotel rooms. The service operates from 8:00 a.m. until 11:00 p.m. There is a MediClinic at the intersection of highways I-4 and U.S. 192. MediClinic's hours are 9:00 a.m. to 9:00 p.m.

Visitors should know something about the hospital serving the area. The Sand Lake Hospital accepts major credit cards and they require payment before you leave the hospital, unless you are formally admitted. However, they will provide care, regardless of a person's ability to pay. The hospital is off highway I-4, at exit # 29 (Sand Lake Road) if you are going west on I-4. If you are going east, take exit #27A.

>Sand Lake Hospital
>9400 Turkey Lake Road
>Orlando, FL 32819
>(407) 351-8550 (Emergency Room) or
>(407) 351-8500 (Switch Board)

There are two places for filling prescriptions. Loomis Drugs is near the Buena Vista Walk-In Medical Center, 828-3434. Gooding's supermarket is in the Crossroads shopping center and contains a pharmacy.

Telecommunications Devices for the Deaf (TDDs): These are available in the Magic Kingdom at City Hall, in the EPCOT Center in the Earth Station, and at the Disney-MGM Studios in the Guest Services Building. Amplified telephones for hearing impaired people are found in several places in each theme park. In the EPCOT Center, Disney offers personal translator units amplifying the audio portion of some of the attractions. Visitors can find these in the Earth Station. They also have units translating some shows into Spanish, French, and German. Disney provides written descriptions of most attractions for people requesting them.

TRAVELING WITH CHILDREN

Taking children to see Mickey Mouse is the excuse many people use for visiting Walt Disney World. Of course we know, and you will learn, there are many more reasons. Children get excited with the mere mention of the words Disney World. Children should not be a burden, they should be a joy. However, we all know how their energy and lack of inhibition can wear on our nerves. There are a few things parents can do to minimize the stress.

It helps if you pack snacks and drinks for the kids. Just like puppies, they can whine mercilessly when they are hungry. It helps having some healthy snacks to pacify them. If you are flying with children, it is advisable to choose the least busy time. Some airlines offer special meals for children. Make sure the kids have the right clothing. Also, they benefit from sunglasses and sunscreen lotion as much as adults.

Walt Disney World caters to families with children. The entire area is carefully supervised so older children can be turned loose to explore on their own. It adds to their feeling of adventure and there are few ways they can get into trouble. The dozens of game rooms hold children's attention for hours. Many of the resorts and hotels have child care facilities. This frees children's parents so they can enjoy their vacation. It is a good idea to put name tags on your children in case they become separated. You can find these at City Hall in the Magic Kingdom, the Earth Station and Baby Services in the EPCOT Center, and at Guest Services in the Disney-MGM Studios.

Visitors can save about six dollars per day by bringing their own baby strollers. They can rent strollers at Strollers — Wheelchairs on the east side of the entrance to the Magic Kingdom, on the east side of the EPCOT Entrance Plaza, and at the International Gateway (near the French pavilion) in the EPCOT Center. A replica gas station called Oscar's, rents strollers at the Disney-MGM Studios. The strollers have a way of disappearing while guests are inside an attraction. To prevent this, it helps to tie an inexpensive scarf or balloon to the stroller. Other guests seem reluctant to make off with a stroller obviously belonging to someone else.

There are facilities for parents with infants. Each theme park has a Baby Services center. There are comfortable and private rooms with rocking chairs for nursing mothers. They have highchairs and bibs for feeding toddlers. The Baby Services centers have places for changing diapers, warming bottles, and preparing feeding formulas. Many kinds of baby food, bottles, pacifiers, and diapers are available. Parents should also be aware that many of the women's restrooms, and, in a nice touch of equality, some of the men's rooms, have diaper-changing tables.

Disney has well-trained and essentially invisible security forces roaming the grounds in the Magic Kingdom, EPCOT Center, and the Disney-MGM Studios. They may not be the Secret Service, but they do an excellent job of keeping everything in order. The Disney employees are experienced in dealing with children and they know exactly how to protect and calm a lost child. The Guest Relations windows at the entrances and the Baby Services centers in all three parks, have information on lost children.

ADVICE FOR SENIOR CITIZENS

Walt Disney World has something for everybody, including senior citizens. However, they also face a few handicaps. The crowds, sun, heat, sounds, and apparent confusion can be stressful. Please consider some of these ideas. First, there are group tours at the Magic Kingdom and EPCOT Center offered by Guest Relations. These are four-hour guided walking (or rolling) tours and they only cost $5. Admission to the parks is extra. For more information, visitors can call (407) 560-6233.

Private guides are available for people who can afford the service. Several non-Disney companies provide individual guides. Incentive Meeting Planners, (800) 827-0028; International Tours & Travel, (800) 822-1318; and Florida Convention Services, (800) 356-7891, all offer private guides. The cost runs from about $17 to $20 per hour or $120 to $200 for a full day.

Everyone should make every effort to visit during the slower periods. Some people feel so strongly about this that they prefer taking their children out of school for a week, rather than visiting during the summer rush. Familiarize yourself with all the information before leaving. Reading this book is a good start. This will minimize the confusion when you arrive. Make a point of eating either before or after the regular meal times. You will avoid most of the crowd. A clever idea is taking the monorail to one of the Disney Hotels, like the Grand Floridian or the Polynesian Resorts, for an elegant, relaxing, full-service lunch or dinner.

Everyone should avoid becoming overheated. This is especially true for elderly people and disabled visitors. Be aware that disabled people, like paraplegics and quadriplegics, do not perspire below the level of their injuries and are susceptible to overheating. Drink plenty of fluids and when you feel tired, find a shady spot and take a break from the action. The EPCOT Center can require people to walk or push a wheelchair at least two miles in the course of a day. Finally, remember that just as it makes no sense trying to swim against the tide, relax, take your time, go at your own pace, and enjoy the details of Disney World.

TRAVEL — PLANES, AUTOMOBILES, TRAINS, AND BUSES

Wheelchairs are wonderful mobility aids for disabled people, but they will not get them to Walt Disney World. Visitors have four options for traveling from their homes to Walt Disney World. They can fly in an airplane, ride in an automobile or van, take a train, or travel on a bus.

Air travel is fast and convenient. Most airports are more accessible than bus or railroad terminals. Travel by automobile offers the ultimate in convenience, privacy, and flexibility. Train and bus travel are the least expensive, but they also present the most problems. For disabled people traveling long distances, we recommend flying and renting an automobile or van upon arrival in Florida.

Air Travel — General Information For Disabled Travelers

Disabled air travelers should first decide when they want to visit Walt Disney World. Then they can contact a travel agent by telephone, mail, or in person. Many travel agencies are in locations accessible to people using wheelchairs. They should ask the travel agents which airlines fly to central Florida. Most people visiting Walt Disney World fly to Orlando, but Tampa is nearly as convenient. The travel agents usually obtain this information from a computer. Try finding a direct or non-stop flight so changing airplanes is not necessary. The airlines do not offer special rates for disabled people but there are discounted fares for everyone.

The U.S. Government passed a law in 1986 prohibiting airlines from denying disabled people access to American aircraft, as long as the traveler's conditions are stable, and they present no exceptional safety hazards. Canada has similar regulations. The law applies to people with physical, sensory, and mental disabilities.

The International Association of Airlines (IATA) regulates foreign air carriers. Travel agents should offer assistance to visitors to Walt Disney World from countries outside the U.S.

If travelers are inexperienced and unfamiliar with the accessibility of their chosen airport, they should ask the airport authorities or their travel agents for more information. This applies to parking and restroom facilities, the accessibility of airport transportation, rental wheelchairs, and the locations of elevators. Early planning can prevent unpleasant surprises.

The author has been using a wheelchair for nearly 15 years. During that time, he has flown in small, twin-engine airplanes and been lifted and carried aboard. He has made transatlantic flights in 747 jumbo jets and flown on smaller jet aircraft operated by all the major domestic airlines. He has traveled with companions and traveled alone. The airline employees always treated him politely. They never denied him access because of his disability, refused to take his folding wheelchair, demanded that he travel with an "attendant," and never requested he have a medical certificate allowing him to fly. In general, his flying experiences have been positive and he recommends flying as a means of transportation for other disabled travelers. However, there are exceptions.

The airlines have broken his wheelchair, they've lost his wheelchair, and they've lost parts to his wheelchair. He doesn't deny coming a bit un-glued when these events occur. His wheelchair is a **very** personal item. Without his wheelchair, he is like a fish out of water. If you can recall the way a dog behaves when someone tries taking its bone, you have an idea how the author reacts when someone damages or loses his wheelchair. He hasn't bitten anyone, but he growls.

Now when he travels, he makes certain the airline attendants understand how important his wheelchair is. One of his rules for traveling is: "assume nothing, double check everything." He does not wait for someone to ask; he tells them. When he calls for reservations he tells them he uses a wheelchair and cannot walk. He tells them how he will get on the plane and he tells them what to do with his wheelchair. Of course he is always polite and friendly, but if they don't get the message, he growls and shows his teeth.

Truly, the airlines appreciate the direct approach. They hate surprises and they appreciate honesty. Often, they comment, "Oh, you've flown before?" The routine usually goes something like this. He makes reservations, informs them he uses a wheelchair, and explains his inability to walk. When he checks his baggage at the airport, he asks for a baggage tag for his wheelchair and explains he can push himself up to the doorway of the plane. Then he transfers to an "aisle cart" or special boarding chair. This is a narrow, high-backed chair with two wheels. It is nearly identical to the device movers use with heavy boxes or furniture. He sits on the aisle cart and an attendant straps him in. Then they tilt him back, pull him on to the plane and down the aisle to his seat. The author transfers onto the cart and into the airline seat unassisted, but those needing help would receive it. The attendants take his wheelchair and usually stow it with the other baggage.

When he arrives at his destination, the other passengers get off the plane first while he patiently waits, trying to hide his anxiety. Eventually, they bring his wheelchair up to the doorway of the plane, and another aisle cart for him. He transfers to it and they take him to his wheelchair. Once he's back in his wheelchair, he's free and off to find his baggage. The process has become routine and he rarely has problems. It might take a few extra minutes, but he plans for it. Planning is the key.

On some of his trips, a cart was unavailable, there was a rush, or there were stairs and no "jet-way" to the plane's doorway. In these cases, the attendants often stand around acting like they don't know what to do. He tells them. He makes it clear he has places to go and things to do. If need be, he curls his upper lip.

He tells them he doesn't mind being picked up and carried and he tells them how to do it. Physical therapists are masters at this maneuver and they taught the author. Other disabled people can use the same technique. One person stands behind the disabled individual and reaches under their arms and grasps their wrists, one in each hand. The other person stands in front of the disabled person and with their arms, grabs the disabled person's legs under their knees. This method allows two people, and they don't need to be weight-lifters, to pick up and carry a heavier disabled person. It is very quick and effective. Being carried doesn't sound dignified, but the author left his false pride in an emergency room in Switzerland in 1978. He has places to go and things to do.

Battery-operated wheelchairs: Many physically disabled people use motorized, battery-operated wheelchairs. They use them because they lack the arm and hand strength needed for pushing a manual chair. These chairs are large and heavy, but offer an unprecedented degree of freedom for their users. Unfortunately, they present problems for the air traveler.

The chairs are expensive, complicated, relatively delicate, and easily damaged. They use batteries containing acid that, if spilled, could pose a danger to an airplane and its passengers. Airlines transport them as checked baggage if the batteries are non-spillable, if the batteries are disconnected, and the terminals insulated to prevent short-circuits. The airlines carry spillable batteries if they can always be stored in an upright position. Travelers must disconnect the batteries, insulate the terminals, and securely attach them to the wheelchairs. In other words, there are many potential problems associated with traveling with an electric wheelchair. There is only one good way of avoiding these problems, and that is leaving the battery-powered chair and traveling with a manual chair.

Indeed, this is exactly what many disabled people do. If they don't own a manual wheelchair, they can temporarily rent one for their trip. Of course this necessitates having a companion with them capable of pushing them. We don't see this as a problem because most people travel with a companion anyway. In cases where a disabled person's companion can't or doesn't want to push a wheelchair, the major theme parks in Walt Disney World rent battery powered, three-wheeled carts. This might provide a solution for some people. However, the carts are not really designed for many disabled people. The other drawback is people become adjusted to and comfortable with their own wheelchairs. Many are custom-designed to fit an individual. Using another chair might be uncomfortable and even dangerous. For people in this situation, we recommend an extra level of preparation and research. Eventually, they might decide it is worth the trouble of transporting their electric wheelchair.

Traveling with oxygen: Some disabled people require a respirator and oxygen. The Federal Aviation Administration (FAA) considers bottled oxygen a hazardous material and restricts its transport. If someone uses a battery-powered respirator and needs oxygen, they can still travel. They must inform their airline when making reservations. The airline can provide the oxygen for a nominal fee. People can only bring oxygen if it is bottled according to FAA regulations. Airlines recommend using their oxygen and shipping your own, if it is properly packaged. People traveling with oxygen should discuss their needs with their airline when making reservations.

Air travel for blind and deaf people: Blind people fly with few handicaps. On domestic flights they can sit anywhere with a leader dog at their feet. Leader dogs are by definition, well behaved and pose few problems. The same applies to visiting Walt Disney World; Disney accepts leader dogs and blind people nearly everywhere. Flight attendants will assist blind people. They tell them when the seat belt signs go on and off and explain the seat controls. If requested, they will explain the foods served and offer assistance in any other way they can.

One of the difficulties deaf people face is the fact that their disability is invisible. This partially explains how and why other people can be rude. Deaf people can not hear announcements concerning their flights or instructions for evacuation. Misunderstandings result from someone speaking to them when they're unable to see the speaker. People with hearing impairments should inform the airline about their situation, especially if they're traveling alone. Fortunately, most people visiting Walt Disney World are with a companion. Many deaf people use a typewriter-style machine (TTY) allowing them to communicate over the telephone. Most airlines allow them to obtain flight, hotel, and auto reservations using their TTY devices.

Air Travel for Diabetics: People with diabetes can travel like everyone else. They can arrange to store their insulin on an airplane in its refrigerator. The same thing applies to train travel. Diabetics should consult with their doctors about specific problems. They should make absolutely sure they have enough insulin for their entire vacation.

Air Travel for People on Dialysis: People requiring regular dialysis can also travel. They can arrange to have their dialysis done at many locations. Again, they should consult with their doctors and have concrete arrangements made before leaving home. There are various tours available for people needing dialysis.

Air Travel for Mentally Impaired: Mentally impaired people can usually travel without problems. The only rule is that they be independent. If they need assistance, they should make careful plans in advance. Again, there are tour operators offering trips designed for mentally disabled people.

Special food requirements: Many airlines offer as many as 30 different menus for people on specialized diets. These diets range from vegetarian and kosher, to those eaten by diabetics or people with ulcers. The only way of knowing whether an airline can accommodate them is by calling and asking. Generally, the airlines are helpful. The time for making these inquiries is when making your reservations, but sometimes, 24-hours before the flight is adequate.

In summary, we recommend air travel for disabled people. They should make their reservations early. They must clearly state their disability and define what they can and cannot do. This gives the airlines a chance to accommodate them, and they usually make every effort to do so; besides, it is the law. The airlines must make "a reasonable effort" to accommodate all disabled travelers.

Disabled travelers should arrive at the airport early, anticipate problems finding parking, and finding their way around the airport. Everybody should remember one of Murphy's Laws, "If anything can go wrong, it will." If they are using their own wheelchairs, it is important they be tagged as luggage going to the same destination as their occupants. After checking baggage, they should move directly to their departure gate. At the gate, an attendant should be told of the disabled person's situation, the need for an aisle cart both coming and going, and any other needs of that disabled individual.

Finally, we recommend that disabled people take care of their bathroom functions before getting on the plane. Unless a person can stand and walk, it is essentially impossible to use the bathrooms on an aircraft. The airlines are apparently trying to remove this handicap, but our advice is — don't count on it.

Air Travel Information For Everyone

Many aspects of air travel apply to anyone. It is the fastest means of travel, and if your vacation time is limited, flying makes economic sense. Walt Disney World and central Florida are major holiday destinations and the airline service is frequent and diversified.

There are more than 21 airlines and 30 charter flights to and from Orlando International Airport. They fly to over 100 U.S. cities and to most major cities in Europe, South America, Canada, and Asia. Delta Airlines is the "official" airline for Walt Disney World and they have approximately 70 daily flights in and out of Orlando. Delta offers travel packages to Disney World. For information, call Delta at 800-872-7786.

When making airline reservations anywhere, there are several key terms to understand. Nonstop flights require no plane changes. Direct flights have one or more stops but no aircraft changes. Connecting flights have one or more changes of planes at one or more stops. Naturally, in flying as in life, there's no such thing as a free lunch. More covenience usually means a higher price and vice versa. We highly recommend that disabled people fly nonstop. The minimal hassles are usually worth any added price. Other airlines serving Orlando include American, Bahamasair, British Airways, Continental, Icelandair, KLM, Mexicana, Midway, Northwest, Pan Am, TransBrasil, TWA, United, and USAir.

Carry-on Luggage: As of January 1988, airlines allow passengers two carry-on bags. The airlines are usually flexible in terms of the size of the bags. On crowded flights they can limit this to one bag. In addition, passengers can carry aboard a purse, an overcoat, an umbrella, camera, reading material, an infant-care bag, and crutches, a cane or braces needed for walking. Infant safety seats are acceptable if parents have a ticket for the child or if there is available space.

Foreign airlines usually allow only one item of carry-on luggage and of course, bags full of duty-free goodies. Passengers in first or business class can bring an additional garment bag.

Checked Luggage: U.S. Airlines usually allow passengers to check two suitcases with dimensions (length + width + height) not exceeding 62 inches, and a weight of less than 70 pounds per bag. If you have any doubts about meeting these requirements, call your airline beforehand. The author has always been able to check his manual, folding wheelchair as luggage, in addition to two suitcases, for no additional fee. The airlines always seem polite, cooperative, and take his wheelchair for granted.

Automobiles, Vans and Recreational Vehicles

A private vehicle is a good way of traveling to Walt Disney World. For many disabled people, it might be the best way. It offers flexibility and privacy. You can take more gear with you than if you fly. You can easily bring your electric wheelchairs, three-wheeled electric carts, oxygen, ventilators, and other needed equipment. Once in central Florida, you save money by avoiding the cost of flying and renting an automobile. You have the benefit of staying at a hotel or motel some distance from Disney World and saving money with lower room rates and eating in less expensive restaurants. Finally, (we know this is a sacrilege to Disney) you can visit other attractions besides Walt Disney World.

Last, and certainly not least, a private vehicle offers the fastest and surest way of traveling within Walt Disney World. There are alternate means of transportation such as the Monorail, buses, vans, and boats. Invariably, they are crowded and involve confusion and long waits. This will be inconvenient for disabled people. If you don't drive your own vehicle, we strongly recommend renting either a car or van.

The greatest handicap facing the largest number of physically disabled people is a lack of mobility. Wheelchairs provide a beginning to the solution. Their value is immeasurable. Without them, many disabled people would be unable to get out of bed and simply move across a room. However, there's more to life than moving around a room or up and down a hallway.

In America, we take automobiles and our ability to drive them for granted. The right to own and drive an automobile is not guaranteed as part of our right to "Life, liberty and the pursuit of happiness," but it might as well be. We assume it. Physically disabled people often lose that ability and the result is traumatic. Fortunately there are ways disabled people can enjoy the freedom of driving their own vehicles.

Reliable, safe and simple, mechanical hand controls can be added to a normal automobile, van, or recreation vehicle. Physically disabled people, even those with limited use of their hands and arms, can learn to drive. The clearest way of understanding the process is by describing how the author handles his automobile.

First, he has a two-door car with an automatic transmission. The steering column supports the hand controls that operate the gas and brake pedals. With his right hand, he steers. There is a round knob attached to the rim of the steering wheel allowing him to easily turn it with one hand. He has been using the same hand controls for 14 years, driving to and from work and making numerous cross-country trips. He has difficulty imagining life without the freedom of driving wherever and whenever he wants. His automobile is almost as important to him as his wheelchair and he does not take it for granted. We think other disabled people feel the same.

For the author, driving is easy; getting in a vehicle is the hard part. Like many other wheelchair users, he slides into the driver's seat, folds his wheelchair, and pulls it into the car. He can only do this with a two-door car. The driver's seat must be similar in height to the seat of his wheelchair, the hand controls only work on a car with an automatic transmission, and the bigger a car's interior is, the better.

Beyond those requirements, he can drive and take trips just like anyone else.

CAR RENTALS

The author routinely rents automobiles with hand controls when he travels. There is no added charge and the service has been without serious problems. All the major rental companies offer automobiles with hand controls. The following is a list of companies renting cars out of Orlando:

> Alamo (800) 327-9633
> Avis (800) 331-1212
> Budget (800) 527-0700
> Dollar (800) 800-4000
> Hertz (800) 654-3131
> National (800) 328-4567
> Superior (800) 237-8106
> Thrifty (800) 367-2277

These are nation-wide toll free numbers. We know Hertz, Avis, and National have cars with hand controls. The others might have them by the time you read this. The only sure way of knowing is by calling. If these numbers change, consult your telephone book. Car rental agencies appreciate a two-week advance notice. They might ask if you prefer the hand controls on either the left or right side of the steering column. As with the airlines, it is helpful if you are honest and assertive in expressing your needs and wishes.

Hertz has a brochure describing its services for travelers with disabilities. They have hand-controls for cars at 900 U.S. outlets and reservation numbers for people with hearing and speech impairments. For more information write: **Services for Disabled Travelers**, Hertz Corp.; Public Affairs; 225 Brae Blvd.; Park Ridge, NJ 07656.

The rental rates for automobiles in Orlando are among the least expensive in the U.S. One proven, money-saving strategy is renting for an entire week and avoiding the daily rates. Car rental companies are competitive in the same way the airlines are. They offer a confusing array of incentives and gimmicks. Think of it as a game; call around and compare prices. Before renting, check with your insurance agent and see if your policy covers rental cars; if not, we recommend the additional Collision Damage Waiver Insurance. Be forewarned — it can be expensive.

VANS AND RECREATIONAL VEHICLES

Many physically disabled people cannot transfer into an automobile the way the author does. They do not have the same strength and flexibility in their arms and upper body. Quadriplegics are examples of people needing help with transfers. The solution for them is a van. These have become popular for everyone; for people unable to transfer, they're a blessing. Usually, they have a motorized lift. The disabled drivers or passengers open a door on the side of the van. The lift folds down and lowers to the ground. They simply roll their wheelchairs onto the lift platform, press a button, move up, and roll into the van. Some of the vans are set up so a person can drive them with hand controls while sitting in their wheelchairs.

Rental vans for disabled people using wheelchairs are becoming more available every day. **Wheeler's Accessible Van Rentals** has 60 vans available at 30 locations in 12 states, including Arizona, Arkansas, California, Colorado, Florida, Hawaii, Nevada, New Jersey, New Mexico, Ohio, Pennsylvania, and Tennessee. Prices are approximately $90 per day and $500 per week. They offer 100 miles per day free mileage and charge 25 cents a mile from then on. Call (800) 456-1371 or (602) 878-3540 for more information.

Wheelchair Getaways has 125 vans at 41 locations in 14 states. Most of the franchises are near vacation destinations like Atlantic City, New Orleans, San Francisco, Denver, Los Angeles, and Orlando, Florida. They charge approximately $80 per day and offer unlimited mileage. Travelers can reach them at (800) 642-2042 or (215) 579-9120.

The more expensive vans come outfitted with sinks, couches, beds, refrigerators, and even mini-kitchens. The benefits for disabled travelers are numerous. They can get in, travel comfortably, and have the privacy and equipment needed to care for themselves. If people wish to sleep in the vans, they can stay in numerous campgrounds and avoid the cost and hassle of finding an accessible motel. Vans equipped to this degree approach the category of recreational vehicles.

Recreational vehicles, or RVs, include elaborate vans and range upward to those the size of a bus. Wouldn't that be nice? At the higher price range, they can be total living units containing electrical, gas, and water storage systems. They have stoves, refrigerators, televisions, stereos, dishwashers, microwave ovens, air conditioning, and more. They might be the ultimate means of travel for anyone, especially disabled people. At the end of this guide, we offer a listing of rental recreational vehicles or motor homes, and companies that build them.

Bus Travel

Traveling by public bus is an option for disabled people, but it is usually not a good one. Bus travel lacks the speed of air travel and the flexibility and privacy of an automobile. However, bus travel is inexpensive.

Physically disabled people can be divided into two categories: those who can stand and walk and those who can not. If a person can climb and walk to their seat, they can enjoy the money-saving benefits of bus travel. For disabled people using wheelchairs who can not stand and walk, there are some major problems.

Most buses do not have wheelchair lifts and the aisles are too narrow for wheelchairs. A disabled person must be lifted and carried to their seat. This might be all right for a disabled child or light-weight disabled adult. For everyone else, it is inconvenient if not impossible. In addition, the restrooms are small and in the back of the bus. Many disabled people have special bathroom needs and the tiny restrooms on buses (and airplanes and trains) are completely inadequate.

In fairness, the bus companies do their best accommodating disabled people. Greyhound and Trailways provide special services for disabled travelers. For more information, we recommend contacting the nearest company office or writing to **Helping Hand Service**; Greyhound Lines, Inc.; 1810 Greyhound Tower; Phoenix, AZ 85077. You can also write to **Handicapped Services;** Trailways, Inc.; 1500 Jackson St.; Suite 1400; Dallas, TX 75201.

Both bus companies allow a disabled person and a companion to travel for the price of one ticket. To qualify, the disabled person must have a written statement from a doctor saying they can travel by bus with the physical assistance of a companion. The companion must provide assistance to the disabled person getting on and off the bus and care for any of their needs during the trip. The bus drivers might help lift and carry a disabled person, but no one should depend on it. The bus companies offer special fares for blind people with doctor's statements. Believe it or not, some people try faking a disability to get lower priced tickets.

There are many bus terminals and some are more accessible than others. The newer ones have ramps, wider doorways, accessible restrooms and food service areas, and lowered telephones and water fountains. Of course none of those features mean much if a disabled person can not get on the bus.

Train Travel

Traveling by train to Walt Disney World is also an option. Amtrak makes three stops in central Florida: in Winter Park (150 Morse Blvd.), in Orlando (1400 Sigh Blvd.), and 20 minutes later, in Kissimmee (416 Pleasant St.). Amtrak offers blind and physically disabled passengers a 25 percent discount; however, unlike the bus companies, their companions pay the full rate. Traveling by train is similar to using a bus. We do not recommend it for physically disabled people who can not stand and walk. The restrooms are just as inconvenient as those on an airplane or bus.

Amtrak has trains with minor modifications for disabled people. The entrances to the railroad passenger cars are wide enough for a wheelchair, but passengers must then transfer to a regular seat. The "accessible" restrooms are in the food service car. As on all the trains, people using wheelchairs can not move from one car to another. We suppose someone would have to carry them; that is not what we consider accessible.

Amtrak has some cars set up for long distance travel. These contain special sleeping cars with facilities for disabled people. Each has a private bathroom large enough for a person using a wheelchair. As on the other trains, people can not move from one car to another in their wheelchairs. Therefore, an attendant handles all food and beverage service. There is none of the elegant group dining you see portrayed so romantically in movies and ads. Disabled people who can and want to contend with these handicaps should obtain more information by calling Amtrak's information hotline, (800) USA-RAIL. Telex. for the deaf is (800) 523-6590. They can write for a free booklet, *Access Amtrak: A Guide to Amtrak Services for Elderly and Handicapped Passengers*. Write the Office of Customer Relations, Amtrak, P.O. Box 2709, Washington, DC 20013.

ACCOMMODATIONS (LODGING)

> *"The service we render others is really the rent we pay for our room on earth."* ——— Wilfred Grenfell

Nothing is more important and more misunderstood about disabled people than their need for accessible lodging. A home is a person's castle. How people live and take care of themselves is a private matter and rarely talked about in detail. The fact remains, before they can do anything else, they must have a place where they can sleep, bathe, dress, and take care of their bathroom functions. They want to be clean, comfortable, and as independent as possible. It is just as important that these needs be met when they travel as when they are at home.

Before anybody can define accessible lodging, they must answer the question, "Accessible to whom?" As we have said before, disabled people fit into two broad categories. There are those who can stand and walk and those who can not. If a person can stand and walk, even with difficulty, they can usually stay in any hotel or motel. Their problems are little different from anyone else's. They try to find a place to stay that is within their budget and close to the places they choose to visit. The more qualitative things like atmosphere, cleanliness, and size of the rooms are ordinary questions, and any reservation clerk can answer them.

However, disabled people who can not stand and walk must use wheelchairs. They face problems in taking care of themselves that non-disabled people never dream about, except possibly in their worst nightmares. Where, for example, do you sleep if you can't even get into a bedroom? How can you shower or use the toilet if you can't get in the bathroom?

The author is a paraplegic; he can not stand and walk and he's used a wheelchair for almost 15 years. During that time, he's dragged himself up stairs to a bedroom, gotten out of his chair, and pulled himself across a floor and into a bathroom because the doorway was too narrow for his wheelchair. There are thousands of variations on this theme, and they are all uncomfortable and potentially dangerous. He deals with the hardships because he wants to travel. To him, it is not a question of winning or losing; it's not a question of how he plays the game — all that matters
is IF he plays the game.

Everybody's situation is different and their abilities vary. With the foregoing in mind, we describe the various types and places to stay in and around Walt Disney World. We describe what we know about "accessible" rooms and we offer a few recommendations. Ultimately each individual must make their own inquiries and decisions.

We strongly urge everyone to confirm the amenities mentioned here, especially when it comes to facilities for disabled people. We also suggest that visitors confirm their room rates. We have made an effort to provide accurate information; however, rates vary by season and applicable discounts.

People visiting Disney World can either stay in Disney World or outside. There are advantages to both. Some of the advantages to staying at one of the Walt Disney World Resort hotels or complexes are:

- Visitors can reduce their travel time by using the Disney World transportation system of buses, boats, and monorail. However, some authorities still feel that driving your own car is preferable.

- Sometimes, guests staying at the Disney resorts receive preferential treatment in making dinner and show reservations, and gain access into the theme parks ahead of others, especially on crowded days.

- Each of the hotels connected by the Monorail system has day care set-ups so parents can leave their children while they go out to play.

- Disney resort guests can leave pets overnight in the kennels. Non-resort guests can only leave their pets for the day.

- Disney resort guests can park their cars without the daily fee at the theme parks.

- People staying in the Disney resorts receive first choice in selecting tee-off times at the Disney golf courses.

NOTE: Many of these benefits will not apply for disabled people. Few of them will be playing golf, leaving children, traveling with pets, and hopefully not visiting on crowded days. If they follow our advice, they will be driving their own vehicles, buying extended-day passes, and getting free parking anyway.

Lodging In Walt Disney World

The most convenient, luxurious, and expensive of the Disney hotels are around the Seven Seas Lagoon and within view of the Magic Kingdom. They offer a variety of water sports like water skiing, sailing, swimming, or sun bathing on the white sand beaches. They connect to the Magic Kingdom and the EPCOT Center via the Monorail System. The Monorail is accessible to people using wheelchairs at the Polynesian resort and the Grand Floridian, but ironically, not at the Contemporary resort.

We attempt to describe all the services and amenities Disney hotels and resorts offer. However, we were unable to get information on their facilities for disabled people.

- **The Grand Floridian Beach Resort** looks like one of the opulent Victorian-era hotels built in Florida around the turn of the century. It is the most elegant and romantic of the Disney hotels. The Victorian-era theme is seen everywhere, from the costumes the staff wear, to the restaurants and room decor. The rooms are about 400 square feet in size, and contain two queen-size beds and a day bed. They allow up to five people in each room. The suites contain a parlor and one, two, or three bedrooms. The Grand Floridian has 900 rooms, five restaurants, two lounges, two snack bars, four shops, an arcade, a child-care facility, a health club, and a marina. Room rates range from $215 to $420 per night and the suites cost $385 to $1,400 per night. The Grand Floridian's telephone number is (407) 824-3000.

- **The Contemporary Resort** is east of the Magic Kingdom and between the Seven Seas Lagoon and Bay Lake. Disney is spending nearly $100 million remodeling The Contemporary Resort. We hope they make the Monorail entrance more accessible to disabled people using wheelchairs. It has two restaurants, two snack bars, two lounges, meeting rooms, six shops, a health club, a marina, a beach, two swimming pools, and a new convention center. The Contemporary Resort has over 1,050 rooms. Some have king-size beds, the others have queen-size beds, and all have a day bed. Each room accepts up to five people. Suites are available for 2 to 12 people. Rooms vary from $180 to $295 per night and suites cost from $640 to $1,430 per night. The Contemporary Resort's telephone number is (407) 824-1000.

- **The Polynesian Resort** is on the south side of the Seven Seas Lagoon. As its name implies, the Polynesian presents an atmosphere of a relaxing, exotic, South Pacific tropical paradise. A three-story garden, filled with lush foliage and crowned with a waterfall, dominates the lobby in the central building. The resort's 855 rooms are in adjacent "longhouses" bearing the names of Pacific islands. Most rooms have two queen size beds, a day bed, and can sleep up to five people. The Polynesian contains three restaurants, two snack bars, two lounges, a marina, two swimming pools, a children's playground, a gameroom, and several shops. Rooms cost from $190 to $275 per night and suites in the Bali Hai longhouse range from $300 to $750 per night. The Polynesian's telephone number is (407) 824-1391.

Fortunately for those of us blessed with neither the Midas Touch nor the silver spoon, there are hotels in Walt Disney World offering convenience and relative economy. Three resorts offer rates ranging from $85 to $99 per night. They are situated around the EPCOT Center, but none have direct access to the Monorail system. Personal or rental cars are the best way of getting around, although Disney shuttle buses are available. Disabled people using wheelchairs can call for vans equipped with lifts, but expect to wait at least 20 minutes for the service.

- **The Caribbean Beach Resort** is southeast of the EPCOT Center and east of the Disney-MGM Studios. The 200-acre complex consists of five "villages" around a 42-acre lake. Each village has the name of a different Caribbean Island: Martinique, Barbados, Trinidad, Aruba, and Jamaica. In total, there are 2,112 rooms. Each village has a swimming pool, guest laundry, and its own beach. A central area called Old Port Royale, contains six counter-service style restaurants, two shops, a gameroom, and a lounge. There is a 1.4 mile path around the lake for walking, jogging, biking, or pushing wheelchairs. The 400 square foot rooms usually contain two double beds and can accept up to four people. Rooms are identical, except for their views, and cost from $85 to $99 per night. The Caribbean Beach Resort's telephone number is (407) 934-3400.

- **The Port Orleans Resort** is northeast of the EPCOT Center off the Bonnet Creek Parkway. Port Orleans imitates the French Quarter in New Orleans, Louisiana. A central building known as The Mint, contains the reception area, a shop, the food court, and a restaurant. The 1,008 rooms are in seven buildings; each has three floors serviced by elevators. Each room has two double beds. There is one full-service restaurant, four counter-service restaurants, one lounge, and a poolside bar. Port Orleans has a swimming pool and a boat rental area at the Port Orleans Landing. Rooms vary from $85 to $99 per night. The Port Orleans Resort's telephone number is (407) 934-5000.

- **The Dixie Landings Resort** is northeast of the EPCOT Center and just north of the Port Orleans Resort. The setting is reminiscent of the Mississippi River country upstream of New Orleans. The 2,048 rooms are in many different buildings, with names like Plantation and Bayou guest rooms, Magnolia Bend Plantation rooms, and Alligator Bayou rooms. The decor varies, but they all evoke life in the old south. There is a recreation area with a pool, playground, and fishing hole. There is a shop called Fultons General Store, one full-service restaurant, five fast-food restaurants, one lounge, and a poolside bar. Dixie Landings contains five swimming pools and walk-ways designed for jogging, biking, and wheelchairs. Room rates range from $85 to $99 per night. The Dixie Landings Resort's telephone number is (407) 746-6385.

The Westin Walt Disney World Swan and Sheraton Walt Disney World Dolphin hotels combine in a large convention-resort complex to the southwest of the EPCOT Center. They are built around the 50-acre Crescent Lake. They connect with the EPCOT Center by a motor tram and walking path, and to the Disney-MGM Studios by boat or bus. The remainder of Walt Disney World is accessible by bus, van, or automobile. Room rates are pushing the expensive to out-of-sight range of our scale.

- **The Swan** has 758 rooms in a modernistic, 12-story building, topped by what else — two enormous swans. The Swan has 46 rooms for disabled guests and they seem eager to accommodate them in any way possible. The bathrooms have wide doors, grab bars, raised commodes, benches, and hand-held showers. They have

TTD/TDY phones, alarms, and closed caption decoders for hearing impaired people. They have handicapped parking, a ramped entry, and a free, accessible shuttle. The architect of the Swan calls his creation "entertainment architecture," and his vision is followed in the interior decor. Fitting for a business meeting center, amenities include safes in the rooms, clock radios, cable television, voice mail service, mini-bars, hair dryers, bathrobes, daily newspapers, and 24-hour room service. There are two full-service restaurants and two lounges. For recreation, The Swan offers boat rentals, a swimming pool, a health club, eight tennis courts, a gameroom, a clothing shop, and a children's center with supervised activities. Standard rooms run from $159 to $375 per day and suites from $425 to $1300 per day. AAA and senior citizen discounts apply to the room rates. The Swan's telephone number is (407) 934-3000.

- **The Dolphin** consists of a 27-story tower rising over a 14-story central building and four subsidiary guestroom wings. Not to be outdone by the neighboring Swan, The Dolphin hotel has two enormous dolphins perched on its roof. The Dolphin has 1,509 rooms, 140 of which are suites. Forty-three of the rooms are for disabled guests. The bathrooms have wide doors, grab bars, and raised commodes. There are TTD/TDY phones and other services for hearing impaired people. There is handicapped parking, a ramped entry, and a free, accessible shuttle. They feature the same business-like amenities as The Swan. There are four full-service, accessible restaurants, one cafeteria, an ice cream shop, a poolside bar and grill, and three lounges or bars. The Dolphin also has boat rentals, a swimming pool, a fitness room with personal trainers for people needing motivation, a children's center, a game room, and several shops. Standard rooms cost $199 to $349 per night and suites, presidential we assume, range from $450 to $2,750 per night. The Dolphin's telephone numbers are (407) 934-4000; (800) 227-1500 and FAX: (407) 934-4099.

Disney's Yacht Club and Beach Club Resorts, like twins, have many features in common. Both have seaside New

England as their primary decorative theme, and share restaurants and recreational activities. They are southwest of the EPCOT Center and between it and The Dolphin. Visitors can walk or roll to the EPCOT Center and sail to the Disney-MGM Studios by boat. The remainder of the World can be reached by bus, van, or automobile.

The Yacht and Beach Clubs share one restaurant and an ice cream and soda shop. They also share the same meeting and convention facilities. The joint recreational activities include boat rentals, a swimming pool the scope of a mini-water theme park, a health club, two tennis courts, a game-room, a children's center, a croquet court, a sand volleyball court, a barber/beauty shop, and two shops.

- **The Yacht Club** has 635 rooms with color TVs, ceiling fans, mini-bars, and tables with inlaid checkerboard tops. Chess and checkers sets are included. It has one full-service restaurant, a buffet, a snack bar, two lounges, and 24-hour room service. Room rates vary between $195 and $365 per night. The telephone number at the Yacht Club is (407) 934-7000.

- **The Beach Club** has staff members dressed in beach outfits from the 1870s providing a bit of good-humored fun. It contains 580 rooms with the beach as the central theme. The rooms have ceiling fans, two double beds, double sinks, and hairdryers. They have 11 rooms for disabled guests. The bathrooms have wide doors, grab bars, raised commodes, some roll-in showers, and some tubs with hand-held showers. They have TTD/TDY phones and other services for hearing impaired people. There is handicapped parking, level or ramped entries, and valet parking. There is a free accessible shuttle, and a Disney ticket desk. The Beach Club has two full-service restaurants, a snack bar, two lounges, and 24-hour room service. Rooms at The Beach Club cost from $220 to $250 per night and discounts are available to Disney shareholders. The telephone number is (407) 934-8000.

FORT WILDERNESS RESORT AND CAMPGROUND

This is a self-contained, all-inclusive resort. It occupies 780-acres north of the EPCOT Center and southeast of the Magic Kingdom. It is crossed by canals and roads and forested with native cypress and pine trees. The atmosphere is relaxed and less glittery than other Disney resorts. There are fields where children or adults can play, and the smell of barbecues is always in the air. There is a marina and beach, a nature trail, and waterways attracting canoeists and fishermen. The Meadow Recreation area contains two tennis courts, a swimming pool, an arcade, and snack bar. There are 1,190 regular campsites for people bringing their own gear. Visitors seeking a kinder and gentler "camping" experience can rent one of 363 air conditioned trailers. The trailers come fully equipped with cooking and eating utensils, color television, and maid service.

Some of the campsites are set up for tents and the remainder accommodate trailer campers. Each site is wired for 110/220 volt electricity and has a barbecue grill and picnic table. The trailer sites have sanitary-disposal hookups, and there are regularly spaced restrooms, private showers, ice machines, telephones, and laundry rooms. Is this camping? Actually, guests welcome the conveniences after a hard day in Walt Disney World.

Most visitors cook their own meals in the campgrounds. This is part of the money-saving appeal and it adds flexibility to people's schedules. A Gooding's supermarket is located nearby. A building named Pioneer Hall offers a cafeteria, and Crockett's Tavern serves beer, cocktails, and complete meals. Entertainment occurs three times each night in the form of the Hoop-Dee-Doo Musical Revue. Make reservations in advance by calling (407) 934-7639. Visitors can also place their names on a waiting list at the Pioneer Hall Ticket Window. Each night there is a campfire program near the center of the campground. There is a sing-along and a marshmallow roast, and later a canoe excursion to see the Electrical Water Pageant.

The activities at Fort Wilderness seem endless. There are two tennis courts and two nearby golf courses. Two swimming pools and a large beach on Bay Lake provide cool and wet fun. There is a Petting Farm and horse barn where people can see real animals if they tire of the cartoon variety. Boats are available for rent at the marina, and fishing and guided horseback rides are popular. There are horseshoe pits, jogging trails, tetherball, and volleyball courts. Finally, River Country, a major Disney water theme park, is nearby and south of the Fort Wilderness Campground.

Boats take people from Fort Wilderness to Discovery Island and the Magic Kingdom. Regular buses take visitors from Fort Wilderness to the other attractions in Walt Disney World. Personal automobiles or vans remain the most convenient form of transportation. The campsites in Fort Wilderness cost between $34 and $48 per night. The fully equipped trailers range from $165 to $180 per night.

Disney's Village Resort is a ten-minute drive east of the EPCOT Center and close to Interstate Highway 4 (I-4). The Village resort is part of a large lodging, dining, entertainment, and shopping complex. The unique aspect of the Village Resort is many of the villa-type rooms offer kitchen facilities. They might cost more than hotel rooms, but they can accommodate more people and provide them with the money-saving option of cooking their own meals. The villas are quiet, secluded, and provide an escape from the hustle of the large hotels. Access to the Walt Disney World attractions by automobile is quick and convenient.

There are five types of villas and they all require a check-in at the Reception Center. There are one and two-bedroom villas. The one bedroom units accept four people and the two bedroom units can sleep six. The Villa Center is the recreation area. It has a swimming pool, and bike and electric golf cart rentals. The golf carts might be a treat for people using wheelchairs, if they can get in them. There is a laundry, snack bar, and game room. The one-bedroom suites only have a small refrigerator, sink, and coffee machine. They lack the full kitchen facilities. The two-bedroom deluxe villas are near the Lake Buena Vista Golf Course. They are spacious and contain a queen-size bed in one bedroom, two double beds in another, and a double fold-out sleeping sofa in the living room. They can sleep six and two children under 12. Disney claims some of these units are for disabled people. We suggest calling and asking for details.

The two-bedroom resort villas with studies are secluded along the western side of the villa area. The kitchens are upstairs with the living room, TV, a sleeper sofa, two bedrooms, and two bathrooms. In this unusual design, the study is on the ground floor, and contains a double bed and a utility room with a washer and dryer. There is bass fishing in the nearby canals and lakes. The shady, flat and quiet roadways are nice for walking, jogging, biking, or pushing wheelchairs. The Grand Vista Suites are essentially "ultra-luxurious" homes. There are daily newspaper deliveries, the refrigerators contain food when guests arrive, and a golf cart and bicycles come with the price of the rental.

Visitors to the Villas can buy groceries at the nearby Gourmet Pantry, and have them delivered at no extra charge. They can also order by telephone. There is a Gooding's supermarket at the Crossroads of Lake Buena Vista shopping center. There are nearby lounges with attractive names like Cap'n Jack's Oyster Bar, the Baton Rouge Lounge aboard the Empress Lily, and many night clubs at Pleasure Island. Room service is also available at the Villas. There are six swimming pools around the Villas, and three tennis courts. The par-72 Lake Buena Vista golf course is nearby and so is a driving range. The Villas might be a bargain for a large family with the time and desire for relaxation. Rental rates vary. Most of the villas range from $175 to $345 per night while the Grand Vista Suites are indeed grand, costing from $725 to $800 per night. The Villas' telephone number is (407) 827-1100.

DISNEY VILLAGE HOTEL PLAZA
There are seven hotels located on the east side of Walt Disney World, near the intersection of highway S.R. 535 and Interstate 4 (I-4). The seven hotels contain a total of 3,825

rooms, and Disney grants them official status. This means that although Disney does not own the hotels, their guests enjoy the same privileges as regular Walt Disney World visitors. The privileges include transportation and first choice for dinner and show reservations. The Walt Disney World Central Reservations facility accepts their bookings, and they are included in some Walt Disney Travel Co. and Delta Air Lines travel packages. The seven hotels in the Disney Village Hotel Plaza are as follows:

- **The Grosvenor** contains 629 rooms in a 19-story tower. Ten of the rooms accommodate disabled visitors. The bathrooms have wide doors, grab bars, raised commodes, and tubs with hand-held showers. They offer TTD/TDY phones and the restaurants are accessible. They have handicapped parking and a level approach to the lobby. Each room has a VCR and a refrigerator-equipped bar. Rental movies are available. There are two restaurants, a lounge, two tennis courts, racquetball and shuffleboard courts, a basketball court, two heated pools, a playground, and a gameroom. They also have substantial convention facilities. Room rates range from $99 to $160. For more information, contact Grosvenor; 1850 Hotel Plaza Blvd.; Lake Buena Vista, FL 3283; 828-4444 or (800) 624-4109.

- **The Travelodge** has 325 rooms and suites. There is a gameroom, pool, playground, two restaurants, and a nightclub with a nice view from the 18th floor. There are two rooms for disabled travelers. Their rates vary from $119 to $139. For further information, contact Travelodge; 2000 Hotel Plaza Blvd.; Box 2220; Lake Buena Vista, FL 32830; 828-2424 or (800) 348-3765.

- **The Royal Plaza** contains 396 rooms in a 17-story building. There are ten suites available, including, for the celebrity-conscious, the Burt Reynolds and Barbara Mandrell. Ten rooms are for disabled guests. The bathrooms have wide doors, grab bars, raised commodes, and tubs with hand-held showers. They do not have TTD/TDY phones. They have handicapped parking and a ramped entry. There is a heated pool, spa, game room, shuffleboard, putting green, four tennis courts, a tanning salon, and saunas. There are two restaurants and a dinner show. There is a lounge with a late-night (midnight to 2:30 a.m.) happy hour. A nightclub named the Giraffe, features live entertainment and attracts a local crowd. There is a barbershop, beauty salon, and one-day film processing service. They have convention facilities and hospitality suites. They offer a free, accessible shuttle. Room rates are from $160 to $180 per night. For more information, contact Royal Plaza; 1905 Hotel Plaza Blvd.; Lake Buena Vista; FL 32830; 828-2828; (800) 248-7890; FAX: (407) 827-6338.

- **The Howard Johnson Resort Hotel** has 323 rooms in a 14-story tower and attached 6-story building. There is a central atrium lounge with a waterfall. The lounge is accessible via glass-walled elevators. There are three heated pools, a playground, gameroom, and exercise room. The hotel contains an accessible Howard Johnson restaurant, and a meeting room for 200 people. They have six rooms for disabled visitors. The bathrooms have wide doors, grab bars, and raised commodes. There is handicapped parking and a ramped entry. There is an accessible, free shuttle, a Disney ticket desk, and they offer a discount for seniors. Nightly rates are from $85 to $160. For more information, contact Howard Johnson; Box 22204; 1895 Hotel Plaza Blvd.; Lake Buena Vista, FL 32830; 828-8888; (800) 223-9930; FAX: (407) 827-4623.

- **The Buena Vista Palace** is the largest hotel in the Disney Village Hotel Plaza. The Palace contains 1,028 rooms, and each has at least two telephones, one of which is a bedside, Mickey Mouse telephone. The Buena Vista Palace has 13 rooms accessible to physically disabled people. They have handicapped parking spaces and a ramp to the lobby. The bathrooms have wide doors with grab bars and raised commodes. They have TTD phones and warning lights in the rooms for hearing impaired visitors. There are two pools, a health spa, three tennis courts, and a large gameroom. They also have a program for children, 24-hour room service, gift shops, a self-service laundry, and hairdressers for men and women. There are four restaurants. Arthur's 27 won four awards as one of Florida's 12 best restaurants. Arthur's Wine Cellar in the Sky stocks 800 bottles. The Laughing Kookaburra Good Time Bar presents live entertainment and 99 different brands of beer. We can see why it's called the Good Time Bar. They have large convention facilities with 40 meeting rooms, 127 suites, and 9 breakout rooms. There is an exhibit hall with 23,000 square feet of space, and two others of similar size. They have in-house convention planners and caterers, and can handle any function. Rooms cost from $99 to $295 per night. For details, contact Buena Vista Palace; 1900 Buena Vista Dr.; Lake Buena Vista, FL 32830; 827-2727 or (800) 327-2990.

- **The Hilton** hotel is across the road from the Disney Village Marketplace. It has 813 rooms, and offers a digital telephone system controlling the air conditioning and television; it contacts the valet, room service, or operators — all with just the touch of a button. The Hilton has 125 rooms for disabled guests, handicapped parking, and a level entrance. The bathrooms have wide doors, grab bars, and tubs with hand-held showers. They have TTD/TDY phones and the restaurants are accessible. They have a free shuttle to Disney World, a Disney ticket desk, and by the summer of 1993, they say people can roll into their swimming pool. The hotel occupies 23-acres and contains nine restaurants and lounges. There are two tennis courts and two swimming pools. There are special services for children, including supervised activities. They have 52,000 square feet of convention space, accommodating up to 2,350 people. Rooms cost from $119 to $249. For more information, contact Hilton at Walt Disney World Village; Box 22781; 1751 Hotel Plaza Blvd.; Lake Buena Vista, FL 32830; 827-4000 or (800) 782-4414.

- **The Guest Quarters** hotel has 229 suites and 12 of these are for disabled visitors. The bathrooms have wide doors, grab bars, raised commodes, and tubs with hand-held showers. They have TTD/TDY phones, handicapped parking and a ramp to the lobby. Each suite contains 600 square feet, has a separate living room and bedroom, and can sleep up to six people. The suites contain two remote controlled TV sets and a third in the bathroom. They also have a wet bar, stocked refrigerator, coffeemaker, and optional microwave oven. The hotel has a heated pool, whirlpool, pool bar, a gameroom, children's play area, and an exercise room. There is one restaurant, an ice cream parlor, and a two-story tropical bird aviary. They have meeting facilities for up to 50 people. They offer complimentary shuttles to Disney World and every other one is accessible. The suites rent for $119 to $215. For further information, contact Guest Quarters Suite Resort; 2305 Hotel Plaza Blvd.; Lake Buena Vista, FL 32830; 934-1000 or (800) 424-2900.

Lodging Outside Walt Disney World

The primary reason anyone stays in a motel or hotel outside Walt Disney World is cost. With some detective work they can find a motel with a pool, pay as little as $25 per night for a room, and still be within a 20 to 30 minute drive from Walt Disney World. Anyone, including physically disabled people, can drive their own vehicle, stay in an inexpensive motel, watch what they spend on food, drink, and souvenirs and make a visit to Walt Disney World an affordable adventure.

With $25 per night as the low end for room rates, prices and amenities range upward, eventually rivaling anything in Walt Disney World. There are a bewildering number of options. Disabled traveler's primary concerns usually relate to accessibility. Our objective is providing the information disabled people need for doing their own research. They or their travel agents, should call, describe their needs, and ask detailed questions about the rooms, facilities, and rates. The rates especially, can vary.

We called more than 35 hotels and motels and asked about their accommodations for disabled people. Not surprisingly, we got a varied response. Some places were helpful, knowledgeable, and polite. Sometimes the people answering the phones did not know what we were talking about. If someone says they have "handicapped accessible" rooms, but know little else, you should speak with someone in charge of housekeeping. They usually know more about the details of the facilities. If you receive vague answers, like "I'm not sure," or "I think the bathroom door is wide enough for a wheelchair," nine times out of ten, the rooms will not be accessible. The best question is, "Have other people using wheelchairs stayed in your rooms?" The lesson is: disabled people, their companions, or travel agents must do their own comparison shopping. Of course they must know what questions to ask. We offer the following questionnaire as a guide.

ACCESSIBLE LODGING QUESTIONNAIRE
1. Is there a reserved parking area for disabled people?
2. Do you have valet parking?
3. Are there stairs leading to the entrance? If so, how many?
4. Do you have portable ramps?
5. Are the restaurants, lounges, bars, meeting rooms, and other facilities accessible?
6. Are the public restrooms accessible?
7. Are there stalls in the restrooms large enough to accept people using wheelchairs?
8. Are the elevators accessible? Do the doors open at least 32 inches?
9. Does a voice announce the floors serviced by the elevator?
10. Are the elevator controls in Braille?
11. Do you have special "handicapped accessible" rooms?
12. Are all the doors in the room at least 32 inches wide?
13. Are there any steps in the rooms?
14. Do the bathrooms have grab bars, and if so, where?
15. Are there roll-in shower stalls?
16. Do the bathtubs or showers have hand-held showers?
17. Can people using wheelchairs fit under the sinks?
18. Are any instructions written in Braille?
19. Are there telephones for the deaf (TTD/TDY)?
20. Are guide dogs allowed?

NOTE: We modified the above questionnaire from one in *Access to the World*, by Louise Weiss, (Facts on File; 460 Park Ave. South; New York, NY 10016.)

Travelers can obtain additional information on lodging from:

    Orlando/Orange County Convention & Visitors Bureau, Inc.
    7208 Sand Lake Road, #300
    Orlando, Florida 32819.
    Telephone: (407) 363-5800
    Telex: 4977247
    FAX: (407) 363-5899

    Kissimmee-St. Cloud Convention & Visitors Bureau
    1925 E. Irlo Bronson Memorial Highway
    P.O. Box 422007
    Kissimmee, Florida 34742-2007
    Telephone: (407) 847-5000, (800) 432-9199 (Florida) or (800) 327-9159

LODGING IN THE LAKE BUENA VISTA AREA

- **The Comfort Inn** has 640, basic motel rooms, each with two double beds and small bathrooms. There is one restaurant, two heated pools, a gameroom, and a gift shop. Room rates vary from $29 to $67 per night. Contact: Comfort Inn; 8442 Palm Parkway; Lake Buena Vista, FL 32830; 239-7300 or (800) 999-7300.

- **The Doubletree Club** has 167 rooms and one restaurant. A breakfast comes with the price of the rooms. There is one swimming pool and an exercise room. Rates vary between $65 and $95 per night. Contact: Doubletree Club; 8688 Palm Parkway; Lake Buena Vista, FL 32830; 239-8500 or (800) 228-2846.

- **The Embassy Suites** hotel offers 280 suites; each contains a bedroom and separate living room. Six of the suites are for disabled guests. The bathrooms have wide doors, grab bars, raised commodes, and roll in showers, but no tubs with hand-held showers. They say a paraplegic designed their accessible suites. They have a dining and kitchen area with microwave ovens, refrigerators, and coffeemakers. The bathrooms are large and contain two sinks. There is one restaurant and a deli that are accessible. They have handicapped parking spaces and a ramp leading to the lobby. The price of the suites includes a free buffet breakfast, and evening cocktails from 5 to 7:00 p.m. There are indoor and outdoor pools, tennis, basketball and volleyball courts, a fitness course, and playground. Rental rates range from $145 to $280. Contact Embassy Suites; 8100 Lake Ave.; Lake Buena Vista, FL 32830; 239-1144 or (800) EMBASSY.

- **The Holiday Inn — Lake Buena Vista** hotel is approximately 1.5 miles from the Disney Village Marketplace. Each of the 507 rooms has a mini-kitchen with a refrigerator, microwave oven, coffeemaker, and VCR. They have two rooms for disabled guests. The bathrooms have wide doors, grab bars, raised commodes, and tubs with hand-held showers. There is handicapped parking and a ramped lobby entry. There is a children's center, one pool, two spas, and a playground. The Holiday Inn has three accessible restaurants, a free shuttle to Disney World, and a Disney ticket desk. Rooms cost from $99 to $135 per night. Contact: Holiday Inn — Lake Buena Vista; 13351 S.R. 535; Lake Buena Vista, FL 32830; 239-4500 or (800) HOLIDAY.

- **The Howard Johnson Park Square Inn** is near the Disney Village Marketplace and contains 222 rooms and 86 suites. The rooms contain two double beds, and the suites come with microwave ovens and refrigerators. There are two heated pools, a playground, and game room. Meeting rooms accommodate up to 144 people. Rooms cost $65 to $105 and suites vary from $70 to $120 per night. Contact: Howard Johnson Park Square Inn; 8501 Palm Parkway; Lake Buena Vista, FL 32830; 239-6900 or (800) 635-8684.

- **The Hyatt Regency Grand Cypress** hotel forms the core of this 1,500-acre resort. It is next to the Disney Village Hotel Plaza and three miles from the EPCOT Center. The 18-story building contains 750 rooms and 72 of them are suites. A large swimming pool has waterfalls and a 45-foot water slide. Guests can rent sailboats, wind surfers and canoes to use on the 21-acre lake. There are 12 tennis courts, racquetball, and volleyball courts. They have walking and jogging trails, a health club, and an equestrian center. The area also contains a 45-hole golf course. The convention facilities can handle up to 2,500 people. The Grand Cypress has five restaurants and three lounges. The hotel has 12 rooms designed for disabled people. Room rates range from $155 to $370 and the suites begin at $340. Contact: Hyatt Regency Grand Cypress; One Grand Cypress Blvd.; Orlando, FL 32819; 239-1234 or (800) 233-1234.

- **Marriott's Orlando World Center** has 1,503 rooms in a 27-story tower. The Marriott offers 26 rooms designed for disabled guests. The bathrooms have wide doors, grab bars, raised commodes, and seats so people can slide from their wheelchairs into the shower. The complex occupies 200 acres surrounded by an 18-hole golf course. It has three heated swimming pools, 12 tennis courts, a health club, a beauty parlor and barber shop, a gameroom, and several shops. There are seven accessible restaurants and three lounges. The convention facilities are large, with 46 possible meeting rooms. They have a $4.50 shuttle to Disney World, a Disney ticket desk, and they accept AARP (retired people) discounts. Room rates vary from $139 to $219 per night and they often have promotional discounts. Contact Marriott's Orlando World Center; World Center Drive; Orlando, FL 32821; 239-4200 or (800) 228-9290.

- **The Radisson Inn Lake Buena Vista** has 200 rooms, each with two double beds, a table and chairs, and a stocked mini-bar. Twelve of the rooms are for disabled visitors. The bathrooms have wide doors and grab bars. They have TTD/TDY phones, TV, and alarms for hearing impaired people. There is handicapped parking and a ramped entry. There is one pool, a spa, playground, gift shop, and gameroom. There are two accessible restaurants and a free, accessible shuttle. Room rates vary from $69 to $109. Contact: Radisson Inn; 8686 Palm Parkway; Lake Buena Vista, FL 32830; 239-8400; (800) 333-3333 or FAX: (407) 239-8025.

LODGING ALONG HIGHWAY U.S. 192

Highway U.S. 192 (also known as the Irlo Bronson Memorial Highway) runs in an east to west direction, south of Walt Disney World. Many small motels can be found along the highway as it leads into the town of Kissimmee. Many are close to Walt Disney World and offer some of the lowest rates around. These are but a few examples of the motels and hotels in the area.

- **The Best Western — East Gate** is three miles from Walt Disney World's main gate and has 13 rooms for disabled guests. The bathroom doors are wide enough for wheel chairs and have grab bars. They offer phones and warning lights for deaf people, and their restaurant is accessible. Their room rates vary from $48 to $71 per night. Contact: Best Western — East Gate; 5565 Irlo Bronson Memorial Highway; Kissimmee, Florida 34736; 396-0707, (800) 223-5361 or (407) 396-6644 (FAX).

- **The Hilton Inn Gateway** is one mile from the entrance to Walt Disney World. They have 13 rooms for disabled visitors. There is handicapped parking and a level lobby. The bathrooms have wheelchair-wide doors, grab bars, raised commodes, and roll-in showers. There are TTD/TDY telephones and two accessible restaurants. Rates vary between $55 and $80 per night. Contact: Hilton Inn Gateway; 7470 W. Irlo Bronson Memorial Highway; Kissimmee, FL 34746; 396-4400; (800) 455-8667; FAX: (407) 396-4320.

- **The Holiday Inn — Main Gate East** is 3 miles from the Walt Disney World main gate. It has 670 rooms with mini-kitchens containing microwave ovens, refrigerators, and coffeemakers. Each room has a VCR. There are two swimming pools, a day-care facility for children, and six eating areas. There are three rooms equipped for disabled people. The bathrooms have wide doors, grab bars, raised commodes, and roll-in showers. There is handicapped parking and a level entry. There is an inaccessible, free shuttle to Disney

World, and a Disney ticket desk. Rates range from $85 to $97. Contact: Holiday Inn — Main Gate East; 5678 Irlo Bronson Memorial Highway; Kissimmee, FL 34746; 396-4488 or (800) 465-4329.

- **The Holiday Inn Main Gate — West #1** is one mile from Walt Disney World and they have ten rooms for disabled visitors. The bathrooms have wide doors, grab bars, and tubs with hand-held showers. There is handicapped parking and a ramped entry. They have three accessible restaurants, a shuttle to Disney World, and a Disney ticket desk. The room rates vary from $84 to $123 per night. Contact: Holiday Inn Main Gate — West #1; 7300 W. Irlo Bronson Memorial Highway; Kissimmee, FL 34746; (407) 396-7300; (800) 465-4329 or FAX: (407) 396-7555.

- **The Hyatt Orlando** is the closest hotel to the Walt Disney World main gate. It has 924 rooms in four buildings. Eight of the rooms are for disabled visitors, but they say they are not suitable for quadriplegics. The bathrooms have wide doors, grab bars, raised commodes, and they can attach hand-held showers in the tubs. They have TTD/TDY phones and warning devices for hearing impaired people. There is handicapped parking and a level entry. The area has three tennis courts and a 1.3 mile jogging trail. There are four swimming pools and playgrounds. There are three accessible restaurants, an accessible shuttle for $7, and a Disney ticket desk. Room rates vary between $79 and $134; suites cost $180 to $470 per night. Contact: Hyatt Orlando; 6375 West Irlo Bronson Memorial Highway; Kissimmee, FL 34746; 396-1234; (800) 233-1234; FAX: (407) 396-5090.

- **King's** motel is one of the many privately owned establishments in the area. It has 122 rooms and one swimming pool. They have standard rooms and "efficiencies" accepting up to six people. There are two rooms for disabled guests. Rates vary from about $50 to $75 per night. Contact: King's; 4836 West Irlo Bronson Memorial Highway; Kissimmee, FL 34746; 396-4762 or (800) 327-9071.

- **Knight's Inn** is distinguished by its purple, crushed velvet bedspreads. It contains standard rooms and efficiencies with completely furnished kitchens. There is one small pool, and room rates are around $55 per night. Contact: Knight's Inn; 2880 Poinciana Blvd.; Kissimmee, FL 34746; 396-8186 or (800) 722-7220.

- **The Ramada Resort Main Gate** offers 400 rooms and is just west of Interstate Highway I-4. There are two swimming pools, two tennis courts, a gameroom, an accessible restaurant, and one lounge. The Ramada has two rooms for disabled visitors. The bathrooms have wide doors, grab bars, raised commodes, and shower chairs. There is handicapped parking and a ramped entry. There is a free, inaccessible shuttle and a Disney ticket desk. Room rates vary from $49 to $115. Contact: Ramada Resort Main Gate; 2950 Reedy Creek Blvd.; Kissimmee, FL 34746; 396-4466; (800) 228-2828; FAX: (407) 396-6418.

- **The Ramada Hotel Resort — Maingate E at The Parkway** has six rooms for disabled guests. The bathrooms have wide doors, grab bars, and raised commodes. There are TTD/TDY telephones and eight accessible restaurants. There is handicapped parking and a ramped entry. Rooms vary from $49 to $102 per night. They offer an accessible shuttle for $6.50 and there is a Disney ticket desk. Contact: Ramada Hotel Resort — Maingate E at the Parkway; 2900 Parkway Blvd.; Kissimmee, FL 34746; 396-7000; (800) 634-4774; (800) 225-3938 (Florida); FAX: (407) 396-6792.

- **The Residence Inn by Marriott** is four miles from Walt Disney World. They have eight suites for disabled guests. The bathrooms have wide doors, grab bars, raised commodes, and two rooms have tubs with handheld showers. There is handicapped parking and a level entry. The rooms have queen-size beds, a fully equipped kitchen, fireplace, and a sofa/sleeper. They provide accessible shuttle service for $7. Rates range from $109 to $115 per night. Contact: Residence Inn by Marriott; 4786 W. Irlo Bronson Memorial Highway; Kissimmee, FL 32741; 396-2056; (800) 331-3131 or FAX: (407) 396-2909.

- **The Sheraton Lakeside Inn** is west of I-4 and near the Ramada Resort. It has 651 rooms in several buildings and has two pools. Seventeen of the rooms accommodate disabled guests. The bathrooms have wide doors, grab bars, and hand-held showers. TTD/TDY phones are available upon advance request. There is handicapped parking and a level entry. They offer a free, accessible shuttle, and there is a Disney ticket desk. There are play grounds, four tennis courts, and a miniature golf course. There are four accessible restaurants. Room rates vary from $79 to $119. Contact: Sheraton Lakeside Inn; 7769 West Irlo Bronson Memorial Highway; Kissimmee, FL 34746; 239-7919; (800) 848-0801 or FAX: (407) 828-8250 ext. 7888.

- **The Wynfield Inn Main Gate East** is three miles from Disney World. They have ten rooms for disabled guests. The bathrooms have wide doors, grab bars, raised commodes, and five of the rooms have tubs with handheld showers. There is handicapped parking and a level entry. They have a Disney ticket desk and accept discounts from AARP, AAA, the military, the Government, etc. The standard room rate is $79 but might be lower. Contact: Wynfield Inn Main Gate East; 5335 W. Irlo Bronson Memorial Highway; Kissimmee, FL 32741; 396-2121; (800) 468-8374 or FAX: (407) 396-2121.

As we said, there are many motels along Highway 192; the following offer some of the least expensive rates:
- **Econolodge Maingate East**, $29-59 per night, (407) 396-7100.
- **Gold Star Maingate East**, $50-56 per night, 396-1748.
- **Howard Johnson's Fountain Park**, $45-75 per night, (407) 396-1111.
- **Larson's Lodge — Kissimmee**, $35-65 per night, (407) 846-2713.
- **Larson's Lodge — Maingate**, $39-75 per night (407) 396-6100.
- **Park Inn International**, $47-97 per night, (407) 846-7814.

CHAPTER 3

THE MAGIC KINGDOM

"The sound of laughter has always seemed to me the most civilized music in the universe" —— Peter Ustinov

INTRODUCTION TO THE MAGIC KINGDOM

The Magic Kingdom may be the heart of Walt Disney World because it contains everything people love about Disney. It combines the elements of an amusement park with the fantastic characters and themes from Disney's movies and cartoons. It may be the place where "dreams come true and fantasy becomes reality." However, it's not equally "magic" for everyone.

The Magic Kingdom presents challenges to people with physical disabilities. There are many inaccessible rides and attractions. Physically disabled people might wonder if visiting is worth their effort — we think it is.

So What Is The Magic Kingdom And Why Go There?

The Magic Kingdom is an elaborate entertainment complex consisting of seven parts. Laid out in a semi-circular plan, the seven lands surround the Cinderella Castle. Each area has an imaginative name and maintains a distinctive theme throughout its part of the Magic Kingdom.

The first area is Main Street U.S.A., the entry point to the Magic Kingdom. Clockwise around the park are Adventureland, Frontierland, Liberty Square, Fantasyland, Mickey's Starland, and Tomorrowland. We describe each area in order and in more detail. Look at the accompanying map now. The map makes our discussion easier to understand.

The themes of each land are expressed in the rides and shows, the ride attendant's and worker's costumes, the restaurants, the food, the shops, merchandise, and even the music. The effect is the creation of an atmosphere, a sense of involvement in space and time. This is Disney's trademark accomplishment and it works well. As an example of how far Disney goes to create this atmosphere, they refer to their employees as "cast members." They truly put on a show. Disney's talent for capturing your attention and stimulating your senses is the main reason why it's an ideal place for disabled people, young or old. There is entertainment and fun for everyone.

For example, if someone uses a wheelchair and can't or doesn't want to get out of it, they still experience the atmosphere of each area. This is possible because the environment draws you into it. It surrounds you with delightful sights and sounds and delicious smells and tastes. There is always something going on. Around every corner is something new. You may run into Mickey Mouse or Goofy in costume. You may even get caught in a cowboy shoot-out in the street. There's a feeling of adventure and fun for everyone.

The author saw and talked with many disabled people. He learned they shared his feelings. One memorable encounter was with two brothers; both have muscular dystrophy and use electric wheelchairs for mobility. They visit Walt Disney World often and were candid about their opinions. When asked about their feelings in regard to the inaccessible rides and attractions, they said they didn't mind. One of the brothers said, "We enjoy getting out, seeing the crowds, the parades, and movies. It's enough just being here." They may be handicapped by more obstacles than the author due to the differences in their disabilities, but the point is — they get out and do it. They demonstrate that because they have the will, there is a way. If we can do it and have fun, everyone can.

How Big Is The Magic Kingdom?

The Magic Kingdom is about three and one-half percent (98 out of 27,800 acres) of the area Walt Disney World occupies. It may seem small when compared to the EPCOT Center, or all of Walt Disney World; but don't get the wrong impression. There are over forty-five attractions, adventures, and rides, along with many restaurants, shops, and street vendors. Even with so many things to see and do, the park is compact. It's relatively easy for physically disabled people to get around. With the proper planning, you won't become excessively tired by long distances. You will appreciate this feature the most on hot and humid summer days.

When measured against the EPCOT Center and the Disney-MGM Studios, the Magic Kingdom offers more barriers to people with physical disabilities. This is partly due to the fact that it's an older park. It opened October 1, 1971, before there

The Magic Kingdom®

- Wheelchair/Stroller Rental
- First Aid
- Accessible Rest Rooms
- Railraod
- Monorail
- Skyway

Map not to scale

1. Cinderella Castle
2. City Hall
3. WDW Railroad
4. Jungle Cruise
5. Pirates of the Caribbean
6. Big Thunder Mountain Railroad
7. Country Bear
8. Tom Sawyer Island
9. Fort Sam Clemens
10. Haunted Mansion
11. Hall of Presidents
12. 20,000 Leagues
13. It's a Small World
14. Space Mountain
15. American Journeys
16. Grand Prix
17. Mickey's House
18. Mickey's Hollywood Theatre
19. Grandma Duck's Farm

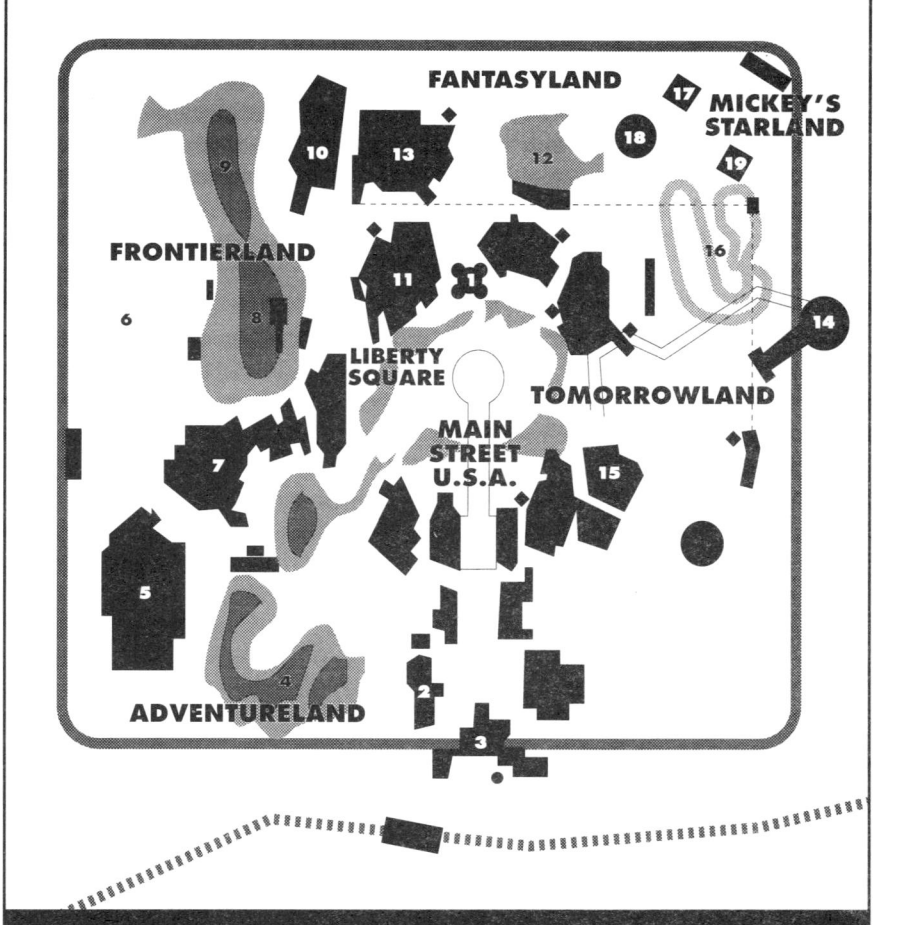

FANTASYLAND

MICKEY'S STARLAND

FRONTIERLAND

LIBERTY SQUARE

TOMORROWLAND

MAIN STREET U.S.A.

ADVENTURELAND

was an awareness of the needs of physically disabled people. To be fair, the handicaps are also due to the nature of some of the rides. Disney could remove most of the obstacles. We hope they will, and we discuss this when we describe them in detail.

Getting To The Magic Kingdom

To get to the Magic Kingdom, the best bet is taking the third exit on I-4 out of Orlando. The first is marked "S.R. 535/Lake Buena Vista," the second is "EPCOT Center/Disney Village," and the third is "192/Magic Kingdom."

Taking this exit, you will be heading west on Highway US 192. You go that way for approximately two miles, turn right, and head north past the Disney-MGM Studios Theme Park.

After traveling two miles north, you reach the Magic Kingdom Main Entrance Toll Plaza. There is a $4 parking fee for each vehicle, except for people staying at one of the Disney resorts, with an identification card to prove it. Parking is also free for people with an Annual Passport.

Disabled visitors should enter the Toll Plaza in the far right lane and ask the attendant for directions to the handicapped parking area. The attendants give them a handicap parking pass for their dashboards. It is important to remember this. It would be more than embarrassing to return to your vehicle and find it towed away for being illegally parked.

From the toll plaza, proceed straight ahead, track the blue line on the road, and follow the blue handicap signs to the designated handicap parking.

What To Take With You

Before leaving their vehicles, everyone should think about their needs. A visit to the Magic Kingdom is usually a day-long affair and it's across the Seven Seas Lagoon from the parking area. Disabled visitors must have everything needed for a lengthy trip. At the same time, don't overload yourselves. Traveling light means going farther and faster, seeing more and doing more. Walking with a disability or pushing a wheelchair is work enough.

Admission Tickets And Passports
From the handicapped parking area, the Transportation and Ticket Center is under the Monorail and to the right. Here, you purchase your admission tickets or passports. If you leave the park during the day and wish to return, you must have your parking and admission tickets to get back in. Please put them in a secure place.

Wheelchair Rental
There are two places for renting wheelchairs when visiting the Magic Kingdom. The first is at the Transportation and Ticket Center, at the gift shop on the left side of the ticket booths. You find this after leaving your vehicles and before boarding the Monorail or the Ferry. If you know you need a wheelchair, it's wise checking here first.

The second place for renting wheelchairs is on the other side of the Seven Seas Lagoon, in the Magic Kingdom. The Wheelchair and Stroller Rental Shop is just inside the main entrance and to the right. If planning on visiting more than one park in the same day and wanting a wheelchair in both places, you should have your deposit tickets validated before leaving the first park. You can borrow another chair at the next park without an additional charge or deposit. It's doubtful many people are that ambitious, but the option exists.

Locker Rentals
Visiting the Magic Kingdom is like going on a day-long hike. Visitors leave their vehicles for four, six, or eight hours. Here, more than at the other Disney World parks, you are likely to carry a lot of gear. It might take an hour to leave the Magic Kingdom, go back to a vehicle in the parking lot and return. No one wants that kind of hassle, but nobody should be a pack mule either. One way you can avoid being overloaded, is by temporarily storing some of your equipment. There are rental lockers for this purpose located just inside the main entrance. These are on the ground level, to the right, under the Train Station. Perhaps you have a heavy video camera and don't want to lug it around all day. You can take your pictures, put the camera away, hustle around to the more thrilling rides, and pick it

up again when you leave. Enjoying your visit to the maximum includes traveling as light as possible.

Restrooms

Restroom accessibility is the least of the problems in the Magic Kingdom. The restrooms have stalls designed for people using wheelchairs. Sometimes people using wheelchairs find it difficult closing the doors behind them, or reaching the flush handles. Usually, disabled people have experience with these problems and adapt to them. At least they can get in and the restrooms are clean. The restrooms are better than many places outside Disney World. One final bit of advice: refer to the accompanying map of the Magic Kingdom and while orienting yourself, take note of where the restrooms are. This might save you anxiety later.

Monorail Or Ferry?

Now, you have another choice. You still aren't in the Magic Kingdom. You must decide how to get there. You can take a ferry boat across the Seven Seas Lagoon or the Monorail around it. It's the most fun to try both, one going and one returning. There's a steep ramp, about 100 feet long, to get up to the Monorail station. The author had to strain a bit to push his wheelchair up the ramp, but the effort wasn't excessive. If you or members of your party are using a wheelchair, keep this in mind.

Monorail

The attendants help those using wheelchairs get on the Monorail. They spot a disabled person and direct them to a waiting area. When the cars come into the station, the doors open, passengers get off, and the attendant lays down a portable ramp from the platform into one of the cars. They take the handles of the wheelchair and pull it backwards into the car, locking it in place. They are very careful.

Once it starts, the Monorail provides a pleasant, five-minute ride to the Magic Kingdom. You have a lovely view as you quietly circle the Seven Seas Lagoon. Disabled passengers shouldn't feel any fear or discomfort while on the Monorail.

Ferry

The author's favorite way of getting to the Magic Kingdom is on the large ferry boats sailing across the Seven Seas Lagoon. They take a few minutes more than the Monorail, but the trip is more enjoyable. It's possible to sit outside without feeling confined or locked in place.

At this point you realize you're in for something special. Looking across the Seven Seas Lagoon, you see the white sand beaches and palm trees of the Polynesian resort. You feel you are leaving central Florida and entering paradise. There are sailboats, wind surfers, water skiers, and speed boats. Everyone is having fun. It's magical.

Getting on and off the ferry is uneventful and easy. It's only a short roll to the entrance to the Magic Kingdom. Straight ahead is Main Street, U.S.A., which is usually busy with people. Directly in front, farther away, is the Cinderella Castle. No matter how many times you visit, it's exciting.

Ramps

Main Street U.S.A. and Frontierland are the only areas in the Magic Kingdom where the streets have curbs or raised sidewalks. This means people using wheelchairs must search for the ramps. Don't do what the author almost did. In front of City Hall, the sidewalks are the same dark color as the street, and he almost went off the curb without noticing the drop-off. In other places, he has fallen out of his wheelchair. We want everyone to be careful. The ramps are easy to find. Ramps for wheelchairs exist at each corner around the town square and at each corner along Main Street.

Information

The City Hall, to the left when entering the Magic Kingdom and Main Street, U.S.A., is the place for obtaining information. They have schedules for special events, entertainment, parades, and transportation. When discussing their strategy for "doing" the Magic Kingdom, many people talk about racing around and beating the mass of other people. That simply isn't very practical for physically disabled people. A wiser approach is determining what you want to see and what you can do. The parades and other shows occur at pre-arranged times and places. Disabled people need to plan so they get there early, ensuring themselves of a good view. There's no point to waiting in line for an attraction and then discovering that it's not accessible.

MAIN STREET, U.S.A

This is the introduction to the Magic Kingdom, appropriately named Main Street, U.S.A. After all, this is America. Main Street, U.S.A. represents small-town America early in this century. Supposedly they were gentler, happier times. There is the Town Square with its City Hall, train station, cinema, and fire station. Everyone enjoys the cleanliness of the streets and the perfection and detail of the buildings. Double-decker buses, horse-drawn trolleys, an old fire engine, and horseless carriages take people up and down the street. These vehicles are not accessible to people using wheelchairs unless they have the ability to get up and walk short distances, or have the means of being lifted. Resist the temptation to race through Main Street, U.S.A. Take your time. There are some interesting things to see and it's a good place to prepare for the adventures ahead. Unlike most real small towns in America, Main Street, U.S.A. is accessible to anyone using a wheelchair.

Orientation

Main Street, U.S.A. is a great place to look at your map again and orient yourself. From your vantage point after entering Main Street, you see Cinderella's Castle. At this point, you are looking to the north. On the left is Adventureland and to the right is Tomorrowland. The area in front of the Castle is the Central Plaza. All seven of the Magic Kingdom "lands" radiate from this central hub. Everyone should discuss the lay of the land with their companions. Take a few minutes and discuss strategy. Do not wander aimlessly, however strong the temptation. This place can, and will, frustrate people who are unprepared. We recommend that you take this guide and refer to it often.

Walt Disney World Railroad — An Overview Of The Magic Kingdom

The quickest way of grasping the size and design of the Magic Kingdom is by taking a ride on the Walt Disney World Railroad. There are two authentic steam engines pulling open-air cars around the Magic Kingdom. The trip takes 21 minutes. Visitors board the train at the Main Street Station; people using wheelchairs must get out of their chairs or have someone in their party lift and carry them aboard the train. An attendant folds and places the wheelchairs on the train, or visitors leave them at the station and hope they will be there when they return. We recommend that people take their chairs with them. Sometimes the wheelchairs get commandeered by other opportunistic visitors.

If people prefer or need to remain in their wheelchairs, there are only two places to get on the train — Frontierland and Mickey's Starland. The train engineer helps them aboard with a small ramp attached to one of the cars. They lock the wheelchairs in place for a secure ride. Getting off the train is just the reverse. It's a gentle, pleasant ride and well worth the effort, at least once.

There are four engines or locomotives and the story behind them is interesting. They were built in the United States in the early 1900's and used in Mexico. Disney discovered them in 1969, brought them home, and rebuilt them. They kept and used many of the original components, like the heavy cast iron wheels, slide rods, and the frames themselves. Disney converted them to burn diesel fuel instead of coal or wood. They still produce steam and operate as originally designed, just more cleanly and efficiently.

The Walt Disney Story

If you are new to the Magic Kingdom, curious about Walt Disney, and how he built his empire, this attraction offers a refresher course.

The Walt Disney Story is a film shown in a theater on the east side of the Town Square. The theater is on the right as you enter Main Street, U.S.A. There's a ramp on the right side of the building. Attendants direct people using wheelchairs to a pair of doors, avoiding the turnstiles. They remain in their wheelchairs throughout the 22-minute show. The show provides a way to relax while gaining an appreciation for the founder of the Magic Kingdom.

Main Street Cinema

You find the Main Street Cinema on the right side of Main Street, on your way toward the Cinderella Castle. People using wheelchairs can easily get in and out and move at will around the theater. Inside, Disney continuously shows old Disney cartoons and tells the story of a silly mouse meeting his lady friend, Minnie. In 1928, the cartoon *Steamboat Willie* introduced the world to the mouse we know as Mickey. Visitors to Walt Disney World see and feel his presence and that of the other famous cartoon characters everywhere. Walt Disney's wife had the foresight to name him "Mickey" instead of his original name of "Mortimer." Who knows what might have become of Walt Disney with a mouse named "Mortimer."

Penny Arcade

The Penny Arcade is a game room similar to those in motels and malls around the country. They appeal mainly to teenagers, but as usual, Disney adds a twist. They have modern electronic games and antiques, such as a vintage football game, a Kiss-O-Meter, and tests of strength. Most interesting are a few devices showing the first "moving pictures." They consist of a series of cards with sequential drawings. Flipped manually or automatically, the images come to life and move. Each sequence tells a story and most are comedies. This is an excellent way of learning or teaching animation.

You create the same effect by drawing characters near the outside edge of the pages of a book. Flipping through the pages rapidly, by bending the pages with your fingers, you make the characters move. It causes your eyes to trick your brain. Perhaps this is how Walt Disney got his inspiration. Playing with these old-time cartoons while explaining them to children, adds to everybody's appreciation of Walt Disney and the art of animation.

ADVENTURELAND

Moving down Main Street and entering the Central Plaza, you find yourself in front of the Cinderella Castle. Turning left, you cross a small bridge and enter Adventureland. There are four attractions in Adventureland. Three are well known and popular. Unfortunately, they are inaccessible to many people with physical disabilities. We describe each attraction and provide disabled people with information on access.

Swiss Family Treehouse

Entering Adventureland from the east, the first attraction is the Swiss Family Treehouse. It's modeled after the treehouse occupied by the family in the 1960 Disney movie, *Swiss Family Robinson*. The movie depicts the adventures of a family shipwrecked on their way to America. They struggle to survive on a deserted island and build a fantastic treehouse. The treehouse is a display of ingenious devices made by the family, and shows how they lived comfortably under primitive conditions. This was a good movie and stimulates the imagination in all of us. The movie and the treehouse seem especially attractive to children. For some reason, they all enjoy climbing trees.

The Swiss Family Treehouse is a passive exhibit. It requires the ability to walk up and down stairs. Many people using wheelchairs will not be able to enjoy this attraction. People using wheelchairs because they have difficulty walking might try it, but it won't be much fun. There's no way Disney can make the treehouse more accessible, short of installing elevators. We think it's best that disabled people forget the attraction, save their energy, and move on to something else.

Jungle Cruise

The Jungle Cruise is popular and well known. It involves a gentle boat ride through a jungle fantasy land. The ride is one of the "not to be missed" attractions in the Magic Kingdom. Once again, physically disabled people may be disappointed.

People using wheelchairs must get out of them and step or

be carried down in to the boats. One person can carry a small child, but lifting and carrying a disabled adult takes two strong people. Remember, the Disney "cast members" can not and will not help. The author looked at the boats, noticed four or five attendants standing around, and knew they could easily lift him into one of the boats. If they put a ramp into the boats, people using wheelchairs could roll aboard and remain in their wheelchairs, or transfer into one of the regular seats.

This type of arrangement works well on other rides in the Magic Kingdom. People using wheelchairs are comfortable making this kind of transfer. They do it every day when they fly on an airline or get in and out of an automobile. It might not be the most dignified way of gaining access but it's better than having no access.

> *"There is no exercise better for the heart than reaching down and lifting people up."* —— John Homer

Passengers who can, board a small boat similar to the *African Queen* used by Humphrey Bogart and Katherine Hepburn in the famous movie. They depart from a make-believe jungle boat station. The atmosphere reflects excitement and muted danger. Passengers sit in shaded comfort and glide along the river through a live jungle. Disney cultivates an array of tropical plants and adds to the realism with waterfalls and artificial rocks.

The captain of the boat adds to the fun and suspense by telling stories. African animals excite and amuse the passengers. There are elephants bathing in the river, a hippo, lions, zebras, giraffes, antelope, and even vultures. The animals and threatening natives are AudioAnimatronic models. They don't seriously frighten anyone. If disabled people can not get on the Jungle Cruise, we suggest they roll on by and forget it. There's a lot more to do and see that will make up for it.

Pirates of the Caribbean
This is an adventure-type, ten-minute boat ride, and the next attraction in Adventureland. It's popular, and another

guide book ranks it as the "best attraction at Walt Disney World." Once again, like the Jungle Cruise, Disney handicaps many disabled people. Disney's description of the ride in their *Disabled Guests Guide Book* is inadequate. They say,

> "Folding wheelchairs may be lifted into the boat; a nonfolding chair may be exchanged for a folding one at the entrance. A limited number of wheelchairs are available, so a short wait may be necessary. NOTE: Guests wearing back and neck braces should be aware that this attraction contains a sequence in which ride vehicles accelerate rapidly down a short, steep waterfall."

The description is not clear. The author can transfer from his wheelchair and thought he could get on this ride. In reality, physically disabled visitors must stand and walk, or have someone lift and carry them into one of the ride's boats. Like the Jungle Cruise, they could put a ramp into the boats, allowing people the opportunity of rolling on, and either staying in their wheelchairs, or transferring from them into one of the ride's seats.

Visitors who can get on the boats, witness a series of scenes depicting a pirate attack on an imaginary Caribbean town. There are cannons firing, shells exploding, rowdy pirates, and drunken pigs. After the battle, the pirates sing and carry on in hilarious fashion. Disney first built the Pirates of the Caribbean at Disneyland in California. When it proved popular, they copied and improved it in the Magic Kingdom.

The author can't stand and walk and he didn't have someone to lift and carry him, so he missed one of the best attractions at Walt Disney World. If the author's situation applies to our readers, we recommend they detour around The Pirates of The Caribbean and move on to the more accessible attractions.

Tropical Serenade (Enchanted Tiki Birds)

This is the only attraction in Adventureland accessible to

people remaining in their wheelchairs. The theater is a comfortable place on a hot, crowded day. The attendants usually spot someone using a wheelchair and politely direct them through the crowds to a convenient viewing area.

Visitors witness more of Disney's AudioAnimatronic characters. Silly but cute, talking, singing, and whistling birds, flowers, and Tiki god statues provide the show. There are over two-hundred of these electronic marvels amazing and entertaining their guests. Small children enjoy the show more than anyone, so if they're members of the group, we recommend seeing the Tropical Serenade.

FRONTIERLAND

Frontierland is Disney's vision of America during its early years. Most of the attractions are familiar due to their widespread depiction in movies. Here again, some of the attractions are inaccessible to physically disabled people. We describe the attractions in light of the author's experience as a disabled person using a wheelchair. This enables everyone to decide what to try and what to avoid.

Diamond Horseshoe Jamboree

This is a live show, sort of an "Old West Vaudeville" act. Physically disabled visitors view it from their wheelchairs while sitting at a table with everyone else. They order food and drinks and enjoy their meals in a relaxing, fun atmosphere.

The show is a professional song and dance routine with a lot of silly jokes. The costumes, dancers, and singers are attractive, clever, and sure to bring a few smiles. Many people feel it is one of the better attractions in the Magic Kingdom.

Remember the show requires reservations. You should make these on the day of the show, early in the morning, as soon as you enter the Magic Kingdom. You (or a member of your party) must appear in person at the Hospitality House, across from the City Hall in Main Street, U.S.A. If you can't get reservations, appear at the entrance to the Jamboree about 45 minutes before the show starts, and hope someone cancels. People using wheelchairs find the ramp on the right side of the entrance. In most cases, attendants notice someone in a wheelchair and direct them to a table.

Country Bear Jamboree

This is a theater-type presentation accessible to people using wheelchairs. The show is pure Disney genius. The cast members are a group of charming, animated, life-size bears. When the lights dim and the act begins, about 20 of these lovable bruins keep their audience laughing and grinning throughout the 16-minute show. There are even talking moose. Their heads, mounted on one of the stone walls, are highlighted by spotlights when they speak.

The author has one critical comment. The Disney attendant directed him to an area off to the left side of the theater. The view from there was poor, and detracted from the enjoyment of the show. This is a popular attraction; you should arrive early. There may be a waiting line, but that shouldn't discourage anyone. Once the lines begin moving, they disappear quickly. Those using wheelchairs should enter from the left and get the attention of an attendant. If they can not reach an attendant, they might ask a companion or stranger for assistance. The attendants courteously direct them to a viewing, or should we say, parking area.

Frontierland Shootin' Arcade

The Shootin' Arcade is next to the Country Bear Jamboree. Instead of real bullets, the Hawken, fur-trapper-era rifles shoot infrared light beams. Otherwise, the heavy guns are like the real thing. The targets are on Boot Hill, in an Old West town. If you hit a tombstone, it disappears or changes its epitaph; when you score the bullseye on the gravediggers shovel, a skull pops out of the ground.

Wheelchair users enter the Arcade using the ramp to the left of the entrance. There are two positions set up for people using wheelchairs. The author tried this and felt silly alongside the kids, but admits he enjoyed it. He held the rifle by leaning on the shooting bench and banged away like everyone else. Someone less able with their hands and arms can still shoot the guns with the aid of a companion. Note that shooters must insert a quarter into the machine for each 15 shots.

If you are lucky, as the author was, you'll get caught in a "gunfight" between cowboys and bank-robbers in front of the Country Bear Jamboree. The cast members are enthusiastic. They run around shouting and shooting their six-guns, falling down, and "dying" when shot. Of course the good guys win. Anyone who has seen a cowboy movie recognizes what's happening. The fun thing is being close to the action. Carefully choreographed, the act gives only the impression of danger. Maybe they aren't John Wayne or Clint Eastwood, but it's still fun. People using wheelchairs enjoy the show as much as anyone.

Splash Mountain
Splash Mountain is a popular, wet, and wild ride typical of other water theme parks. Disney opened the ride on the weekend of October 4, 1992. They bill it as one of the longest flume-type rides in the world. It's 87 feet high and covers 9.2 acres. The theme is a take-off on the animated Disney movie *Song of the South*.

The ride combines a water-borne, roller coaster-type ride with Disney's special effects. The ten-minute ride goes through caves and backwoods swamps, climaxing in a steep (about 60 feet), drop down a water-filled chute. More than just physically thrilling, the ride passes at least 100 animated critters.

Undoubtedly, Splash Mountain will include waiting lines. Visitors will rush to it as they do Space Mountain. People using wheelchairs aren't going to compete with the mad dashers or teenagers. One thing physically disabled people learn, like it or not, is patience.

It's questionable whether physically disabled people can ride Splash Mountain. The author went on the Space Mountain ride, which is similar. He got on by lifting himself out of his chair and into the space vehicle. It wasn't too rough for him and when he knew he survived, he loved it. Presumably, he could do the same thing at Splash Mountain. Physically disabled people lacking the upper body strength to transfer themselves, will require lifting and carrying by their companions. If this isn't possible, then pass on the ride. There are other great attractions.

A note of caution: someone with little or no control over their upper bodies might find these rides uncomfortable and frightening. It is essential that people know their abilities or those of their companions. Combining that knowledge with our descriptions of the attractions in Walt Disney World, they can avoid being disappointed and enjoy the area along with everyone else.

Big Thunder Mountain Railroad

Does a ride through a mountain in a run-away mine train sound exciting? Well maybe, but not necessarily for everyone. The Big Thunder Mountain Railroad goes around and through an artificial red rock mountain with scenery and action reminiscent of the Gold Rush days of the United States. The mountain is 197 feet high and the track is about a half-mile long. The ride passes a flooded mining town named Tumbleweed and uses AudioAnimatronic characters in its skits. Disney made the scenery realistic. They spent over $300,000 collecting antique mining equipment from around the west. People have difficulty seeing all the amusing characters and critters the first time around. At least that's their excuse for riding the run-away train again and again.

Big Thunder Mountain is impressive by itself. Supposedly planned for 15 years and two years in the making, it incorporates 4,675 tons of cement, 650 tons of steel, and 16,000 gallons of paint. Disney designed it like a real rock formation in the American desert. They spent a few dollars making the mountain, like $17 million, almost equaling that invested in building Disneyland in California. Even if physically disabled people are handicapped by being unable to get on the ride, they enjoy the visual effects. Disabled passengers have a good view of the mountain and its activity from the Walt Disney World Railroad as it circles the park.

The Big Thunder Mountain Railroad ride is fast, turbulent, and lasts about four minutes. It's similar to a roller coaster; anyone prone to motion sickness or easily frightened should avoid it. The author asked if he could get on the ride. The ride attendant asked the author if he could stand and walk. This sounds like a stupid question to someone in a wheelchair. More than once, the author felt like replying, "If I could walk, why would I be in this wheelchair?" The point is, the author can't stand and walk and they wouldn't allow him on the ride. Their policy is, in case the ride malfunctions, all passengers must be able to walk at least 300 feet to get off the ride.

Disney policy prohibits people with back or neck braces from riding. They recommend against pregnant women riding. (Do pregnant women consider themselves handicapped?) A person with a visual impairment must be accompanied by a companion other than their guide dog.

As a sideline, the author saw active, strong, and healthy paraplegics turned away from the ride. It's a common misconception that everyone in a wheelchair is weak and fragile. We've all seen men and women pushing wheelchairs in marathon road races. Do they look weak and fragile? We think they could easily handle the Big Thunder Mountain Railroad. A responsible adult usually knows what he or she can and can't do. They know if they mind being picked up and carried. We assume Disney is concerned about everybody's safety. Still, it's a curious fact that the author rode Space Mountain. We wonder why Disney allowed him that opportunity and not the Big Thunder Mountain Railroad.

> "Only those who will risk going too far can possibly find out how far one can go." —— T.S. Eliot

Walt Disney World Railroad

This is the same ride that originates at Main Street, U.S.A. We mention it here because this is one of the stops for wheelchair users to get on the train. They must go up a fairly steep ramp to reach the level of the train. Once there, one of the engineers lowers a ramp from the leading passenger car for access. He pulls them onto the train, and locks their wheelchairs in a forward-looking position. People using wheelchairs can stay in them while safely enjoying the trip. There's room for two people in wheelchairs, sitting side-by-side.

When you ride, you get an overview of the Magic Kingdom. Although not an exciting ride, it is enjoyable. The train goes behind Big Thunder Mountain, providing a glimpse of the old mining camp. It also passes a replica of an American Indian encampment with a teepee and Indians tanning buffalo hides.

The most efficient plan involves taking the train all the way around the Magic Kingdom and returning to the station in Frontierland. Wheelchair users wanting the best view should sit on the right hand side. This allows a view from the open-air cars toward the Magic Kingdom. The author didn't enjoy being locked in a forward-looking position, and found he couldn't see or take photos the way he wanted. However, locking the wheelchairs in place is one of the Disney safety regulations.

Tom Sawyer Island

The Island is in the northwestern corner of the Magic Kingdom. It's surrounded by the Rivers of America and feels isolated and reminiscent of backwoods Missouri. It's a great place for kids between the ages of five and fifteen, but less than ideal for people using wheelchairs.

You take a flat wooden raft across the river. People using wheelchairs might get to the Island, but there won't be much they can do. There are numerous stairs, a dark and narrow cave, hilly and steep dirt paths, a hanging rope bridge, and a floating barrel bridge. The obstacles are unpleasant, if not impossible, when using a wheelchair.

On the Island, among the hills and trees, are Harper's Mill, a windmill, and an old waterwheel. You reach Fort Sam Clemens, a frontier outpost made of logs, by crossing a hanging bridge. There is a guardhouse with an AudioAnimatronic, scruffy-looking drunk, his dog, a few chickens, and a couple of horses. The upper level of the guard house has air guns to fire at imaginary enemies. With a little searching, you find a dark, winding, escape tunnel from the fort.

Adults using wheelchairs can accompany children to the Island. The attractions are self-guided, so older children can wander around by themselves. This requires faith that they find their way back at a pre-arranged time. Children love exploring and playing on the Island. It would be a shame for them to miss it because someone in their group is using a wheelchair. In the following section, we show an alternate way physically disabled people can see and enjoy the Island.

LIBERTY SQUARE

Liberty Square is between Frontierland and the Cinderella Castle. Here, Disney creates an impression of Colonial America. The transition from Frontierland is subtle but unmistakable. The buildings are faced with brick or painted boards, and decorated with fancy wooden moldings. Even the glass in the windows looks old. There are brightly colored flowers in boxes and the landscaping is immaculate. Visitors feel as if they are in Philadelphia in 1776.

If you become hot and tired, Liberty Square offers a quiet place to cool off and relax. Behind the Silversmith Shop, there are tables with umbrellas and trees providing shade. There are times when the crowds and noise become overwhelming, and this might be especially true for physically disabled people. Touring the Magic Kingdom shouldn't become an ordeal. If you sense you or your companions are becoming stressed, we suggest taking a break in Liberty Square.

Liberty Square Riverboat

The Riverboat is the best way of seeing Tom Sawyer Island for people using wheelchairs. It's ideal for people handicapped by the walking and climbing required on the Island. The Liberty Square Riverboat is a steam-driven, paddle-wheel riverboat named the *Richard F. Irvine*. The boat sails around the Island in about 16 minutes. They built the boat at Walt Disney World as a re-creation of the paddle-wheelers moving passengers and cargo on the rivers of America in the 1800's. It is accurate, except that it moves around the seven-foot deep Rivers of America on an underwater steel rail.

You board the boat at the Riverboat Landing on the east side of the Rivers of America, across from Tom Sawyer Island. Access is simple for people using wheelchairs. They wheel freely around on the wooden decks. If it's crowded, they should sit towards the front and along the rail for the best view. The cruise is smooth and pleasant, allowing people to remain in their wheelchairs while enjoying the trip.

You see Fort Sam Clemens and most of what is on Tom Sawyer Island. It becomes obvious why the Island is a poor place for people using wheelchairs, with its hills, stairs, and bridges. Along the way, those with sharp eyes see deer and other animals in the woods. A burning log cabin, presumably torched by marauding Indians, adds to the frontier environment.

Mink Fink Keelboats

Another way of seeing Tom Sawyer Island and the Rivers of America is by riding the Mike Fink Keelboats. The view from the boats, as they circle Tom Sawyer Island, is as nice as that from the Liberty Square Riverboat. Getting on the keelboats is not as nice. People using wheelchairs must climb into the smaller craft or be carried by companions. The keelboat trip takes about ten minutes. It's more intimate and adventurous than the Liberty Square Riverboat, but hardly worth the effort if visitors or their companions are physically disabled.

There are two boats, the *Bertha Mae* and the Gullywhumper. The boats are replicas of the keelboats of the late 1700's and early 1800's. Mike Fink was an infamous captain of these boats, when according to Disney, he met Davey Crockett. The boats are small, perhaps 25 feet long. They were rowed with oars or pushed by poles and could be used on narrow and shallow rivers. They carried settlers and their goods westward from the eastern states and into the wilderness. Roads and wagons came later.

The Hall Of Presidents

> *"Most folks are about as happy as they make up their mind to be."* —— Abe Lincoln

The Hall of Presidents is an example of how the Magic Kingdom is magic and accessible for physically disabled people. The theater holds approximately 700 people and there's rarely a long wait.

The presentation begins with a short film shown on a huge screen. The film discusses the United States of America's Constitution. It serves as an educational and inspiring introduction to the Constitution's meaning and significance.

The complete show takes about 25 minutes. It's a change of pace from the humor and excitement of much of the Magic Kingdom, but the show is impressive. Following the film, a roll call begins, including all of America's Presidents. Disney presents each of our past and present leaders as an animated character. Each responds when introduced while others twitch and fidget, much as they might if really alive. The Disney designers researched and copied minute details, ranging from clothing to hairstyles and facial expressions, making this one of their best animated displays. Following the introductions, President Lincoln provides a few words of inspiration. Older adults appreciate the show the most, but everyone gains from the experience.

The Haunted Mansion

The Haunted Mansion is one of Disney's finest attractions. It is an eight-minute ride in a moving vehicle through a huge Victorian mansion, with dozens of special effects. There are eyes staring from the wallpaper, a suit of armor that comes alive, and a frightened cemetery watchman appearing with his mangy dog. A woman's face appears in a crystal ball while holographic ghost images fly over your head.

The ride is accessible to most physically disabled people. However, if they are using wheelchairs, they must leave them and get into one of the moving vehicles. The author managed this by himself and so could others. The ride's vehicles look like horse-drawn carriages. They're covered and made of hard, black plastic. They seat two or three people.

One of the ride's attendants directed the author to the exit area when he asked how he could get on the ride. During the ten-minute wait, he met a couple from England. They were escorting their daughter who was using a wheelchair. They talked about accessibility and the English father explained how he could lift and carry his daughter into the ride. Noting that the author was alone, the man from England asked if he could lend a hand. The author, although confident of his ability to transfer himself, asked him to stand beside him while he tried getting in one of the cars. He asked the man to help lift his legs only if it was obvious he needed the help. We think it's worth noting the sense of urgency a disabled person feels in this type of situation. Yes, it's as simple as getting into an automobile, but one that's going to start moving in two minutes — whether they're in or not.

They stopped the ride. The author wheeled up to an empty car and locked the brakes on his wheelchair. Swinging the footrests out of the way, he lifted his feet and legs through the narrow (approximately 18-inches), opening into the car. The vehicles are solid and provide a stable lifting surface. With one hand on his wheelchair and the other on the side of the car, he lifted himself in. The moving vehicles at each Disney attraction are slightly different. The ones in the Haunted Mansion are among the easiest for those transferring from a wheelchair. He wasn't terribly graceful, but the author is no gymnast and certainly not a "super" paraplegic.

Once in the vehicle, the Disney attendants took away his wheelchair and placed it near the exit for his return. The ride went smoothly. We think people more severely disabled than the author could enjoy it. Anyone with limited upper body strength, such as quadriplegics, should ride with a companion to help them stay upright. This will also alleviate a bit of the fear associated with being out of their familiar wheelchairs. Exiting the vehicle was the same. They stopped the ride and brought the author's wheelchair. He placed his feet and legs out first, and grabbed on to his chair and the side of the ride vehicle. Then, as it feels to him, he leaped out of the car, sort of crashing into his wheelchair. It wasn't pretty, but it got the job done.

FANTASYLAND

Fantasyland is a favorite of children and everyone can enjoy it. However, people with physical disabilities must work a little harder to find the enchantment. Of the eleven major attractions in Fantasyland, only two are accessible to people remaining in their wheelchairs. People with so-called "limited mobility", that is those able to transfer themselves or be lifted by others, can experience a few more of the attractions. People must carefully consider their own and their companions' abilities. What are their ages? What do they really want to see? Remember, you can always enjoy the overall atmosphere.

Fantasyland is on the north side of the Magic Kingdom, behind the Cinderella Castle. Entering from the Liberty Square area and turning left, the first attraction is one of the best.

Magic Journeys

Magic Journeys is a wide screen, 70mm film producing three-dimensional images. You wear silly-looking polarized glasses to get the effect created by two simultaneously operating cameras. The theater is accessible for everyone using wheelchairs, even if they must or wish to remain in them. Visitors using wheelchairs enter the theater and stay to the left. Attendants guide them to a reserved seating area.

The show runs for 25 minutes. It is stunningly real, so much so it frightens some people. When a flower fills the screen, or lightening flashes, it's hard avoiding a flinch. The film is a time-tested favorite. Originally shown at Journey into Imagination in the Epcot Center, Disney moved it to the Magic Kingdom. There is rarely a waiting line and on a hot day, the cool, air-conditioned theater offers a welcome refuge.

Peter Pan's Flight

The next attraction is Peter Pan's Flight. This is a two-minute ride in a suspended vehicle. Wheelchair-users must leave their chairs. The procedure is similar to that in The Haunted Mansion. They must transfer themselves or be lifted by companions. The ride is gentle, amusing, and fun.

Peter Pan was the boy who would never grow up. He comes from a story written by the Scottish playwright Sir James M. Barrie. Walt Disney made this into a movie, first shown in 1953. Recently, Robin Williams as Peter Pan and Dustin Hoffman as the notorious Captain Hook starred in a remake.

Visitors ride in miniaturized pirate ships through the dark and on to "Never-Never Land." Music adds to the atmosphere, with songs such as *You Can Fly, You Can Fly, You Can Fly*.

It's A Small World

> *"In my belief, you cannot deal with the most serious things in the world unless you also under-stand the most amusing"* — Winston Churchill

Directly across the street from Peter Pan's Flight is an attraction no one should miss. Fortunately, no one has to. Even the most severely disabled people — those who must remain in their wheelchairs — can experience It's A Small World. Small barge-type boats make it easy to roll aboard. The boarding process takes a few seconds and is easy and comfortable. The boats appear to float, but are guided along underwater rails.

In a large, air-conditioned building, you sit back and enjoy the ride through a fantasy world of little people. Moving slowly along, with the theme song, *It's A Small World* playing continuously, you encounter an endless array of animated dolls. They represent people from all corners of the world. It seems silly at first, but grows progressively more appealing.

Looking left and right and back again, around every bend, there are little people. They're dressed as wooden soldiers, bagpipe players, London Tower guards, and Dutch children with wooden shoes. These are a few of the hundreds of small characters delighting visitors to It's A Small World.

Skyway To Tomorrowland

The Skyway is a gondola carrying people over the Magic Kingdom from Fantasyland to Tomorrowland. It is much like the hanging cable-cars used at ski resorts for carrying people up the mountains.

Disabled people using wheelchairs find the best access to this ride in Fantasyland between Peter Pan's Flight and It's a Small World. Still, they must leave their chairs and pick them up on the return. Walking people can get on and off at either end of the ride, but the stairs at Tomorrowland handicap many physically disabled wheelchair-users.

The gondolas of the Skyway provide an overview of the Magic Kingdom. Otherwise, the ride is uneventful and we're not enthusiastic about it because of its inaccessibility. Basically, it's just another link in the Magic Kingdom transportation system. Most people find it faster to walk or roll to Tomorrowland.

Fantasy Faire

On the north side of Fantasyland, there is an open-air show area for live performances. These kinds of shows are always fun and accessible to people using wheelchairs. Visitors wishing to see these shows should refer to the daily schedule of events, or ask an attendant when the next show begins. They should plan on arriving 10 to 15 minutes early, insuring themselves of a good viewing area.

Dumbo, The Flying Elephant

The flying elephants are south of Fantasy Faire and next to the 20,000 Leagues Under The Sea attraction. The elephants are favorites of children under ten years old. Dumbo is inaccessible to physically disabled people unless they are very agile and skilled at getting out of their wheelchairs. Of course small children can be lifted and placed in one of the flying elephants. It's a good idea for an adult to ride with them.

The Flying Elephant comes from a Disney movie made in 1941 called *Dumbo*. This is one of Disney's early animated features. Young Dumbo discovers he can fly with his huge ears after drinking too much champagne. Timothy Mouse, Dumbo's friend, helps him join the circus and become a star. You see Timothy on the mirrored ball in the center of the ride. The ride is similar to others found in amusement parks around the country. Except for the Disney theme, there's little that's exciting or unusual. The elephants contain a seat holding two adults and perhaps one or two children. Attached by steel spokes to the center of the ride, they rotate around in a circle and dip and rise in the air for about two minutes.

The elephant cars are made of sturdy plastic but have narrow, 12 to 18 inch wide doors. These create a very difficult entry for people transferring from a wheelchair. A physically disabled adult might as well pass up Dumbo.

Cinderella's Golden Carousel
Cinderella's Carousel is an old fashioned carnival ride and one of the prettiest anyone will ever see. It is in the center of Fantasyland. The ride consists of a circular platform carrying wooden horses and their riders as the carousel turns. As nice as Cinderella's Carousel is, it isn't for physically disabled children or adults. Riders must climb, or have someone lift them on the horses, and hold on to a pole while the horses turn and slowly move up and down. We suppose an adult could stand next to and hold a disabled child, but even that might prove difficult. We think disabled people should content themselves with watching.

Cinderella's Carousel is worth seeing. Disney found an old carousel in New Jersey that was built in 1917 with the help of Italian woodcarvers. Disney restored the horses, upgraded the machinery, painted everything, and included scenes from the Cinderella story. As the Carousel turns, visitors hear some of their favorite Disney songs, like, *Chim-Chim Cheree* and *When You Wish Upon A Star*. It's especially charming at night when its lights are on.

20,000 Leagues Under The Sea

From Cinderella's Carousel, you move to the northeast and see the 20,000 Leagues Under The Sea Lagoon. You get a view of this attraction at a railing on the north side of the Magic Kingdom. However, unless you can walk or be easily carried, that's all you can do — view it from a distance.

The attraction consists of a blue-green lagoon and submarines allowing a view of an imaginary undersea world. Passengers on the submarines must walk down nine steep steps and negotiate a narrow passageway. Disembarking is just as difficult, involving a climb up a few stairs. A small, light-weight disabled person can be carried aboard by a companion. The effort would be substantial, even if Disney allowed it. The author looked at the submarines and carefully studied how people got on and off. It was obvious he couldn't participate.

Disney obtained their inspiration for the 20,000 Leagues Under The Sea attraction from Jules Verne, who wrote the original story about Captain Nemo, his undersea craft, and his fantastic adventures. Disney made a movie from the novel in 1954 and then created this attraction in the Magic Kingdom.

Disney built graceful-looking submarines, like the one in the movie. They don't actually go under the water, but passengers get that impression as they peer through submerged port-holes. The 61-feet long, 58-ton, 38-passenger submarines are interesting to look at because they appear so real. They travel an underwater track through the lagoon. Passengers view underwater vegetation, coral, fish, clams, seahorses, and are attacked by a giant squid. The creatures aren't real but the effect is fun. Disney shows the lost city of Atlantis and a polar ice cap as Captain Nemo plays his ominous-sounding organ. The total trip time is about ten minutes.

Mad Tea Party

You find a spinning ride in the Mad Hatter's teacups south of the entrance to 20,000 Leagues Under The Sea, and adjacent to the entrance of Mickey's Starland. The novelist Lewis Carroll wrote the story called *Alice in Wonderland*. In

1951, Disney made an animated cartoon from the book and used it as their inspiration for this attraction. Disney derived the ride from a scene in the movie where the Mad Hatter holds a tea party for his guests.

The ride is similar to many found in amusement parks around the country. It involves different colored tea cups on a rotating platform. As the base turns, riders control the rate the individual cups spin with a wheel in the center of the cups. The Mad Tea Party is popular with children and teens, but not those with physical disabilities. First of all, it's difficult getting into the teacups. For people using wheelchairs, this means getting out of them and maneuvering through a narrow doorway and into one of the teacups. A small person can be lifted from their wheelchair and into the ride. Each teacup seats five or six people. An adult should sit with and hold a disabled child.

The rapidly spinning cups present a problem. As they turn, they subject their passengers to considerable centrifugal force. It can be frightening and dangerous for people without good muscle control over their upper bodies. The author didn't try the ride. He was without partners to lift him, and even then, he thought he would have difficulty holding himself in a sitting position.

Mr. Toad's Wild Ride

Mr. Toad's Ride isn't as wild as its name implies. It appeals to youngsters, and although it might frighten some young children, it's fun for everyone — if they can get on. It's similar to other attractions in the Magic Kingdom. Physically disabled people using wheelchairs must leave them and transfer into a seat in one of the ride vehicles. They can use the aid of their companions, but as usual, the Disney attendants can't help. The ride takes three minutes. It's relatively tame, so disabled people can enjoy it without discomfort or danger. NOTE: For more information on access for physically disabled people, see our description of The Haunted Mansion.

The inspiration for the ride comes from a 1949 Disney production called *The Adventures of Ichabod and Mr. Toad*. Disney based their cartoon on the novel *The Wind in the*

Willows, by Kenneth Grahame. In the Disney version, Mr. J. Thaddeus Toad is conned by a group of weasels. They fool him into trading his mansion for an automobile. In the Magic Kingdom, people enter one of these cars and careen along the road to Nowhere In Particular. The ride is like a Disney "spook-house." Its passengers move through darkened rooms lit by black lights and neon paint. The scary parts of the ride occur when the automobiles smash through a fireplace, when a suit of armor falls, and as they crash through a chicken coop.

Snow White's Adventures

This is the last major attraction in Fantasyland and it's found east of the Cinderella Castle. The three-minute ride in a moving vehicle is similar to Mr. Toad's Wild Ride, but with a different theme.

Snow White is a familiar character from one of the Grimm Brother's fairy tales. Walt Disney transformed the story into his first animated full-length movie in 1937 and 1938. Most children know the story and enjoy the ride. You go through darkened rooms and are suddenly confronted by an ugly witch. Young children can be frightened by her spectacle, especially at the end, where she drops a rock and fills their vision with stars.

Access to this ride is similar to other rides requiring a transfer from a wheelchair into a car-type vehicle. As with the others, disabled people make their transfer in the exit area. The attendants stop the ride momentarily and people must transfer themselves or be lifted by friends. It's not a turbulent ride, but people should know their companion's abilities and consider if they are easily frightened. If there is any doubt, have a brave member of the group take the ride and provide a first-hand report.

MICKEY'S STARLAND

Anyone with children should visit Mickey's Starland. Since the opening of the Magic Kingdom, this is the only new area. Disney realized how popular their cartoon characters were and decided to give them their own "land." Located off the beaten track, it's in the northeast corner of the Magic Kingdom, between Fantasyland and Tomorrowland. Best of all, the attractions are accessible to physically disabled people. This includes people who want to, or must, remain in their wheelchairs.

A live stage show featuring Disney cartoon characters, called Mickey's Starland Show, highlights the area. The performers are people (don't tell the kids) dressed like Mickey Mouse, Chip and Dale, or Goofy. Children can hardly contain themselves when seeing their favorite cartoon friends. They bring smiles to a few adult's faces as well. The attractions include Mickey's House, Grandma Duck's Petting Farm, and an abundance of colorful buildings and props.

Grandma Duck's Petting Farm
The Petting Farm appears on the right-hand side as you enter Mickey's Starland from Fantasyland. Disney states the area is "wheelchair accessible," but most of the paths are covered with gravel. Nobody pushing a wheelchair through deep, soft gravel would consider it accessible. However, if someone is insistent about seeing the animals, and there's a wheelchair involved, they can do it, with a little help from their friends.

Grandma Duck's Petting Farm includes a small barn and 10 to 12 live farm animals. There are goats, small pigs, ducks, chickens, and Minnie Moo, a cow with a natural marking on her side shaped like Mickey Mouse's head. You wander among the animals and touch them through their enclosing fences. The animals are unique in a land filled with animated characters. The petting farm offers you the opportunity of teaching children the difference between "real" and "animated."

Mickey's House
While other buildings in the area are miniaturized, Mickey's is life-sized. You find it across and down the street from the Petting Farm. In front of the house, note his funny-looking car with its balloon tires and Pluto's doghouse. When you enter, you see Mickey's bedroom and hear popular Disney songs played from a radio in the den. A television broadcasts

episodes of *The Mickey Mouse Club*. Another room contains photos of Mickey and Walt Disney. Unless it's very crowded, touring this area is easy for people using wheelchairs.

After Mickey's House, you proceed into a waiting area for the live show. Signs point the way to Mickey's Magical TV World. A large screen shows cartoons like *Rescue Rangers, Tale Spin,* and *Duck Tales*. When prompted by Mickey Mouse, you move through a decorated entry tunnel into the theater.

The stage show features characters like Mickey Mouse, Scrooge McDuck, Launchpad McQuack, and Chip and Dale. The show is lively, amusing, and ends with the audience joining in the songs.

Leaving the show, you enter the Mickey Mouse Club Funland Tent and find yourself surrounded by a cartoon skyline. You discover an area where video cameras project your image onto television screens. You encounter other activities, such as audio entertainment, a popcorn shop with boxes that pop, a firehouse, and Mickey Mouse's Walk of Fame, with Disney characters instead of those from Hollywood.

Just outside the exit is Mickey's dressing room. People with patience have a chance of meeting the famous mouse and having their photo taken with him. A photo makes a lasting impression on children and provides a fine souvenir.

There's a playground for children in Mickey's Starland. It is similar to others with ladders, slides, and tunnels, but most physically disabled people find it inaccessible. If a disabled adult is accompanying children, the disabled person can watch and supervise.

Mickey's Starland has the usual vending carts selling drinks, ice cream, and cookies. These are scattered throughout the Magic Kingdom. No one goes thirsty or hungry.

TOMORROWLAND
Tomorrowland occupies most of the eastern half of the Magic Kingdom. Today was tomorrow when Disney designed the

area and built it in 1971. They created an attraction depicting life in the future. The result is as pleasing now as it was then. Best of all, physically disabled people find most of the attractions accessible. For our purposes, we see Tomorrowland as the best of all worlds in the Magic Kingdom.

The author enjoyed the rides and witnessed many disabled people doing the same. Especially memorable were a group of teenagers from Wisconsin. Their baseball caps and lack of hair revealed their ongoing battles with cancer. He watched as they left their wheelchairs and got on the Space Mountain roller coaster. They were going for the gusto, in spite of the handicaps.

Their enthusiasm inspired him and their courage humbled him. Others warned the author against riding Space Mountain. They said, "It's too rough, you'll get sick, and besides, you won't be able to get on it." As readers will see, thanks to those kids from Wisconsin, he tried it, survived it, and loved it. We think many physically disabled people can do the same.

Grand Prix Raceway

The first attraction is the Grand Prix Raceway. This is a reduced-scale Grand Prix-type race track. The race cars are smaller versions of the real thing. They seat two people and are powered by gasoline engines. They boast rack and pinion steering, disc brakes, and run on rubber tires. Hot stuff — except they have a top speed of less than ten miles an hour!

Pre-teenage boys are first in line at the Grand Prix Raceway. Concerned parents can rest assured because of the low speeds and the fact that the cars are guided around the track by steel rails. Drivers control the cars with a steering wheel, but they can't side-swipe the other cars because of the rails. This sounds like a fun attraction for some physically disabled children, or adults, but there's a couple of problems.

First, the race cars have the usual gas pedals and foot brakes. Most people using wheelchairs have problems with muscular control over their feet and legs. They can drive full-sized cars with hand controls, but Disney hasn't thought of the idea. Our suggestion is for an adult to accompany a disabled child. The disabled child can steer, while the non-disabled adult operates the gas and brake pedals. The author thought of reversing the roles. He would ask a child to help him with the gas and brakes while he steered. He didn't, but it is possible.

Disney could equip a couple of the cars with hand controls like the author uses in his car. Hand controls work fine for physically disabled people. The author drives this way and has done so for 15 years.

The ride is very safe. However, the author found it mildly amusing watching the little drivers purposely, and with obvious delight, crash into the cars in front of them while approaching the end of the track. We suspect this is a case of "like father-like son." The cars move slowly and have bumpers to cushion the impact. There's no harm done. It adds to the children's fun.

Physically disabled, would-be race car drivers, must transfer or be lifted from their wheelchairs and into the miniature cars. We have no doubt that disabled children would enjoy this as much as their more able-bodied friends. Getting into and driving these cars would give them the experience of doing instead of watching. We all know positive experiences are important for children's self-confidence.

Space Mountain

A large, futuristic-looking, white building dominates the eastern half of the Magic Kingdom and contains the attraction known as Space Mountain. The building looks like a domed sports stadium, 180 feet tall and about 300 feet in diameter. The roller coaster ride in Space Mountain is a great attraction. However, it is not great for everyone. Some physically disabled people can experience Space Mountain, many can't. We think our description of the ride will help people decide if they want to try the roller coaster in Space Mountain.

Some roller coaster veterans claim Space Mountain is tame. Most other people get all the thrills they can handle. The space vehicles reach speeds of almost 30 miles per hour as they rocket their passengers through the darkness for two minutes and 38 seconds. On most roller coaster rides, passengers see their positions relative to the surroundings; they anticipate and prepare for each movement. Not in Space Mountain; because of the darkness, its riders just hang on, grit their teeth, or scream.

The author approached Space Mountain with a feeling of apprehension. His able-bodied sister wouldn't ride it because of her susceptibility to motion sickness. Disney's guide to Walt Disney World, *The Disabled Guests Guide Book*, says:

> "If you wish to experience the ride, plan to leave your wheelchair outside the attraction entrance. In order to board, you must be able to maneuver across catwalks, 100 feet in height, and down a series of ladders in an evacuation situation. Guests required to wear back, neck or leg braces will be unable to ride this attraction. This ride is not recommended for pregnant women."

From Disney's description, it didn't sound like a paraplegic, unable to stand and walk, and using a wheelchair, could experience Space Mountain. Also, the author wasn't eager to get sick, or hurt, or make a fool of himself. Despite his doubts, he rolled his wheelchair toward the entrance. He watched a group of teenagers get out of their wheelchairs and stand in line. Their enthusiasm inspired the author. He figured that if they could do it, maybe he could too.

An attendant asked if he could get out of his wheelchair. He replied that he could make a transfer and asked to look and decide for himself. The attendant agreed. While waiting in line, the author explained his situation to a man next to him. Mike, manager of *Kincaids*, "the most popular nightclub in Chicago," agreed to help. Mike insisted on pushing the author and his wheelchair up the ramp into the ominous-looking interior of Space Mountain.

On reaching the exit area of the ride, an attendant explained how he could stop the ride for 21 seconds while the author made the wheelchair to rocket transfer. Doubting his ability to make the maneuver in just 21 seconds, the author asked Mike to help if there was a problem. When they stopped the ride, the author rolled up to one of the small rocket-shaped cars and set his brakes, swung his footrests aside, and lifted himself in. Being in a rush, he sort of crashed down onto the bar designed to hold riders in, and then struggled to get his feet and legs back under the bar. He made it. Probably not in 21 seconds, but he made it. He thanked Mike, and the attendant took his wheelchair, keeping it for his return.

The ride began suddenly, plunging into the darkness. It gained speed and abruptly turned left, then right, then down, then up and down again. Stars blinked and lights flashed. There was no warning of when and where the next change in direction was coming.

At first, the author felt a bit panicked. He leaned forward and held on to the safety bar with all his strength, hoping he would survive. He was thankful for having strong arms and hands. Space Mountain would be dangerous for people without substantial upper-body strength and the ability to keep themselves from being whipped from side to side. "It's a good thing I lift weights," he thought.

Eventually, and none too soon, the ride ended. The author exited the car in the same way he got on, by himself. He was "pumped-up" and very happy for having experienced the ride. Leaving Space Mountain and returning to the sunshine, he knew the Magic Kingdom was magic. He knows that if he can do it, so can many other physically disabled people.

> *"I have learned to use the word 'impossible' with the greatest of caution."* — Wernher von Braun

Much is written and discussed about the strategy of how and when to visit Space Mountain. The ride is popular and long lines develop with people waiting to get in. For people with physical disabilities, we think racing around the Magic Kingdom, trying to beat others for access to the rides, is unrealistic. The optimum time for visiting is in the off season. Patience might be a virtue, but here it becomes a necessity. Disabled people usually know that. If they don't, they learn quickly.

Skyway

Visitors leaving Space Mountain see a loading tower for the Skyway. This aerial tram provides a scenic trip to Fantasyland. However, walking or rolling is faster than taking the Skyway, and at this point, disabled people face a stairway to the aerial tram. Unless a person can get out of a wheelchair and negotiate a flight of stairs, we advise forgetting the Skyway.

Starjets

Centered in Tomorrowland, Starjets is one of the few outdoor rides in the Magic Kingdom. A NASA-type rocket acts as the hub for ten or twelve "starjets." The two-passenger space vehicles dip up and down while circling the rocket. The ride lasts two minutes and it isn't up to the same exciting standards of other Disney creations. Starjets receives little notice in guidebooks to the Magic Kingdom. Ironically, these characteristics make Starjets a good attraction for some physically disabled people.

Starjets is a pleasant ride. It is rarely crowded because it can't compete in terms of excitement with rides like Space Mountain. Best of all, a person can approach the starjets and get into them from a wheelchair.

The author, wanting an experience of everything, asked a ride attendant if access to the ride was possible from his wheelchair. The attendant directed him to the exit area of the ride and took him in an elevator up two levels. He waited in line about five minutes.

Once on the loading level, the ride stopped and previous passengers disembarked. The author got directions to one of the small space vehicles and made his move. Rolling up alongside one of the cars, he set the brakes on his chair. A narrow wing surface on the jet made a good preliminary sitting place. Then, lifting his rear end into the ride's seat, he grabbed his legs and swung them into place. The whole maneuver took about one minute. The ride attendant took his wheelchair away, holding it for his return.

The starjets began slowly but soon picked up speed, looping up and down while flying around in a circle. Viewing the Magic Kingdom and enjoying the freedom of flight makes the ride worthwhile. The author enjoyed the ride as much as anyone.

More severely disabled people, like quadriplegics, might enjoy the ride. However, they need lifting into the starjets and the loving arms of a companion holding them in place. With help from a sensitive companion, almost anything is possible.

WEDway PeopleMover

Disney built Tomorrowland in 1971 as their image of what life might be like in the future. Unfortunately, their planning did not take into consideration millions of disabled Americans.

The WEDway PeopleMover is an example. These five-car "trains of the future," provide a pleasant and picturesque view of Tomorrowland. They use state-of-the-art technology, with pollution-free, linear induction motors quietly powering the ride. In our minds, it fails as a solution to our cities' transportation problems because of its inaccessibility. Maybe in a real "Tomorrowland," wheelchairs won't exist. We hope so.

The ride attendants prevented the author from pushing his wheelchair up the moving escalator ramp. The WEDway PeopleMover takes people along a mile of track, reaching speeds of ten miles per hour. It runs around and through most of the attractions in Tomorrowland. It moves through the waiting area inside Space Mountain, providing a view that gives people second thoughts about riding this roller coaster in the dark.

The inaccessibility of The WEDway PeopleMover is a minor handicap to visitors' enjoyment of the Magic Kingdom. There are other, more interesting attractions.

Carousel Of Progress

> *"To wish to progress is the largest part of progress"*
> —— Lucius A. Seneca

You should look for the large, circular building in the southeast corner of Tomorrowland to find the Carousel of Progress. Disney has gotten a lot of mileage from this 21-minute theater presentation. They first exhibited it in 1964 and 1965 at the World's Fair in New York City. In 1975, they moved it to the Magic Kingdom. You sit in a small theater that moves sequentially around six separate stages. Each scene depicts the development of electrical power and technology.

AudioAnimatronic characters tell the story. Viewers follow a typical American family from their first use of electric lights to the wizardry of modern technology. All the while, cheerful music accompanies the story.

This type of entertainment is Disney's real genius. It's clever and educational. Young children might become a bit bored, but everyone else gains a deeper appreciation of how far civilization has taken us. You shouldn't let the lack of thrills deter you from seeing this attraction. People using wheelchairs find it at least accessible, if not perfectly comfortable.

One difficulty experienced in the Carousel of Progress involved the seating arrangement for people using wheelchairs. The Disney attendants ushered the author to a seating area at the rear and to the side of the theater. The view from that angle was poor and he felt a little left out of the action. Another problem was parking his wheelchair on the incline where they directed him to sit. Anyone sitting in a wheelchair will agree on the discomfort of leaning forward for a long time. People using wheelchairs often have little or no control over the muscles in their upper bodies. They hold themselves up with their arms or lean back in their chairs. A simple, level platform for wheelchairs would solve the problem.

As a sidelight, if people have children with them, they should take some time, find a quiet place, and talk with them for a few moments. Encourage them to ask questions and explain the significance of the things they've seen. Technology is our future; it is our Tomorrowland. Children play the key role, disabled or not.

Tomorrowland Theater

If lively dance and music shows appeal to you, head for the Tomorrowland Theater. You find it on the southern side of Tomorrowland, next to the Carousel of Progress. Check for the show times on the billboard in front of the theater. During the author's latest visit, "Rap and Role" was showing.

The theater is an open-air affair, seating several hundred people. Children love the life-sized Disney characters. The performers, dressed as Disney cartoon characters, do their version of contemporary rap music. At other times, the Tomorrowland Theater features acts with jazz or rock music. The performers include members of the group, Kids of the Kingdom.

The theater is accessible to people remaining in their wheelchairs and for anyone else with a disability. If the thrill-a-minute rides and attractions don't suit your needs, you can see one of these shows. They are excellent.

Dreamflight

"The Wright brothers flew right through the smoke screen of impossibility." — Charles Kettering

Aviation enthusiasts should visit this attraction. Dreamflight is located in the large building across from the Carousel of Progress and next to the Tomorrowland Theater. You enter a gently moving vehicle for a five-minute ride. This means people using wheelchairs have to find a way of getting out of them and into the ride vehicles.

The author transferred himself from his chair into the ride vehicle with some difficulty. Again, Disney prohibits their cast members from lifting disabled people. If disabled people can't transfer themselves, they need the help of companions or friends. The moving vehicles rotate slowly and move up and down small inclines, but there's nothing rough. Any physically disabled person gaining access will enjoy it without being frightened by the movement.

We don't think it's unreasonable or unrealistic asking strangers for assistance. It just shouldn't be demanded or expected. Sometimes people are willing to help and other times not. It depends on what they are comfortable with and how they're approached. Most strangers quickly warm to the author when he is friendly and polite. They enjoy helping if they know they can do so without offending.

The presentation traces the history and thrills of man's effort and experience of flying. Special effects and stereo music provide a wonderful, entertaining experience. There are awesome wing-walking scenes, and incredible aerial acrobatics shown on a large screen. From the early days of aviation, riders move to scenes of modern flying feats leading into the jet-age. Near the end, the viewer is treated to a feeling of zooming through canyons and valleys lit by the sun and moon, and over cities of the future.

The ride is thrilling without being physically rough; it doesn't toss people around in their seats. This is important because few disabled people ever experience the thrill of flying in a real, small aircraft. Many can't get on or tolerate the turbulent rides in the Magic Kingdom that others can. If any physically disabled person can get in one of these moving vehicles, either by themselves or by being lifted, they should enjoy this attraction.

Once again, visitors should think about their individual circumstances, and plan accordingly. The experience is fun and educational. It surpasses a common video game on a computer screen or a movie on television. We would like seeing all physically disabled people experience and enjoy Dreamflight. We think everyone can.

Circlevision 360 American Journeys
One of Disney's strengths is making movies. Everyone finds

American Journeys a good example of the art of film making. The theater showing the film is in the same building as DreamFlight. Leaving Tomorrowland, before crossing the bridge leading to the central plaza, you turn left and find the entrance to Circlevision 360 American Journeys. The theater accommodates people using wheelchairs. Everybody should put this attraction high on their list of priorities.

Disney went to great lengths and expense making this film a unique experience. The movie is displayed on nine, 20-feet high by 30-feet wide, encircling screens. It's shown by nine separate projectors, and in effect, the movie places viewers in the center of the action. Looking around, you feel as if you're outside instead of in a theater. You see what is in front of you, to the sides, and to the rear.

A superb sound system enhances the realistic visual effects. It consists of 12 sound channels directed through nine surrounding speakers. Six additional speakers in the ceiling transmit the narration of the film.

Disney spent four years putting the film together. The camera crews traveled to places like Glacier Bay, Alaska, the Statue of Liberty in New York Harbor, and the Colorado Rockies. They took the cameras under water off the Florida coast and captured some great shots of surfers in Hawaii. They managed some spectacular film of Mt. St. Helens, the volcano, just two days after it blew in 1980. The images of the launch of the Space Shuttle Challenger are awesome. This may be the one of the best advertisements for the scenic wonders of America.

In creating these unique images, the photographers simultaneously used nine cameras. The multiple cameras made a recording of the entire 360-degree view, as seen from an airplane, helicopter, train, or whatever point they were filming. The results are breathtaking, so much so that some people suffer from motion sickness while watching. The motion sensed by viewers is a tribute to the realism of the film.
The theater handles over 3,000 people per hour, so waiting lines are short. The only viewers able to sit are those bring-

ing their own chairs. In this case, using a wheelchair has its advantages. Actually, most people have no problem standing for 20 minutes while engrossed in the movie.

People using wheelchairs enter the same place as everyone else. An attendant directs them to the optimum place for viewing. They shouldn't worry about being able to see from a sitting position while everyone else is standing. The surrounding screens are tall and provide a view for everyone.

Mission To Mars

The final attraction is the Mission To Mars. Leaving Tomorrowland and moving toward the Central Plaza, you find it on the right or north side of the street. The name of the attraction sounds exciting, but all of the action occurs in a theater-like environment. It's accessible to physically disabled people, including those remaining in their wheelchairs. The trip takes about 20 minutes.

If visitors are using a wheelchair, they should enter Mission To Mars on the right side of the turnstiles. Usually a host or hostess greets and directs them to a viewing area designated for people using wheelchairs. The simulated rocket ship vibrates slightly, so wheelchair users should make sure their brakes are set.

The special effects used in Mission To Mars may be obsolete when compared to other Disney World attractions, but most visitors enjoy them anyway. First, in a Mission Control Room, there's a pre-flight briefing establishing a feeling of suspense. Then they usher passengers into the flight vehicle.

The vehicle is actually a circular theater, sloping toward a central screen set in the floor. This provides everyone with an equally good view of the trip. Video screens on the walls, sound effects, shaking, and vibrations in the theater add realism to the journey. NASA's Mariner Nine program provided the video images of the planet Mars. These include an area called Mariner Valley and pictures of the largest volcano known in the universe. They named the volcanic feature Olympic Mons, and NASA estimates it's 40 miles in diameter.

LIVE SHOWS, PARADES AND FIRE-WORKS IN THE MAGIC KINGDOM

We described some of the handicaps physically disabled people face when visiting Walt Disney World's Magic Kingdom. Our purpose is providing physically disabled people with the information they need to make their visit more enjoyable. There's no question that many of the attractions are inaccessible. Maybe Disney could remove some of the barriers, but we can't control that. What we can do is show physically disabled people what is possible. Some of the better attractions, accessible to everyone, are the live shows, parades, and fireworks displays.

In contrast to other guidebooks on the Magic Kingdom, we encourage people to seek out live performances. The other guides ignore the fact that many visitors are physically disabled. They suggest that people on tight schedules should avoid lengthy shows and concentrate on action-oriented attractions. We advocate a different strategy. We recommend that physically disabled people allow themselves plenty of time, and actively seek out the accessible events and attractions.

First, it's important to learn what shows are playing and when and where the parades are. This information is available at the City Hall in Main Street U.S.A. You save time by reading this guide and determining what attractions are accessible. Then determine what your priorities are.

Street Shows

Disney changes the character and times of their shows, so this list is not absolute, but it is representative of what visitors experience.

DAPPER DANS

The Dapper Dans offer the four-part harmony of barbershop quartet singers in Main Street, U.S.A. The four men in straw hats and striped vests, sing, tell jokes, and tap dance.

The trick to enjoying this show, and others like it, is position. You need to know when the show starts and get there early. Usually visitors are polite about moving and making room for people using wheelchairs. Sometimes it becomes necessary to be assertive and ask them to move. It is common for people to get caught up in the excitement and be unaware someone behind them is sitting in a wheelchair.

WALT DISNEY WORLD MARCHING BAND

The Magic Kingdom has its own permanent marching band. They perform every morning in the Town Square in Main Street, U.S.A. The Band puts on a great display. Knowing the time they perform allows disabled people the opportunity for finding a good viewing position. Late arrivals find themselves behind a mass of people and unable to see. Sometimes, people using wheelchairs can work their way to the front of the crowd — but don't count on it.

The author once stood six feet, two inches tall. Now, in a wheelchair, he's acutely aware of what short people and children face while trying to view an event from a crowd. In more ways than one, being in a wheelchair provides a different view of the world.

REFRESHMENT CORNER PIANIST

The refreshment corner pianist is on the left and at the end of Main Street, as visitors face the Central Plaza. He entertains on an upright piano while people satisfy their hunger with hamburgers, hotdogs, and soft drinks.

ALL-AMERICAN COLLEGE MARCHING BAND

Disney has an annual summer program featuring marching bands from colleges around the United States. They perform throughout the Magic Kingdom in the afternoons and evenings. The City Hall information center has the exact times and places. They're always excellent. They seem to catch the magic of the Kingdom and rise to the occasion with youthful enthusiasm.

KIDS OF THE KINGDOM

These lively singers and dancers may be "kids", but they're polished professionals. The performer's energy and skill makes everybody smile and puts a spring in their step or in the push of their chair.

The Kids perform every day in the Castle Forecourt, in front of the Cinderella Castle. They sing and dance to popular Disney tunes. Costumed cartoon characters like Donald Duck, Winnie-the-Pooh, and Mickey Mouse join in the fun. The Castle Forecourt is centrally located and quickly found from any of the surrounding "lands." They appear on an elevated stage and their voices and music are amplified, so the show is easy to see and hear from almost anywhere. You get information on performance times at City Hall, near the entrance to the Magic Kingdom. Try making this show a priority.

FLAG RETREAT
In the evening, Disney doesn't just lower the American flag in the Magic Kingdom; they do it with style. In the Town Square, usually around 5:00 p.m., a color guard and small marching band appear and lower the flag. With a beautiful and emotional touch, they release a flock of white pigeons. These symbolize the white doves of peace, a nice wish. Of course they train the pigeons to fly home, where they're cared for and gathered for the next day's routine.

J. P. AND THE SILVER STARS
For an out-of-the-ordinary musical treat, you look for a stage near the Pirates of the Caribbean ride in Adventureland. The band adds the flavor of the Caribbean Islands to the atmosphere. They play a lively brand of music on steel drums. The music is sure to get everyone wiggling and giggling.

BANJO KINGS
This group performs music with a Roaring Twenties theme on banjos and washboards. You find them on Main Street. Again, check the schedule of events at the City Hall information center.

Parades In The Magic Kingdom
Parades are essentially moving street shows. Disney uses them as an integral part of their entertainment package and conducts them two and sometimes three times each day. The parades make ideal viewing for physically disabled people, especially those using wheelchairs.

The parades in the Magic Kingdom are special events, even if they do occur daily. Everyone has the opportunity of seeing dozens of costumed Disney characters and some dazzling special effects. The parades are popular, so plan accordingly. Stake out a good viewing area 15 to 30 minutes before they begin. This ensures an unobstructed view of the festivities.

The parades usually begin near the Fire Station in Main Street, U.S.A. They go around the Town Square and proceed up Main Street to the Central Plaza. They circle the front of the Cinderella Castle, proceed into Liberty Square, and end in Frontierland. Sometimes the parades follow the reverse route, beginning in Frontierland and ending in the Town Square.

The largest crowds are usually around the Central Square. The upper platform at the Walt Disney Railroad Station in Main Street, U.S.A. provides one of the best viewing areas. However, getting there in a wheelchair is difficult. Those using wheelchairs have to go up the three-level exit ramp. If time is available, and viewing the parade is a high priority, plan on getting to the platform 30 to 45 minutes early. In addition to the difficulty of getting to the platform, only a few spots have views not blocked by trees. Watching the parades is more practical from other places.

Disney reserves an area for people using wheelchairs in front of City Hall. Visitors shouldn't feel limited to this area alone. Many other locations are just as good. The key for wheelchair viewers, is establishing a place early and making sure people don't stand in front of them.

A nice place for watching the parades is in the Sleepy Hollow sandwich shop. Look for this on your right after crossing the bridge into Liberty Square from the Central Plaza. If early enough, you can order something to snack on and sit at a table near the rail. Then, you have a good view of the parades crossing the Liberty Square Bridge.

AFTERNOON PARADES
These begin around 3:00 p.m. They treat everyone to the

spectacle of marching bands and colorful floats carrying singing and dancing Disney cartoon characters. It's almost like the Mardi Gras in New Orleans.

EVENING PARADES

It will not be long before Disney is open 24-hours per day. At least it seems that way. Normally, they have one parade in the evening, starting at 9:00 p.m. If they stay open late, they have two, one at 9:00 p.m. and another at 11:00 p.m. For late-niters, the parades at 11:00 p.m. attract the smaller crowds.

Disney expanded the evening parades into hi-tech affairs, keeping with the times. These include huge holographs, fabulous clouds of harmless, colored smoke, and fascinating electrical displays. Combined with the usual Disney characters and music, the parades play a part in creating the magic in the Kingdom. Everyone with use of their eyes and ears enjoys the magic equally. There are few handicaps to watching and listening.

Fireworks In The Magic Kingdom

On the nights the Magic Kingdom is open late, Disney adds a final, dramatic touch. They launch a concentrated, four-minute fireworks display. They use the best of everything. The huge starburst shells come from Japan, and the white sparkles pouring from the sky come from England. This seems like over-kill, but we never see people turn their backs and walk, or roll away.

Special Events

As might be expected, Disney creates some special magic on days like the Fourth of July, Christmas, and New Year's Eve.

On the Fourth of July, celebrating America's Independence Day, they fire off a double-size fireworks display. They light up the sky over the Magic Kingdom and the Seven Seas Lagoon. Even though the Fourth of July brings some of the largest crowds, Disney rewards you with a fabulous visual feast.

At Christmas time, Disney pulls out all the stops in decorating the Magic Kingdom with Christmas trees and lights galore. They put together special parades, shows, and Christmas carolers. More people than usual find themselves drawn to the Magic Kingdom at Christmas, for good reason. No one does Christmas like Disney. The moderate temperatures are a consolation prize for visiting in the winter. Anyone bothered by the summer heat should consider this when planning their visit.

Then of course, there's New Year's Eve. The Christmas decorations are still up. The air still has a little nip in it, and Disney puts on another double fireworks display. They celebrate the old year and welcome the new. For people tolerant of crowds, Disney promises a show to remember.

NOTE: We feel it's important mentioning the effects crowded conditions have on disabled people. At the best of times, moving around is difficult for people with physical disabilities, whether they use a wheelchair, or not. Huge numbers of people magnify the problem. We don't want to discourage people from visiting, we want to warn them of the realities.

For a test of a disabled person's tolerance for crowded conditions, we suggest a short trip in their wheelchair. They can go by themselves, or with their traveling companions, through a busy shopping mall. If they absolutely hate it, we recommend avoiding the Magic Kingdom on its busiest days. However, living in a cocoon, sheltered from the rest of humanity, is not really living. Human beings are social animals, and so are disabled people. There's no difference.

PLACES TO EAT IN THE MAGIC KINGDOM

Sooner or later everyone needs to eat. You may not think this warrants much thought, but from experience, we do. Most people visiting the Magic Kingdom stay inside the boundaries of the park for an extended period of time, usually six or more hours. Traveling back and forth to your vehicles for lunch or dinner is impractical.

Adding to the dilemma, Disney prohibits people from bringing food into the Magic Kingdom. They don't literally search anyone, they just discourage it. This is understandable; it's not a picnic area. When hunger strikes, there are few options other than finding something to eat in the Magic Kingdom.

Eating in the Magic Kingdom presents several problems. We offer several solutions.

First, the food is expensive. Some people find this discouraging. Food is expensive in all of Walt Disney World. You can spend about $8 to $10 for breakfast, $6 for a fast-food lunch, and $15 to $25 or more for dinner. This is per person. It's roughly twice as expensive eating inside the Magic Kingdom as outside. Add this to the cost of your daily passes, motel, and auto rental, and you can feel depressed in a hurry.

The simplest solution is eating before leaving for the Magic Kingdom. An exception is if you plan on riding Space Mountain five times in a row and don't want to lose your lunch. If supervising some wild kids, it pays to monitor their eating habits. You should know yourself and your companions. The Magic Kingdom is quite a distance from your vehicle and lodging. It's a poor place to get sick.

It's easy finding eating places outside the Magic Kingdom. This makes logistical and financial sense. Many hotels, motels, and restaurants, including the Disney resorts, serve adequate and less expensive food. Many places have buffet-style breakfasts where people eat all they want. After a healthy breakfast, some people find they can go without eating until dinner.

Second, waiting in line and obtaining reservations can be excruciatingly time-consuming. A typical sit-down type meal might take an hour and a half. Fast-food takes a slow 45 minutes, at least. Considering the cost of a daily pass, time is money. If you have a surplus of time and money, relax. If you don't, give this a little thought.

Third, the food is mostly typical fast-food fare and not all that great. In fairness, the Magic Kingdom is an amusement park. Expecting fine cuisine is unrealistic. Most people don't mind and many enjoy the food. The author for example, enjoys eating an occasional chili dog, burger and fries, or ice cream bar. It seems to fit the atmosphere and mood of the Magic Kingdom.

Besides eating before leaving, and like a camel, loading up on food and water before the journey, we offer several options.

One solution is breaking the rules. Most people carry some kind of tote sack, purse, or pack. They can store food in these and stash them in the rental lockers. Then when they get hungry, they return to the rental lockers in the Main Street Train Station for a quick snack. Sandwiches or energy bars are ideal for this purpose. This trick is convenient, inexpensive, and possibly healthier than eating the typical fast food found in the Magic Kingdom.

Another idea is snacking from the vending carts. Who can resist a box of popcorn while watching a parade? An ice cream bar coated in chocolate provides energy, if not complete nutrition. Health-conscious people might find chocolate-covered bananas. If someone eats a substantial breakfast and dinner, snacking this way might be enough to keep them going all day.

Finally, if visitors have the time and the money, we recommend trying the restaurants. We think it's a mistake to turn a visit to the Magic Kingdom into a contest or a test of endurance. This is true for everyone, especially physically disabled people.

Traveling, often doing ordinary activities, can be an ordeal for physically disabled people. It's important that non-disabled people try to understand. Sometimes, they want and need a break. Sometimes the author feels exhausted after simply getting up in the morning. Imagine, being disabled and getting out of bed, lifting yourself into a wheelchair, getting into a bathroom, out of the chair, into a bathtub or shower, bathing, back into the chair, back to the bed, out of the chair, onto the bed, struggling to dress, back in the chair, out of the chair, into a car, out of the car, and back into the wheelchair. Whew! It's tiring just reading that. And that's only getting started. We think other disabled people feel the same. Add the stress of maneuvering through a crowd and being denied access to a few attractions, and it's easy understanding why a relaxing lunch in any kind of restaurant is such a pleasure. The restaurants are accessible to people using wheelchairs, and they are an experience all physically disabled people can enjoy.

There are as many opinions about food as there are people. We try to be objective in the pictures we paint of the eating places. This allows you the opportunity for making up your own mind about when and where you wish to eat. We divide the dining options into four categories, then we describe each in some detail. These categories are: street vendors, fast-food, one cafeteria, and the full-service restaurants.

We think "fast-food" receives undeserved criticism in other descriptions of the Magic Kingdom. It is what it is — fast. No one advocates it as a steady diet. It's quick and reasonably nutritious. Disney wants everything in the Magic Kingdom to be fun. The food compliments the festive atmosphere. Best of all, physically disabled people can participate and enjoy it along with everyone else.

Street vendors are everywhere in the Magic Kingdom. They are typical amusement park-type wagons or stands, selling ice cream sandwiches, Mouseketeer Bars, and low fat strawberry yogurt bars. These frozen treats cost from $1.60 to $2.00 each. They also sell sandwiches, hotdogs, chips, soft drinks, and everybody's favorite, popcorn.

NOTE: Physically disabled people sometimes find eating at street-side vendors impractical. Experienced wheelchair-users realize this; for others, let us explain. Non-disabled people often buy a snack, a hot dog, popcorn, or soft drink, and eat and drink while walking. This is impossible while a person is operating their own wheelchair. It's true someone could push the wheelchair while the disabled person eats, but many disabled people like being independent. Also, at a street vendor, people using wheelchairs must eat off their laps, using their legs as a table.

This is impractical for a couple of reasons. First, the author at least, has a talent for spilling food and drink on himself. He feels self-conscious enough, without having ketchup and mustard all over his pants. Second, many disabled people have difficulty sitting up straight in their wheelchairs. The author is paralyzed from his upper chest down. He does not have control of his lower back and abdominal muscles. To sit upright, he holds himself up with one hand and then eats with the other. The alternative is slouching in his chair, leaning back, and using both hands for eating. Either way, it's uncomfortable. It might be like standing on one leg, balanced on a wall, while trying to eat. It's possible, but impractical. This is typical of the problems faced by people with physical disabilities. Disabled people know their limitations, but their companions sometimes forget.

Fast Food Eating Places — Main Street, U.S.A.

Main Street Bake Shop: Visitors follow their noses to this shop on the right-hand side of Main Street, on the way toward the Central Plaza. They can take time out and sit at a small round table while enjoying a cup of coffee and sampling the array of pastries, cakes, pies, and cinnamon rolls. There are also chocolate chip, oatmeal raisin, sugar, fudge, and peanut butter cookies.

Plaza Ice Cream Parlor: Just down Main Street, on the same side as the Bake Shop, is an old-fashioned ice cream parlor. They offer a wide range of flavors, making this a favorite for everyone.

Refreshment Corner: Visitors seeking the epitome of American fast food find it here, at the end of Main Street, on the left, or west side. What is an American baseball game without hotdogs? The same is true in the Magic Kingdom. Visitors sit at a small, outdoor table and enjoy a regular, jumbo-sized, plain, or cheese hotdog. They can satisfy their thirst with soft drinks or get a boost from a brownie and a cup of coffee. The refreshment corner provides a central location for relaxing while eating, and enjoying the spectacle taking place all around; some refer to this as "people-watching." We all do it, and everyone can. During the busiest times, a piano player adds his lively music to the atmosphere.

Cafeterias — Main Street, U.S.A.

Crystal Palace: This is a cafeteria-style restaurant and the only one in the Magic Kingdom. Basically, cafeteria service means the restaurant patrons move in a line with other people and select the food they prefer. The process is relatively fast and allows people to see the food before they order.

From too much experience, the author knows the difficulty people using wheelchairs have in cafeterias. First, they must maneuver around and through the crowds. Second, they have to balance a tray on their laps while pushing their chairs, hoping they don't spill anything in the process.

If the author is alone, he avoids cafeteria-style restaurants. If he is with a companion, he enlists their help. Usually, he prefers sitting at a table and having a waiter take his order. He feels less handicapped that way and less of a burden on his companions. In the Magic Kingdom, there are many choices. You choose what suits your abilities, tastes, and budget.

The Crystal Palace is between Main Street, U.S.A. and Adventureland. It is popular and attracts large crowds. The best advice is avoid the mid-day rush. For example, eat breakfast or lunch either later or earlier than usual. Sometimes, it's wise to march, or roll, to the tune of a different drummer.

The Crystal Palace offers the largest variety of food in the Magic Kingdom. A partial offering includes prime rib, roasted chicken, fish, pasta, vegetables, salads, and desserts. There are many seating areas, but the ones in front overlook a beautiful flower garden. People sitting in the east end of the cafeteria look into a quiet courtyard.

The Crystal Palace deserves special mention for serving a full, American-style breakfast. They have bacon and eggs, with hash-browned potatoes, biscuits, sausage, ham, and pancakes.

Full-Service Restaurants — Main Street, U.S.A.

Tony's Town Square Restaurant: Tony's is in the northeastern corner of the Town Square area in Main Street, U.S.A. The Disney movie, *Lady and the Tramp*, provides the theme for the restaurant. The leading dog in the story, Tramp, meets his Lady in an Italian cafe, similar to Tony's.

As in the film, the food is Italian. For dinner, they offer lasagna primavera, chicken flavored with basil, spaghetti with meatballs, steaks, and grilled fish. The dessert choices include spumoni ice cream and Italian pastries, followed by a cup of espresso or cappuccino coffee.

The lunch menus contain healthy options like pasta salads, a fruit plate, and a deli-platter. They accommodate children and people with special dietary requirements by providing custom menus and foods. Disney, always eager to entertain, provides crayons and menus for children that double as coloring books.

Tony's is a good place for breakfast. They open before the rest of the Magic Kingdom, and serve pancakes and eggs, cold cereals, and pastries. Children can even choose waffles shaped like the Disney characters. Yes, it is Goofy.

The Plaza Restaurant: Another full-service restaurant, the Plaza, lies hidden at the end of Main Street, on the east side, across from the Central Plaza. This is a pleasant place for a sit-down, hot meal. Of course the author is always sitting, but he favors this kind of dining because of its relaxed atmosphere.

The Plaza offers cold sandwiches and fresh salads. Probably due to its proximity to the Ice Cream Parlor, they serve great milk shakes, ice cream floats, and ice cream sundaes. Our favorite is Cafe Mocha, combining ice cream, chocolate, and coffee.

Fast Food Eating Places — Adventureland

Adventureland Veranda: Visitors sit at an outside table on the veranda, with overhead fans cooling them under a red-tiled roof. They can pretend they're in Margaritaville; the only thing missing is the margarita and Jimmy Buffet. On the secluded eastern side of the veranda, there's a nice view of the Cinderella Castle. This is one of our favorite places for eating lunch and relaxing. That's part of learning to live with a physical disability, learning when to push it and when to relax.

They serve hotdogs, hamburgers, and soft drinks, but their specialties are teriyaki steak or chicken sandwiches, and fresh fruit. Guests order and pick up their food at a counter. The servers wrap the food in paper and place it on plastic trays. They serve the drinks in paper cups. It isn't elegant, but it serves the purpose. Fast food is fast.

When the author was there by himself, he had trouble reaching the counter from his wheelchair. He struggled a bit until another visitor stepped in and offered help. The thoughtful man carried the author's tray for him out to the veranda and placed it on a table. The author finds this type of help fairly common and welcome.

Aloha Isle: They sell cool treats in character with the Adventureland setting at this refreshment stand. People have their choice of fresh pineapple, various juices, or Dole Whip soft serve. Visitors find Aloha Isle across from the Jungle Cruise attraction.

Egg Roll Wagon: This vending cart offers a variety of pork and shrimp egg rolls and oriental (?) cheese hotdogs. Not exactly authentic, but they provide a quick snack with a soft drink.

El Pirata y El Perico: In Spanish this means "The Pirate and The Parrot." Again in character, it is across from the Pirates of the Caribbean ride. At this snack stand, they sell hotdogs with cheese or chili toppings, other sandwiches, and soft drinks. For a little spicy fun, they offer tacos, taco salads, or nachos.

Sunshine Tree Terrace: This is the best place in Adventureland for finding cold refreshment. The snack bar sits next to the Tropical Serenade attraction and its Enchanted Tiki

Birds. They offer a selection of tropical treats such as orange slush, frozen yogurt, and our favorite, an orange-flavored yogurt swirl.

Full Service Restaurants — Frontierland

Diamond Horseshoe: We described this as one of the attractions in Frontierland. Visitors must make reservations in person on the day of their visit. They accept reservations at the podium in front of the Disneyana Collectibles shop, on the east side of Main Street, in Main Street, U.S.A. The Diamond Horseshoe Jamboree and restaurant is a popular attraction. Guests should make their reservations early.

The Diamond Horseshoe Jamboree is worthwhile for the show alone. They offer casual food with a western flavor. This includes potato and corn chips, fruit punch, pies, and cold sandwiches. People using wheelchairs find the restaurant and jamboree accessible and enjoyable.

Fast Food Eating Places — Frontierland

Pecos Bill Cafe and the Mile Long Bar: The Pecos Bill Cafe allows people to pretend they are in some wild-west town. They can kick back their boots, or wheelchairs, and enjoy lunch either indoors or outside. The cafe looks like a Hollywood cowboy movie set. They have leather-backed chairs, ceilings made of twigs, and red-tiled floors.

If it's not too hot, sitting outside is nice. If the heat is too much, visitors can sit inside, in an un-cowboy-like, air-conditioned room. The selection of food includes hotdogs and hamburgers, barbecued sandwiches, and a variety of soft drinks. There are no cold beers. Yes, hardly authentic, but Disney prohibits alcoholic beverages in the Magic Kingdom. We guess they want it to be magic without the help of alcohol.

The Mile Long Bar, located next to The Pecos Bill Cafe, serves Tex-Mex food. This includes American-styled Mexican staples, like tacos, nachos, burritos, tortillas, and beans. The waiting lines move more quickly than in the Cafe. Look around for the animal heads on the walls.

Notice how they turn and wink at each other; they might be making fun of someone.

Turkey Leg Wagon: For something a lot different, visitors can pick up a large, smoked turkey leg. Sure, they can make-believe they're pioneers, or cowboys and girls out on the range. Some people enjoy this. For us, well, we described the difficulty of using two hands while sitting in a wheelchair.

Aunt Polly's Landing: People seeking this restaurant must make a visit to Tom Sawyer's Island in Frontierland. It sits along the shore on the eastern side of the island. The menu caters to children and fits the theme of its surroundings. They offer peanut butter and ham and cheese sandwiches, apple pie, cookies, iced tea, lemonade, and soft drinks.

Eating here while overlooking the Rivers of America is a nice change of pace. Diners relax along the covered part of a boat dock while watching the boats go by. Some people find it a nice place for lunch, but there are problems for physically disabled people.

Even if using wheelchairs, disabled people can take the Tom Sawyer Island rafts to the island. The problems begin when they arrive. The island is inaccessible for people using wheelchairs. Unless a person is exceptionally ambitious and has friends willing to help, we advocate avoiding Tom Sawyer's Island and Aunt Polly's Landing.

Full Service Restaurants — Liberty Square

Liberty Tree Tavern: This restaurant presents a colonial-era atmosphere. You find it between the Diamond Horseshoe Jamboree and the Hall of Presidents. Compared to the wild west of Frontierland, the atmosphere is refined. The oak flooring, wooden venetian blinds, ladder-backed chairs, and decorative antiques lend an air of authenticity to the setting.

The lunch menu offers sandwiches and large salads. At dinner they present heartier fare. This includes such early American favorites as prime ribs, lobster, roast chicken, fresh fish, and shrimp dishes. You also find New England specialties like clam chowder and oysters, at lunch and dinner. The Tavern accepts reservations at the door. This helps avoid a wait. The best advice remains eating at off times, either earlier or later than normal.

Fast-Food Eating Places — Liberty Square

Columbia Harbour House: This restaurant is across from the Liberty Square Riverboat Landing. It sports a nautical theme. Dozens of artifacts like harpoons, sailing instruments, and model ships decorate the interior. The food reflects the atmosphere. They offer clam chowder, fresh fish, and shrimp, as well as the usual sandwiches, salads, and drinks.

Sleepy Hollow: The specialties of the house are their Legendary Punch and chicken salad and Reuben sandwiches. Located across from a shop called Olde World Antiques, it's one of the nicer places for lunch. A quiet and shaded area across the street offers a bit of peace while dining.

Sleepy Hollow also serves as a place for catching a snack and watching the parades. If you find a table along the railing, you get a good view of the parades as they cross the bridge to Liberty Square

Full-Service Restaurants — Fantasyland

King Stefan's Banquet Hall: For a special occasion, King Stefan's restaurant in the Cinderella Castle ranks as the best in the Magic Kingdom. A large part of the appeal, of course, is the Castle itself. The banquet room reflects what visitors might expect in a medieval castle, with high ceilings, a huge chandelier, and leaded glass windows overlooking the activity in Fantasyland.

Guests must ride an elevator to the second floor in the castle, but it is accessible to people using wheelchairs. King Stefan's requires reservations. People should secure a place as soon as possible, at the entrance in the rear of the Castle.

The hostesses wear 13th-century-style French dresses. If lucky, diners might see Cinderella in all her beauty. The menu and prices are up-scale. At dinner, they serve prime ribs, filet mignon, seafood, and chicken dishes. During the lunch hour, they offer roast beef sandwiches, seafood salads, and fruit salads. They also provide a children's menu on request.

Again, King Stefan's Banquet Hall is popular and expensive. Visitors should decide, before leaving for the Magic Kingdom, if they want to eat here. We recommend it for special occasions. Dinner time is the best time. The view of the Castle and its surroundings, lit by thousands of lights, adds romance to an already lovely setting.

Fast-Food Eating Places — Fantasyland

Pinocchio Village Haus: The north side of the street between Fantasyland and Liberty Square hosts Pinocchio's restaurant. They serve hamburgers, hotdogs, cold sandwiches, pasta salads, and soft drinks.

The decorations in Pinocchio's are a special treat. We all remember the story of Pinocchio, the wooden puppet with the nose that grows. Guests sit in any of six rooms and enjoy the antique cuckoo clocks, European-style tile ovens, and toy shop atmosphere. Murals on the walls display characters from the Pinocchio story. They show Figaro the Cat, Cleo the Goldfish, Monstro the Whale, and of course Geppetto, the puppet-maker.

Troubadour Tavern: Located across the street from Pinocchio's, The Troubadour is not a tavern in the true sense. Instead, it's a small snack stand serving chips and soft drinks.

Tournament Tent: Visitors find this small refreshment island next to Fantasy Faire, on the north side of Fantasyland. Milk shakes and soft drinks are the excuse for stopping.

Gurgi's Munchies & Crunchies: This snack shop is tailored for children. This is appropriate, here between Dumbo, The Flying Elephant and the Mad Tea Party. They serve their hamburgers and fries in a box covered with cartoon characters and include a small souvenir.

Round Table: Although not exactly what King Arthur would offer his knights, guests to the Round Table choose from a variety of soft-serve ice cream cones, hot fudge sundaes, or root beer floats. We admit a weakness for these cold treats, and on a hot, summer day, we aren't alone.

Enchanted Grove: This is a small snack stand between Tomorrowland and Fantasyland. They specialize in lemonade, lemonade slush, or soft-serve ice cream.

Fast-Food Eating Places — Tomorrowland

Tomorrowland Terrace: This fast-food spot is the largest in the Magic Kingdom. It's also the fastest of the fast. It is on the west side of the street, across from the Grand Prix Raceway. They serve hamburgers and french fries, cold sandwiches, soups, and salads.

Lunching Pad: This snack stand is sandwiched between the Space Port and Mickey's Mart. They serve frozen yogurt, fresh fruit, and "natural foods." Would anyone eat "unnatural" foods?

WEDway Space Bar: A snack bar sits at the base of the StarJets Ride. It features Disney Handwiches, designed to be eaten with one hand. They contain a variety of fillings, and for people in a hurry, they're ideal. They aren't as great for people pushing wheelchairs. They also offer chips, some desserts, and soft drinks.

Plaza Pavilion: This is in the same building as the American Journeys and Dreamflight attractions. They serve heartier fare such as pizzas, pasta salads, and Italian sandwiches. As a bonus, people can sit at a table and look out over the canals surrounding the Central Plaza while feasting on the magic of the Kingdom.

SHOPPING IN THE MAGIC KINGDOM

Some say, "no one travels all the way to the Magic Kingdom just to go shopping." We doubt anyone comes to the Magic Kingdom just to eat. Yet the snack bars, restaurants, and shops are always crowded with people; someone must think differently.

The fact is, a lot of people enjoy shopping. There are Disney souvenirs everywhere. There are Donald Duck key chains, Walt Disney World sweatshirts and T-shirts. Think of the children in the Orlando airport proudly wearing their Mickey Mouse Hats. The author witnessed one little girl wear hers on the airplane, all the way back to Dallas.

The author's favorite is the Goofy Hat, with the long ears hanging to its proud owner's shoulders. Sadly, his wife won't let him wear it in public. Everyone should get a Mickey Mouse lapel pin to wear as testimony to their adventure in the Magic Kingdom.

There's a lot more. The shops maintain items in character with the themes of their respective "lands." Items range from inexpensive to out-of-sight. The shops and boutiques on Main Street sell antiques and jewelry. In Adventureland, they offer items from the far corners of the world. Fantasyland shops specialize in toys. Tomorrowland offers modernistic art and furnishings.

You should note the shops in Main Street, U.S.A, open one hour earlier and stay open one hour later than those in the rest of the Kingdom. You can stash your purchases in the rental lockers on the ground floor of the Main Street Train Station. If you don't trust the lockers, the clerks in the shops will forward items to Parcel Pick-up. Then you retrieve them when you leave the park.

We recognize the fact that many people like shopping, so we describe the options. We describe each area in turn, moving around the Magic Kingdom in a clockwise direction. We recommend that you think of our descriptions as a catalog. Consider the choices before visiting. If there are specific shops of interest, note them and do your shopping more efficiently.

NOTE: All the shops in the Magic Kingdom are accessible to people using wheelchairs. This means there are no steps or stairs. This does not mean it's easy getting around. Sometimes people crowd the shops, making it difficult maneuvering around in a wheelchair. In Dallas, they have a saying, "Shop 'till you drop."

Our advice for disabled people and their companions is that they prepare themselves, at least in terms of their attitudes. Unless, of course, they're from Dallas. If they want to shop and have to use a wheelchair, they need a little patience. Other shoppers can mill around a person in a wheelchair, treating them like a piece of furniture. They will walk in front of them, block their way, and reach over them. They will, on occasion, be rude. Shopping is not the author's favorite contact sport. That is his opinion. Many people, physically disabled people included, love shopping. Since this guide is for everyone, we describe the shopping opportunities in the Magic Kingdom.

Main Street, U.S.A. — East Side

Stroller Shop: Visitors to the Magic Kingdom can rent strollers for children and wheelchairs for disabled people. They rent these at the stroller shop, just inside the entrance to the Magic Kingdom and to the right.

It is fairly obvious why parents choose a stroller for children, even for children quite capable of walking. The little ones get tired, they can wander off, and the strollers make a handy place to store excess gear. Obviously, anyone who is completely unable to walk, will have their own wheelchair. In regard to rental wheelchairs, we strongly recommend that anyone with a walking disability rent a wheelchair. Renting a wheelchair might make the difference between enjoying the visit or being miserable. Hundreds of people, every day, agree. Visitors will see wheelchairs in use all over the Magic Kingdom, and many of the people using them can stand and walk. Visitors should note that they rent the strollers and wheelchairs on a first-come, first-served basis. Visitors should plan for this requirement before arriving in the Magic Kingdom.

The Chapeau: This is the shop on the Town Square for buying personalized Mouseketeer hats with Mickey Mouse ears. They also have visors, straw hats, derbies, and top hats. They display an abundance of lady's hats that are at least fun for trying on while acting silly in front of a mirror.

Disneyana Collectibles: This shop is between The Walt Disney Story and Tony's Town Square Restaurant. As the name suggests, they sell Disney memorabilia.

Kodak Camera Center: If visitors somehow make it to the Magic Kingdom without a camera, they can buy a new one in this shop. They also sell film, offer two-hour film-processing and they can make minor camera repairs. Renting a video camcorder is an interesting idea. They are perfect for recording moving images and the sounds and voices of the Magic Kingdom. They are easy to use and don't require developing of any film. Visitors can take the film cassettes home, slip them in their VCRs, and re-live their adventures on their own televisions.

Main Street Confectionery: Chocolate addicts always find their way to this little shop. Watching the cooks prepare peanut brittle is fun and mouth-watering. They also offer jelly beans, marshmallow crispies, nougats, and mints.

Uptown Jewelers: This shop is noted for porcelain figurines made by Disney and others. Shoppers can part with as much as $3,500 or as little as $3.50. Collectors of Hummel figurines make a point of visiting and browsing. They also offer a selection of inexpensive costume jewelry. If you want a genuine Mickey Mouse watch, you can buy one here. The shop sells other kinds of clocks and even a Mickey Mouse telephone.

Disney & Company: Disney created an elegant, Victorian-style shop by using beautiful wallpaper, intricate woodwork, and overhead fans. The shop features T-shirts, sweatshirts, hats, bags, stuffed animals, and other Disney souvenirs.

Market House: This shop looks like a turn-of-the century general store. They offer pretzels, pickles, honey, and other small items. It is one of the few places in the Magic Kingdom selling tobacco products like cigars, cigarettes, and pipe tobacco.

The Shadow Box: This is a fun place to stop for a few moments. You watch artists as they busily cut silhouettes out of black paper. For about $4.00, they produce framed silhouettes of the guests themselves, their children, or companions.

Crystal Arts: In this shop, visitors watch glassblowers and engravers practice their art. They offer a fabulous array of cut-glass bowls, vases, urns, and plates. They will directly ship the glassware or deliver it to the Parcel Pick-up, allowing you to retrieve your purchases when leaving the Magic Kingdom.

Main Street, U.S.A. — West Side

Newsstand: We guess Disney applied the name to this shop for the sake of authenticity, because they don't sell newspapers in the Magic Kingdom. The Newsstand is across from the Stroller Shop. They sell a limited collection of Disney souvenirs. The location allows you a final opportunity for buying souvenirs when leaving the Magic Kingdom.

The Emporium: This is the largest souvenir and gift shop in the Magic Kingdom. It's considered a landmark in the Town Square and it offers a bit of everything. Best of all, it's close to the rental lockers at the Main Street Train Station. You can quickly stash your booty in the lockers and go on with the rest of your tour of the Magic Kingdom.

The Emporium offers a variety of inexpensive souvenirs. Children always appreciate stuffed animals and toys. They have clever Disney T-shirts carrying pictures of Mickey and Minnie Mouse. If someone wants one of those Goofy Hats with the long ears, this is the place. It's easy spending a lot of time here. The crowds and large selection of souvenirs make the shopping go slowly. You should time your shopping for either early in the morning or later in the day. The shop opens earlier, and stays open later, than the rest of the Magic Kingdom.

Harmony Barber Shop: If you are late for a very important date and your hair is looking a little ragged, you can get a trim in the Harmony Barber Shop. Nostalgia buffs can buy old-fashioned shaving items. These make clever and functional gifts.

Disney Clothiers: Devoted Disney fans can find nearly any kind of souvenir clothing in this shop. Everything carries a Disney character or symbol, and they offer men's, women's, and children's clothes. More fashionable than the usual T-shirt, they sell men's golf shirts with an image of Mickey Mouse embroidered on the pocket. The author liked the jackets with Mickey Mouse dressed as the sorcerer's apprentice from the cartoon movie *Fantasia*.

House of Magic: This is a sort of magician's supply house. Many people find the tricks, props, and jokes amusing. Young boys in particular, think the House of Magic is fascinating.

Main Street Book Store: A book makes an excellent souvenir. Why not give a copy of this book to a friend? In the Main Street Book Store, they have a selection of books about Disney artistry and history. You can find other paper products, like wrapping paper, greeting cards, paper plates, napkins, and tablecloths.

Shopping In Adventureland

Traders of Timbuktu: This shop is across from the Enchanted Tiki Birds attraction. As the name implies, the selection represents what you might find in a tourist shop in Africa. You can choose from inexpensive trinkets and jewelry, or carved, wooden African animals. They make wonderful displays on a coffee table. There is also a modest collection of African-styled clothing.

Bwana Bob's: Animal fanciers find a collection of toys and models in this colorful little hut. They play off the themes seen on the Jungle Cruise ride or in the Enchanted Tiki Birds attraction.

Tiki Tropic Shop: You can find brightly colored, flowered Hawaiian shirts, assorted shorts, and shoes in the Tiki Tropic Shop. The clothes are comfortable in the hot Florida climate and fit the festive atmosphere of Walt Disney World.

Elephant Tales: After the Jungle Cruise ride, you might be motivated by the idea of an African safari. This is the place you can shop for the appropriate clothing. They also offer a variety of accessories to accompany the safari look.

Island Supply Company: To look like a Florida native, you might want some surfer clothing and accessories. The only thing they don't sell is the sun tan; that's free.

Laffite's Portrait Deck: This could be fun. You can dress in loaned costumes and appear in a photo as a rowdy-looking pirate, or a daring pirate maiden. A pirate sitting in a wheelchair would be unique. This shop is worth a visit merely to watch others having fun and posing for their pictures.

House of Treasure: This shop offers pirate hats, flags, rings, and treasure maps for fueling the imagination of would-be pirates.

The Golden Galleon: This is a nautical dream house. They sell model ships and accessories. They also offer a selection of clothing for people wanting to look as if they just got off the boat.

La Princesa de Cristal: You must look carefully to find this little shop across from the Pirates of the Caribbean ride. The shop sells an assortment of cut glass and engraved glass plates, bowls, and drinking glasses.

Plaza del Sol Caribe: This little market, next to the Pirates of the Caribbean, sells candies and snacks. They also offer Mexican styled hats, (sombreros), straw hats, straw bags, pottery, and artificial flowers.

Shopping in Frontierland

Frontier Trading Post: This shop is unique, and in character with the image of the frontier. They offer venison chili, wild boar meat, and buffalo meat. Before heading west in their wagon trains, or wheelchairs, people need equipment. They might need a cowboy hat, or a feathered headdress and moccasins. There are many trade items, like Indian drums, peace pipes, belt buckles, sheriff's badges, gold nuggets, and jewelry.

Tricornered Hat Shop: You find this shop next to the Diamond Horseshoe Saloon; not surprisingly, they sell hats. They specialize in western hats and offer accessories like feathered hat bands. The shop also features items made from leather, such as belts, purses, and wallets.

Prairie Outpost & Supply: This is a new shop in Frontierland. They offer a variety of clothing, gifts, and artwork, with a theme based on the American Southwest.

Wood Carvers: This is a nice spot to shop for hand carved wooden items. They make ideal gifts or household decorations.

Big Al's: This little shop sounds as if it belongs on the South Side of Chicago; instead, visitors can find it along the Rivers of America in Frontierland. At Big Al's, shoppers have a choice of leather goods, harmonicas, hard rock candy, and toy six-shooters.

Shopping In Liberty Square

Olde World Antiques: This is a serious antique shop. Unless shoppers have deep pockets, they just look, but that's part of the enjoyment. It is one of the first shops visitors see when they cross the bridge into Liberty Square. The shop has antique furniture on display, like hutches, tables, and decorative items. They also offer some less-expensive reproductions and they sell jewelry, clothing, and perfume.

Heritage House: The theme for this shop is Colonial America and the goods offered represent that time period. The shop is next to the Hall of Presidents. They sell pewter plates and candlesticks. You can buy a bust of your favorite President, or a painting of an early American sailing ship. Some of the more meaningful items are old-looking copies of historical American documents.

Yankee Trader: You find this shop as you head toward the Haunted Mansion and near the arched entry to Fantasyland. Here, you choose from an assortment of kitchen equipment; again, the theme is early Americana. They sell an incredible variety of jams and jellies. Cookbooks containing historical recipes are also for sale.

Ichabod's Landing: This is a small shop near Mike Fink's Keelboats. If the Haunted Mansion stimulates your imagination, you might look for the monster masks and scary toys at Ichabod's.

Silversmith: This shop might look like Paul Revere's. Cabinets display plated or sterling silver tongs, teaspoons, bowls, tea-sets, candle-holders, and silver-covered roses.

Shopping in Fantasyland

The King's Gallery: This might be the nicest shop in the Magic Kingdom. Most items are expensive but just looking is enjoyable. You find it in the Cinderella Castle, near the entrance to King Stefan's Banquet Hall. It looks like a medieval general store, if there was such a thing.

They sell tapestries, suits of armor, cuckoo clocks, Spanish-made swords, and an assortment of smaller items. You should watch the artists making Damascus steel. They repeatedly heat and pound the steel, producing a strong, durable, and beautiful product.

Mickey's Christmas Carol: Regardless of the time of year, Christmas shopping is a pleasure. At Mickey's, they offer a variety gifts, ranging from tree-top dolls to Disney Christmas tree ornaments.

The Mad Hatter: This shop offers another opportunity for buying Mouseketeer hats. They named the shop after the Mad Hatter, who played a key role in the Disney movie, *Alice in Wonderland*.

Tinkerbell Toy Shop: This is a nice toy store by any standard. They offer stuffed animals, model trucks and cars, wooden toys, and old-fashioned wind-up toys. Little girls may want an Alice in Wonderland or Snow White dress. They also stock a selection of Madame Alexander dolls.

The Aristocats: This shop is northeast of the Cinderella Castle. It offers the chance of picking up one of many, inexpensive Disney Souvenirs. They have Mickey Mouse and Donald Duck key chains, sweatshirts, T-shirts, Disney figurines, salt and pepper shakers, and similar items.

The Royal Candy Shoppe: This is yet another inexpensive souvenir shop. In addition to the usual items, they sell a selection of candy such as jelly beans, peppermint sticks, Tootsie Rolls, lollipops, and hard candy. The shop is next to Gurgi's Munchies and Crunchies, a snack shop.

Shopping in Tomorrowland

Mickey's Star Traders: This might be one of the best places for buying Disney souvenirs. The selection is comprehensive, offering all the usual T-shirts, sweatshirts, and hats.

Skyway Station Shop: This is a small shop located close to the Skyway to Fantasyland ride. It offers a modest selection of Disney souvenirs.

Space Port: They sell contemporary toys in this shop. Not surprisingly, teenagers prefer it over some of the other Disney shops. They offer toys, games, jewelry, watches, and clothing. It's one of the more popular shops in the Magic Kingdom and correspondingly crowded.

Space Place: This is yet another small shop. It's claim to fame is its variety of souvenir Disney hats.

CHAPTER 4

THE EPCOT CENTER

"I like the dreams of the future better than the history of the past"——Thomas Jefferson

INTRODUCTION TO THE EPCOT CENTER

E.P.C.O.T. is an abbreviation for Experimental Prototype Community Of Tomorrow. If the Magic Kingdom is "the heart of Walt Disney World," then the EPCOT Center is the brain. The Magic Kingdom is similar to an amusement park. Its rides and whimsical Disney characters focus on entertaining children. The EPCOT Center has something for everyone. It is educational and entertaining. In our opinion, it qualifies as a "community of tomorrow" because it is accessible to everyone.

Tomorrow's world will demand more of our mental abilities. It will handicap us less for our physical disabilities. Jobs requiring purely physical labor are disappearing. More than ever, we need advanced scientific and technical training. The EPCOT Center demonstrates the progress we have made and reminds us of the importance of our intellect. It shows how a physical disability can be less of a handicap than anyone ever dreamed.

> "Out yonder there is a huge world, which exists independent of us human beings and which stands before us like a great, eternal riddle, at least partially accessible to our inspection and thinking. The contemplation of this world beckons like a liberation."
> —— Albert Einstein

What Is The EPCOT Center

The EPCOT Center is Disney's version of a huge world's fair. It is twice as large as the Magic Kingdom. With help from corporate sponsors, foreign governments and over one billion dollars, Disney created a showplace with no equal. The EPCOT Center consists of two parts. One is Future World and the second is World Showcase.

Future World presents the best of American technology and innovation while World Showcase presents condensed versions of eleven countries of the world. The EPCOT Center offers an idealistic view of the world, but that is the point. Ideals are like stars in the sky. They guide us through the darkness.

Future World, the first part of EPCOT Center, has pavilions devoted to energy, life, communication, transportation, imagination, agriculture, and the oceans. Each pavilion presents complex subjects with humor and elegance.

The second part, the World Showcase, features the cultures of eleven countries. Each country shows its character in the buildings, shops, food, costume, and music. Visiting the World Showcase is like taking a trip around the world and seeing a little of everything. Best of all, disabled people see it, smell it, hear it, and taste it without leaving their wheelchairs.

Getting To The EPCOT Center

You can take your car, the Monorail, or buses to the EPCOT Center. The Monorail and buses are accessible to people using wheelchairs. However, the Monorail system is slow and inconvenient. Riding the Monorail is interesting, but only if you have a surplus of time. The bus service is worse. We strongly recommend that disabled people use their own or rental vehicles. This saves time, prevents frustration, and provides much needed flexibility.

Getting to the EPCOT Center is easier, by any means, than to the Magic Kingdom. For our discussion, we assume people are using their own vehicles. You should locate Interstate Highway I-4 on your maps. Travelers to Walt Disney World frequently use I-4. It crosses the Florida peninsula from southwest to northeast. It links the cities of Tampa, Orlando, and Daytona Beach. The exit leading to the EPCOT Center lies about half way between the exits marked U.S. 192 and the other indicating Route 535.

When exiting I-4, you merge into a four-lane, divided highway termed the EPCOT Center Drive. This leads directly to the entrance. We recommend that all disabled people use the handicapped parking area.

Disabled guests should stay in the right hand lane while approaching the toll plaza. Normally, parking costs $4.00 per day, but it's free for holders of annual passes and guests at the Walt Disney World resorts. Guests must have the proper identification. A toll booth attendant issues a handicapped parking pass for display on the vehicle's dashboard or windshield. The first turn to the right, clearly marked by signs, leads to the handicapped parking area.

Visitors using the 9,000 space Main Parking Lot have the option of riding a tram to the entrance. They can fold and place their wheelchairs on the trams.

Admission To The EPCOT Center
The Main Entrance Plaza is to the left, or east of the handicapped parking area. If visitors don't already have an admission ticket, they must stop here and buy one.

Wheelchair Rentals
When disabled people absolutely cannot walk, they bring their own wheelchairs. However, many disabled people find walking painful or dangerous. They might get by without using a wheelchair in their daily lives, but we recommend they rent one in the EPCOT Center. The EPCOT Center covers a lot of territory. It is more than a mile around the World Showcase Lagoon and everything involves walking or rocking and rolling. We can almost guarantee if someone has trouble walking, they will regret not using a wheelchair in the EPCOT Center. The same rationale applies to parents with small children. Rent a stroller.

Visitors rent wheelchairs and strollers on a first-come, first-served basis. They find wheelchairs and strollers on both the west and east sides of the Main Entrance Plaza. If someone is half-way around the World Showcase Lagoon and wishes they had a wheelchair, they can still get one near the French Pavilion. If people have the stamina for visiting more than one of the Walt Disney World theme parks during the same day, they should save their rental receipts. They can use them again at the Magic Kingdom or the Disney-MGM Studios.

Another popular option at the EPCOT Center is renting a motorized, three-wheeled cart. These are for people needing a wheelchair who do not have a companion to help push them. In the author's experience, pushing the average rental wheelchair by himself is difficult and uncomfortable. The same holds true for the type of wheelchairs loaned out in airports and hospitals. They are poorly designed for self-propulsion. If pushing a wheelchair is impractical, disabled people should consider one of the motorized carts.

Locker Rentals

The author found the rental lockers very useful in the Magic Kingdom. At the EPCOT Center, he found returning to his car was a simple matter and a locker wasn't necessary. In the situation where a disabled person arrives at the EPCOT Center by Monorail or bus, and wants to stash something for a while, they provide rental lockers. These are in two places. The first is in the Bus Information Center. This is directly in front of the handicapped and bus parking areas. They have other rental lockers on the west side of the Main Plaza, underneath Spaceship Earth.

Information — Earth Station

This is the place for information and reservations in the EPCOT Center. It is comparable with City Hall in the Magic Kingdom. You find it near the exit of Spaceship Earth, on the south side, towards the World Showcase Lagoon.

If you are visiting the EPCOT Center for only a day or so, you can skip the Earth Station. If you have more time, make a point of learning about the WorldKey Information Service at the Earth Station. This involves playing with a "user-friendly" network of touch sensitive video display terminals. The monitors display instructions and information in either English or Spanish; German and French may soon be available.

The system offers an index to information about the EPCOT Center. On the television screens, by pointing and touching, you can bring up descriptions of the various attractions with maps and pictures. You can get information on shops, services, and entertainment. WorldKey also allows you to make reservations for dining in many of the EPCOT Center restaurants.

The area is accessible for people using wheelchairs. However, be aware that reaching and seeing the screens can be difficult from a wheelchair. Also, people with limited use of their arms and hands can have difficulty with the touch sensitive, interactive video display screens. For anyone impaired in such a way, we suggest working with a companion. There are many means and levels of communication; communication requires cooperation.

If you desire some human interaction, you can see an attendant on the two-way television screens. The attendants can answer most questions; many speak Spanish and some speak other languages.

Finally, if all else fails, there is another option. There are hosts and hostesses available to talk with across a counter. If you have the time, learn about WorldKey. It represents a sample of our near-future communication systems. Like all of the EPCOT Center, it's educational as well as entertaining.

Orientation

When you enter the EPCOT Center for the first time, take a few minutes and orient yourselves. The maps are an invaluable time-saver. If you forgot, or don't have them, they are available in Spaceship Earth.

At the Entrance Plaza of Future World, you see Spaceship Earth to the south. Spaceship Earth is the large, spherical trademark structure of the EPCOT Center. If you go to your left and proceed clockwise, there are eight major attractions in Future World. They are **Spaceship Earth, Universe of Energy, Wonders of Life, Horizons, World of Motion, Journey Into Imagination, The Land, and The Living Seas.** In the center of Future World, two large buildings house a variety of exhibits. These buildings are Communicore East and West. We discuss them in greater detail later in this chapter.

The other half of the EPCOT Center is the World Showcase. Clockwise around the World Showcase Lagoon are pavilions displaying the characteristics of the following countries: Mexico, Norway, China, Germany, Italy, The United States, Japan, Morocco, France, the United Kingdom, and Canada.

There are boats that take you across the World Showcase Lagoon, and they are accessible to people using wheelchairs.

Epcot® Center

WORLD SHOWCASE

WORLD SHOWCASE LAGOON

FUTURE WORLD

Main Entrance Plaza

Group Tickets and Information

Monorail Station

1. Earth Station
2. Spaceship Earth
3. Universe of Energy
4. Wonders of Life
5. Horizons
6. World of Motion
7. Journey into Imagination
8. The Land
9. The Living Seas
10. Communicore West
11. Communicore East
12. Mexico
13. Norway
14. China
15. Germany
16. Italy
17. American Adventure
18. Japan
19. Morocco
20. France
21. United Kingdom
22. Canada

Map not to scale

▲ WorldKey Information Satellites
● Wheelchair/Stroller Rental
✚ First Aid
◆ Accessible Rest Rooms

Bus Parking | Handicapped Parking

They are slow, but riding the boats once for the view is nice. You can board them at four locations. Two of these are on the north side of the World Showcase Lagoon, another is between the German and the Italian Pavilions, and the last is in front of the Moroccan Exhibit.

There are also several double-decker buses carrying people around the World Showcase. We don't recommend them for wheelchair-users. They require that people leave their wheelchairs and climb or have someone lift them aboard. Then someone must fold, lift, and place their wheelchairs on the bus. In addition to their inaccessibility, they are slow. Our recommendation is admire them from a distance for the antiques they are. It's far easier rolling around at whatever pace a person chooses.

FUTURE WORLD
Spaceship Earth

> *"The most important fact about Spaceship Earth: An instruction book didn't come with it."*
> —— Buckminster Fuller

The EPCOT Center's golf-ball-shaped structure is one everyone recognizes. Its "geospherical" shape, gleaming silvery color, and immense size set it apart from everything else. It is beautiful. Many first-time visitors pause for a few moments and stare in awe.

The geosphere houses an appropriately named attraction, Spaceship Earth. It stands 180 feet high, is 164 feet in diameter and has a volume of 2,200,000 cubic feet. It is large enough, and its aluminum skin brilliant enough, that people see it from the air while flying along either coast of Florida. Its name is fitting because the Earth is truly our spaceship. It holds onto all of us as we speed through the darkness of space. It is the universally recognized symbol of the EPCOT Center. The story inside gives us a hint of where we've been and where we're going.

> *"We are not going to be able to operate our spaceship earth successfully nor for much longer unless we see it as a whole spaceship and our fate as common. It has to be everybody or nobody."*
> — Buckminster Fuller

You witness the show inside Spaceship Earth while seated in moving vehicles. If someone uses a wheelchair, they must transfer from it to the ride. These vehicles take their passengers back in time, to the earliest human history. Using all of Disney's resources, with detailed animated characters and stunning visual effects, the show depicts the history of communication. It shows Cro-Magnon people (cave-men) 40,000 years ago, first learning to speak, and moves forward to the miracles of computers and satellites.

As marvelous as the world seems, we haven't perfected our communication or accepted everybody. Spaceship earth is not complete. The *Disabled Guests Guide Book* to Walt Disney World is an example. It states:

> "Partial mobility is required to experience this attraction."

What exactly does "partial mobility" mean?

Well, it means you must step through a narrow doorway in a slowly moving vehicle and sit in a hard plastic seat. That sounds easy enough. Countless people do it every day. The author found out the hard way that it's not quite that easy for everybody. Despite the fact that he can't stand or step, he got on the ride. If he can, we believe many similarly disabled people can get on the ride and enjoy it as much as he did. The following experience illustrates exactly why we wrote this book.

The author rolled around the usual entrance to Spaceship Earth and went inside the geosphere. He found the ride's exit and asked an attendant if he could get on the ride from his wheelchair. The attendant asked him if he could stand, which as usual, seemed an odd question. The author replied, "No, but can I at look at the ride and see if I can do it?"

The ride attendant patiently and politely explained how he could stop the ride for a few minutes. He also explained how the Disney employees can't help lift disabled people, "for insurance reasons." The author knew he had to make the transfer himself. His sister was with him, but she would not be able to lift him by herself. Our advice for disabled people who anticipate a similar problem is, if possible, travel with two or more companions.

Transferring into these and several other rides in the EPCOT Center is similar to getting into an automobile. The difference is, it's more difficult. The reason is because the doorway to the Spaceship Earth ride vehicle is only about 18 inches wide. They designed the doors for standing people's legs, not whole bodies.

Fortunately, they stopped the conveyor belt that normally moves with the ride vehicles. The author rolled his wheelchair up to one of the cars. He locked his brakes, swung his footrests away, and placed his feet on the ground. One at a time, he placed his feet into the car. The ride vehicles are like those on a roller coaster, made of smooth, hard plastic. They are solid and provide a good lifting surface. Their smoothness made it unlikely that some of his clothing or part of his body would catch on anything. The hard part was lifting himself about 18 inches, up and over the side of the car. The author managed it and then sort of fell into the seat. He wished he had remembered to put his wheelchair cushion in first.

The lesson for all disabled people and their companions: think about the situation and be prepared. We think many disabled people can make this kind of transfer, with or without help. Lifting small, physically disabled children or adults from their chairs and into the ride is possible. Lifting heavier disabled people usually requires two people. Once in the ride, they can enjoy the show without danger or discomfort. If disabled people can get in and out of an automobile, with or without a little help from their friends, they should give Spaceship Earth a try. Regardless, onward to the "future."

The Show Inside Spaceship Earth: Disney consulted with science fiction writers and scientists while creating this history of communication. The ride begins with primitive men and women, dressed in skins, learning to speak. You pass an Egyptian temple with its "hieroglyphics." These are ingenious pictorial representations of sounds and objects, a crude but effective, early form of communication. There is a Greek theater scene. Then, as we do now, the Greeks used the theater in communicating their cultural values. The ancient Romans had a sophisticated network of paved roads linking their empire and providing communication with far-off provinces.

In the 11th and 12th centuries, Benedictine monks hand-copied religious, philosophical and scientific texts. They preserved ancient knowledge and passed it on to future generations. Another scene depicts the first printing press. All through history, technological advances eliminated jobs and created new ones. Think about it. Adapt and survive or stop learning and become extinct.

Every scene incorporates historically accurate detail. In the Greek theater the actor is quoting Sophocles in *Oedipus Rex*. They copied the markings on the walls of ancient Rome from those preserved in the ruins of Pompeii. The depiction of Islamic culture includes a replica of a quadrant. This is an instrument from the 10th century used for celestial navigation. The page on the printing press is a copy from a 15th century Bible.

Later scenes show excerpts from radio and television shows. The original *Lone Ranger*, *The Shadow* and commentary by Walter Winchell are from old time radio. There is a film clip from the 1938 Joe Louis-Max Schmeling boxing rematch. Of course there is a film scene of Walt Disney introducing *The Wonderful World of Color*. All of these are forms of communication.

Finally, the ride takes you to the top of the inside of Spaceship Earth. Here, Disney treats you to a breathtaking night sky, complete with stars and planets. It feels like a calm and cloudless night on a ship at sea. As you gaze at the heavens, Walter Cronkite's narration explains the significance of the experience and our existence.

Communicore
The name is an abbreviation for "Community Core". The attraction consists of two buildings in the center of Future World, arcing away from Spaceship Earth toward the World Showcase Lagoon. The two large, curved buildings, Communicore East and West, surround a beautiful three-level fountain.

Like the Earth Station, Communicore is something to experience if you have the time, perhaps on your second or third visit to the EPCOT Center.

The Communicore buildings are accessible, if not always convenient, for people using wheelchairs. The crowds of people and some of the ramps make moving around difficult, but not impossible. The exhibits are more educational than entertaining, so think about your priorities before committing to Communicore.

COMMUNICORE WEST
This is the building to the right, looking toward the World Showcase Lagoon. It contains a popular fast-food restaurant and an attraction called FutureCom. Here, you get an idea of how people gather information. The information sources range from satellites and telephones to newspapers, ticker tape, and traffic lights.

One exhibit provides information on different areas of the country using touch sensitive video terminals. Another demonstrates teleconferencing, the technology allowing people in two or more meetings, at widely spaced locations, to see as well as speak with one another. It allows people to meet and share ideas without physically traveling. The idea is a good one, especially for disabled people. A person could work at home and still communicate with and see their co-workers. The technology exists, but at present, the cost for common use is prohibitively high.

Another exhibit includes a device called the Phraser. The computer speaks the words a user types on a keyboard. The benefits for speech-impaired people are obvious. The reverse technology also exists. People can talk to computers and have their spoken commands recognized. This allows people with little or no use of their hands, the ability to interact with computers and other people in a way that was not possible just a few years ago. Someday the phrase, "Your wish is my command," may become reality.

Expo Robotics: This is a new exhibit demonstrating the talents of computer controlled robots. You can watch robots juggling, spinning a top, have your portrait drawn, or your photograph put in an EPCOT Center, postcard-like scene. Once again, the possibilities for disabled people are nearly infinite.

EPCOT Outreach and Teacher's Center: You find this display in the FutureCom area. It shows the variety of EPCOT developments. It includes a library of information on any aspect of the EPCOT Center. Teachers can find hand-outs to supplement their visit and provide study material for future projects.

COMMUNICORE EAST

> *"The only thing more expensive than education is ignorance."* —— Benjamin Franklin

EPCOT Computer Central: On the north side of the Communicore East building, near Spaceship Earth, is the EPCOT Computer Central exhibit. It has an array of the familiar touch sensitive video displays. The exhibit demonstrates how computers aid in the design and control of mechanical functions. One example allows a sitting or standing person to design a roller coaster. Disabled people are more appreciative of this capability than other people because of their limited mobility. Computer-aided design eliminates the need for inaccessible tables, large sheets of drawing paper, and cumbersome drawing tools. Computers can remove many of the handicaps disabled people face in the workplace. Technology to increase their productivity already exists. Disabled people just need access to the tools.

Travelport: This is an opportunity for playing with more touch sensitive screens, accessing information, and planning a variety of vacations. It's amazing how quickly the information appears. Disabled people could easily serve as travel agents with such a system. They can talk on hands-free telephones and obtain and transmit information with a computer.

Energy Exchange: This exhibit provides information on worldwide energy sources and issues. Some of the sources are solar, coal, oil, and nuclear. The issues are conservation of resources and pollution. These topics might not always be front page news, but the problems are always there, lurking behind the scenes, waiting to spawn another crisis. This is a valuable exhibit. The author sat in front of one of the touch sensitive screens in his wheelchair and scanned through the data. Everyone using a wheelchair can do the same.

Electronic Forum: This contains an area called the World News Center. Television sets show live broadcasts from different parts of the world. In the Future Choice Theater, visitors can express their opinions by pushing buttons in the armrests of the chairs. Computers relay their response to questions, compare them to others, and display the results on a video screen.

Backstage Magic: This partly televised show provides a basic introduction to computers. It allows a look into the EPCOT Center Computer Control Room and shows how Disney manages their operation. A Disney character called "I/O" provides a little light-hearted entertainment. The exhibit offers an opportunity to better understand and appreciate the role computers play in our daily lives.

If someone is disabled and young, or disabled and facing a career change, Communicore provides a wealth of ideas for future employment. Computers and technology hold the key to the removal of handicaps and the solution of problems that sometimes seem impossible. We enthusiastically encourage everyone to visit these attractions.

Universe Of Energy

> *"The universe begins to look more like a great thought than like a great machine."* — Sir James Jeans

Consult your map of the Future World section of the EPCOT Center and look in the northeast corner for the Universe of Energy pavilion. Mankind's use and abuse of energy are such important subjects that we feel everyone should visit this exhibit. The ability of human beings to harness the energy of the universe makes almost anything possible. The misuse of energy can lead to our destruction.

Experiencing the Universe of Energy takes 45 minutes. It involves a ride in a moving vehicle, back about 100 million years, to the land of the dinosaurs. It includes watching three spectacular motion pictures. The theater and vehicles are accessible to people using wheelchairs. We wish all the attractions at Walt Disney World were this easy.

People using wheelchairs can stay in them throughout the presentation, with the exception of people using the three-wheeled electric carts. The carts are probably too large to fit in the ride vehicles. This is one of the disadvantages of the electric carts and a reason for not using them. However, we realize many people can walk, but use the carts for "convenience." They get off them when needed and walk to a regular seat.

The author remained in his conventional, manual wheelchair. We believe people using electric wheelchairs can do the same. After entering the Universe of Energy pavilion, an attendant directed him to a designated seating area in the rear of the theater. They lowered a short ramp and he wheeled his chair into what became the ride vehicle.

The presentation begins with a motion picture shown on a wide screen. It illustrates the types of energy used around the world. You see shooting flames, glowing coal, stacks of logs, and cascading water.

The next movie shows the formation of fossil fuels in prehistoric times. You see dinosaurs roaming over a strange looking landscape with active volcanoes, lush tropical vegetation, and bizarre insects. Then things get even more interesting.

Without warning, the seating area begins rotating and separating into six segments. Each segment seats 96 people, is 18 feet wide and 29 feet long. The movement is a bit startling, but soon you realize you are going on an adventure. The vehicles move slowly without jerking anyone around. People sitting in wheelchairs find it as comfortable and enjoyable as anyone else.

The lower half of the screen opens and the vehicles slide silently into the cool darkness of a primitive landscape. Pale blue moonlight and fiery volcanoes provide the only light. The jungle vegetation is wet with falling rain while the warmth, humidity, fog, and a faint odor of sulfur fills the air. Passengers blink, gasp, and point, wondering what is happening.

Monstrous dinosaurs appear out of the mist. Gigantic brontosauruses feed in a lagoon, while a ferocious allosaurus goes after a stegosaurus defending itself with it's spiny armor. Lurking above are the strange, winged reptiles called pteranodons. Disney built these creatures with the help of paleontologists — scientists who find and study the fossilized remains of ancient animals. They used the expertise of paleobotanists in creating accurate reproductions of prehistoric plants.

Too soon, the trip ends and the vehicles enter another theater for a third and final movie. This one takes 13 minutes and is projected on a huge, curved screen. The movie brings you back to the present and examines some future sources of energy. Nothing is free. Today, oil, gas and coal are relatively inexpensive and plentiful. Burning them pollutes the air. Nuclear energy is clean in some ways and hazardous in others. Hydroelectric power often requires the damming of wild rivers. Solar and wind power are limited to small scale applications. Disney is at its best when it educates and entertains — it is even better when it makes attractions accessible to everyone — like it does in The Universe of Energy.

Wonders Of Life

Next in clockwise order around Future World is the EPCOT Center's newest attraction. Appropriately, a 72-foot DNA molecule marks the entrance to the Wonders of Life pavilion. Disney spent around $100 million building this tribute to life and the human body. Some of us would rather not think about our frailties, but Disney makes the process of learning about life fun, as well as educational. Everyone benefits by knowing more about their bodies and minds. Best of all, everybody has access to the Wonders of Life. Most of the attractions are accessible to disabled people and those using wheelchairs. We discuss the exceptions in the following paragraphs.

Once inside the building, you are in a place called the Fitness Fairgrounds. You encounter a variety of activities designed for both adults and children. The author's favorite Disney character stars in a short film called, *Goofy About Health*. The show presents Goofy making the transition from lazy slug to health nut. They use old cartoon stories of Goofy's escapades and end with him visiting his doctor. They show the movie in an open, 100-person theater. This allows everyone easy access.

The Anacomical Players Theater offers an improvisational comedy show. The cast members encourage the audience's participation. This guarantees a few laughs. The theater holds about 100 people and enables people using wheelchairs to fit in with everyone else.

Finally, there is an enclosed theater showing a 14-minute movie called *The Making of Me*. The comedy actor Martin Short is the central character. The show begins as he wonders about the miracle of his creation. In a flight of curiosity, he travels back in time and witnesses his parents meeting, making the decision to have a child, and finally, he watches his own birth. The film uses scenes from the birth of a human baby. The images are accurate and graphic, but tasteful. Consider the emotional make-up of your companions before watching the film, although we doubt many people find it offensive.

The Making of Me is a popular show. Waiting lines can be quite long; try watching the show at an off time. The theater is accessible to physically disabled people using wheelchairs.

There are many other activities in the Fitness Fairgrounds. Physical fitness is as important for disabled people as it is for anyone, but not all the activities are accessible to them. For example, non-disabled visitors can try the Wonder Cycles. Riding these requires sitting in them and pedaling with their legs and feet. Most people using wheelchairs have something wrong with their legs and must pass it by. The author wonders if they could set up one of these bikes so disabled people could pedal them by hand. Our guess is some disabled people are more "fit" than their non-disabled friends, and the results might dispel some of the myths about their fragility.

Another attraction goes by the name of the Coach's Corner. It is fun for young athletes, but not disabled athletes. They video-tape people swinging a golf club, baseball bat, or tennis racket. After taking a few swings, they replay the tape. Then a "coach" steps in and offers some constructive criticism. The author enjoyed watching children taking their cuts. We imagine some physically disabled people might enjoy the same interaction. Some people using wheelchairs play tennis and others swing a baseball bat. There are people who play basketball and compete in marathon road races while using wheelchairs. Many disabled people are healthy and active. It is just a little different, that is all.

If you want a taste of reality, there is the Met Lifestyle Revue. You sit at an interactive computer and answer questions about your age, weight, height, and exercise habits. The computer thinks for a few minutes and then offers advice on leading a healthier and less stressful lifestyle. Everyone can participate in this exhibit since it is accessible by wheelchair.

Body Wars: Try to imagine being reduced to the size of a molecule and sent on a mission through a human body. Well, that is what Body Wars is about, a simulated, exciting, high-speed trip through the inside of a human being.

The author was apprehensive about going on this ride because someone told him it was fairly violent. Disney's description in their *Disabled Guests Guide Book*, only increased his anxiety. They describe it like this:

> "Guests in wheelchairs must be able to transfer into a ride seat. Due to the motion of Body Wars, good upper body strength is needed. An extra restraint, fitted over the shoulders, may be used if requested. Guests should be in good health, free from neck or back injuries, heart problems and motion sickness. This ride is not recommended for pregnant women. Contact a host or hostess at the attraction entrance for assistance."

Hopefully our description helps readers understand why a 40-ear old paraplegic, paralyzed from his chest down, might be a little apprehensive. He knew he could transfer himself to another seat. He does that every day getting into his car. But does he have "good upper body strength?" Will he need an "extra restraint"? If he does, should he, or does he really want to go on the ride? Is he in "good health?" Does a broken back and a damaged spinal cord, even if it happened 14 years ago, qualify as a "back injury?" He asked himself those questions and a few others.

Even two years after his injury he would have been afraid to try a ride like Body Wars. In the years since, he has gained confidence in his abilities through experience. He decided to try it. The point is, a disabling accident does not change a person's basic personality, and almost everyone enjoys a little excitement and challenge.

The author approached an attendant at the entrance to Body Wars and asked if he could get on the ride. It's not really a ride. Participants don't really go anywhere. It only seems that way. The attendant was skeptical. He sort of cocked his head, gave him a curious look and said, "Are you sure? This is a pretty rough ride."

The author acted confident, so they agreed to let him look and see if he could get into one of the chairs. He felt a little embarrassed and frightened, yet encouraged, by the presence of children waiting to get on the ride. He remembered similar anxiety while riding a chair lift to the top of a ski run. They were good feelings, alive feelings.

The attendant ushered him into a theater-like room with high-backed seats sloping up towards the rear. In one glance, he knew he could get in to one of the seats. They were just like any other chair in a movie theater. He stopped his wheelchair in front of one and locked his brakes. Swinging the footrests away, he placed his feet on the ground. With one hand on the seat of his wheelchair and the other on an armrest of the ride's chair, he lifted himself from one to the other. The attendant rolled his wheelchair out of the theater. He didn't need any encouragement to fasten his seatbelt. He figured it had a purpose.

The adventure only lasts five minutes, but it is intense. The theater darkens. The host explains how they miniaturize and launch everyone into a human body on a routine medical exam. Suddenly, it begins. A believable video image fills the screen at the front of the theater. You feel the acceleration and the sense of turning left, then right, then up and down. The movements are real. They are the same as the flight simulators used in training commercial and military airplane pilots.

The author held on to the armrests with all of his strength. After about a minute, the author realized he could hold on. Is that an exaggeration? No. When someone is paralyzed from their chest down, like the author, or higher, they have no control over their abdominal or lower back muscles. They must always use their arms and hands for holding themselves upright. It is still tiring for the author to hold himself up while sitting at a table and eating or working.

After a couple of minutes, the initial fear passed and he began enjoying the sensations. Again, we can make an analogy with downhill skiing. The author remembers the ecstasy of flying down a mountainside, turning, feeling in control, but just. These are not ordinary feelings for someone spending all of their time in a wheelchair. Yes, the EPCOT Center, yes, Walt Disney World is great!

Five minutes was enough. The adventure ended with a flourish after several simulated "close calls." He unbuckled his seatbelt. The attendant brought his wheelchair back and he lifted himself back in. He felt excited in a way that only happens after a thrilling physical experience. He did not feel handicapped. He felt strong; he felt good.

Having expressed that excitement and optimism, we recognize Body Wars is not for everyone. Disabled people using wheelchairs must transfer from their chairs to a movie theater seat. More importantly, they must hang on tightly during the adventure. A quadriplegic, or anyone with limited strength or control of their hands and arms, will have problems. A restraint over the shoulders, in addition to the seat belt across their laps, might help. Even then, we think Body Wars will frighten and be dangerous for people more severely disabled than the author. None of us can do everything and there are plenty of other attractions everyone can enjoy.

Cranium Command:

> *"Life would be infinitely happier if we could only be born at the age of eighty and gradually approach eighteen."* —— Mark Twain

Can anyone understand the way a 12-year old boy thinks and feels? The final attraction in the Wonders of Life pavilion offers some clues to a boy's behavior and it might be "one of the best-kept secrets" in the EPCOT Center. Best of all, it is completely accessible for people using wheelchairs. They can comfortably remain in their wheelchairs throughout the 12-minute show. It is fun and educational for everyone.

Initially, attendants directed the author in his wheelchair to a waiting area. He had a good view of a pre-show cartoon. Then he rolled into the theater for the start of the main show. From where he sat, the visibility and the audio portions of the show were excellent.

Cranium Command takes you inside a 12-year old boy's head. You see how and why he reacts to a series of common experiences. An AudioAnimatronic character named Buzzy controls the boy, acting as his brain. Buzzy gets his orders from General Knowledge. Together, through the eyes of the boy, they explain the functions of the left and right brain. Buzzy and General Knowledge explore the functions of the heart, the adrenal gland, and the stomach. Readers recalling Norm, on the TV sitcom *Cheers*, appreciate the humor involved with him acting as the boy's stomach.

Cranium Command is an example of the way Disney teaches us about our bodies and keeps us laughing while doing it. Everyone should make a point of seeing Cranium Command, especially if they are physically disabled.

Horizons

> *"The farther backward you can look, the farther forward you are likely to see."* — Winston Churchill

A horizon is something to look back upon, or forward to. The Horizons pavilion in the EPCOT Center offers both for most of us, but not all of us. The exhibit involves a ride through the past and the future in moving, suspended, four-passenger vehicles. The ride in the Horizons pavilion handicaps physically disabled people because they must get out of their wheelchairs and into the ride vehicles.

The author managed the transfer by himself, without assistance. Some disabled people can do this with a little help from their friends. Others, who must remain in their chairs, have to pass on the attraction. In this respect, the Horizons ride is similar to that in Spaceship Earth and several others. The ride itself, although moving, is not violent. Even severely disabled people can enjoy it, if they can find a way to get in.

The author explained to an attendant that he felt confident about transferring into one of the vehicles. They directed him to the exit area. Normally the ride vehicles continually move and passengers disembark onto a conveyor belt-like walkway. They agreed on stopping the ride for a few minutes so the author could make his transfer.

He wheeled his chair up to one of the cars and locked his brakes. With the same technique as before, he set his feet on the ground and lifted himself through a narrow doorway. The distance from a wheelchair seat is about 18 inches. This was not easy and the fact he felt rushed, did not help. To anyone trying this, we recommend resisting the urge to hurry. In the author's case, one of his shoes was pulled off and he had to put it back on once in the ride. He forgot his wheelchair cushion, which he regretted when he sat on the hard plastic seat. The trip itself was relatively tame and he had no trouble holding himself in the vehicle. Normally a physically disabled person will be with a companion to steady them. The ride is well worth the effort. The author found it interesting.

Horizons has a series of animated and video scenes illustrating how things taken for granted today, were once considered impossible. Science fiction writers envisioned rockets carrying us like bullets. They wrote of machines that would cool us. They dreamed of robots to work for us, lamps to tan us, and televisions to entertain us.

After viewing visions of the past, you move into a theater and witness the thunderous launch of the Space Shuttle. You see some of the applications and benefits of living and working in space. The film shows satellites launched and recovered, and crystals and organic molecules grown in a weightless environment.

Then the ride moves farther into the future. You see progressive transportation and communication systems. There are telephones using holographic images so people see one another as they speak. Trains move along a track, held in the air by magnetic forces. A futuristic farm flourishes in an arid environment, where crops are planted, harvested, and moved to market by robots. Another scene has people living underwater. They farm and mine and build in familiar ways.

The best experience comes at the end of the ride. A voice instructs you to choose one of several adventures by pushing buttons on a console in front of you. Majority rules. The author was alone so he chose a flight through the desert. Of course the ride vehicles don't actually fly, but the sensation is real, almost frightening. The cars tilt back and vibrate, but not uncomfortably. The sensation of rapid movement in the 30-second sequence comes from the vision-filling video screens. We emphasize the experience because we think all physically disabled people can share it — if they can get on the ride.

We believe that physically disabled people gain confidence and inspiration by experiencing this and other attractions in the EPCOT Center. Disabled people are well suited for developing ideas. They have obvious and valid reasons for improving their situations. A simple ramp in the right place can make all the difference. Of course that is only a beginning. Necessity breeds innovation. If society handicaps our ability to contribute, society loses.

World Of Motion

> *"All the tools and engines on earth are only extensions of man's limbs and senses."* —— Ralph Waldo Emerson

The World of Motion pavilion is appropriately wheel-shaped. You find it in the southeastern part of Future World, next to the Odyssey Restaurant. In it, Disney traces the evolution of human transportation systems. They show the past, present, and what they think the future promises. The presentation requires a 16-minute trip in a moving vehicle. They call the ride, "It's Fun to Be Free." The concepts of freedom and motion have special meaning for disabled people.

People using wheelchairs have access to the World of Motion ride. A couple of modified ride vehicles allow people to roll wheelchairs aboard and see the exhibits with everyone else.

This accessibility is a welcome improvement over other EPCOT Center attractions. They do not allow the three-wheeled, not-so convenient carts on the ride. If using one of these, people must either transfer into a regular wheelchair, or into a seat in the ride.

Some people say mankind's progress can be measured in terms of improvements in mobility. However, walking is always preferable to using a wheelchair. Perhaps it is time to perform some human engineering and cure people's disabilities.

We are intimately familiar with the mobility problems faced by physically disabled people. If the above statements are true, we must say the progress of mankind is short of what it could and should be.

Returning to the World of Motion and the history of transportation, the ride moves through 22 entertaining exhibits, filled with AudioAnimatronic characters. Many contain antique or accurate reproductions of wagons, bicycles, carts, cars, and trains. They even have a 150-year old Wells Fargo Stagecoach.

The ride begins with a look at the original form of human transportation, foot-power. The domestication and use of animals represents a great advancement. Somewhere, someone invented the wheel, allowing the movement of greater loads. Wheels led to carts, which led to engines, then automobiles. Wings, propellers, and engines led to airplanes. Rockets paved the way for jet aircraft and the Space Shuttle. Sailing ships gave way to steam ships and the nuclear-powered ships of today. Try imagining the genius involved in developing the helicopter. The trip through the World of Motion concludes with a film showing a futuristic city, with trains going through the air from one tall building to another.

Transcenter: After getting off the World of Motion ride, you enter a sort of automobile showroom. It is that and more. General Motors sponsors the exhibit and they show off their latest models. They display a robot used in assembly functions, like welding and painting. Another area demonstrates new designs being torture-tested to detect flaws. Finally, "Dreamer's Workshop" presents experimental cars of the future. The Transcenter is a fine place for automobile enthusiasts to escape the sun and heat and enjoy this multi-faceted showroom. People using wheelchairs can easily see all of the exhibits.

Journey Into Imagination

> *"The mightiest lever known to the moral world, Imagination."* — William Wordsworth

It is hard to imagine, spending millions of dollars on an attraction without making it accessible to everyone. However, that is what happened. The highlight of Journey Into Imagination is a 13-minute ride in a moving vehicle. As Disney says in their *Disabled Guests Guide Book*,

> "partial mobility is required to experience this attraction."

The author assumed people using wheelchairs must find a way of getting out of them and into the ride vehicles. The author tried and succeeded, but we realize many disabled people find themselves handicapped by the ride's inaccessibility.

Journey Into Imagination is in the southwest part of Future World, in a building marked by two large glass and steel pyramids. The attraction consists of three parts. These are the partly accessible Journey Into Imagination Ride, Image Works, and Michael Jackson's *Captain Eo* — a 3-D musical video.

Journey Into Imagination: The hosts on this journey are Dreamfinder, a happy, red-haired professor and a dragon named Figment (of your imagination). Figment appears throughout the ride, reminding visitors of his importance in creativity.

The ride shows how our senses gather information and send it to our brains. Our brains use an ability called imagination, processing information and producing miraculous results. The ride's passengers see the products of people's imaginations in the form of literature, visual and performing arts, science, and technology. In one scene, letters of the alphabet pour from a typewriter while laser beams accent the scene, like bolts of lightening.

The author tried getting on the ride. When an attendant at the entrance asked if he could get out of his wheelchair, the author replied, "I imagine I can if you'll give me a chance by stopping the ride for a couple of minutes." They reluctantly agreed, but said he had to be quick. If they stop one of the vehicles for more than a couple of minutes, the whole ride shuts down.

The ride vehicles are similar to others in the EPCOT Center. The cars have hard, blue plastic bodies, and two doors about 18 inches wide. Normally, the vehicles continuously move and people step into them from a conveyor belt. They stopped one car for the author. Feeling rushed, he raced up, screeched to a stop, and locked his brakes. Following a familiar routine, he placed his feet into the car, lifted himself from his chair, through and partly over the side of the vehicle and into the seat, falling on his side in the process. His performance was not worthy of an Olympic medal. When the ride ended, he reversed the procedure and returned to his chair. The attendants act as spectators. They can not and will not help lift disabled people. For people needing help, like the author, we recommend bringing a couple of friends and practicing the routine before the show begins.

The Image Works: This is an area in Journey Into Imagination where everyone can exercise their imagination. Who doesn't enjoy that? The electronic games are accessible to anyone using a wheelchair. An elevator brings them to the level of the activities.

In the Dreamfinder's School of Drama, you have the chance to be in a television show. This may be difficult for someone using a wheelchair, but it's possible. It's fun simply watching others. Using pre-recorded video effects, they superimpose the actors on other images, similar to the way TV weathermen have maps projected behind them.

In another area, the Sensor produces lights and sounds when detecting your presence and allows individual expression of style and rhythm. Numerous other electronic gadgets allow you to create light displays, colors, and sounds. Naturally, children and uninhibited adults love these interactive games.

Imagine conducting an orchestra. With the Electronic Philharmonic, you can raise and lower your hands over discs on a control console and direct the music. You can combine woodwind instruments, or the brass, strings, and percussion sections. It helps having a partner. It allows the joining of two people's imaginations.

Captain Eo: Last and not least, is a musical video starring Michael Jackson. It appeals to children and teenagers but the special effects are superb and appreciated by everyone. They show this rock and roll space fantasy in the Magic Eye Theater. Francis Coppola directed the action. Michael Jackson and his friends seek to change a bleak planet into a happy place, using song and dance as their weapons. Michael Jackson wrote two of the songs, *We Are Here to Change the World* and *Another Part of Me*. The sounds of cannons, lasers, fiber optics, and other special effects in the theater, compliment the singing and dancing on the screen. People using wheelchairs and all other physically disabled people, enjoy this show as much as anyone. We recommend it for everyone.

If anyone wants to see imagination at work, they should make a point of finding the fountains in front of Journey Into Imagination. Some people refer to these as "jumping water" and they always attract a crowd. Children delight in watching and playing with the blobs of water as they pop up from one fountain, float through the air, and land in another. Then they go up again and on down the line.

The Land

> *"Whoever could make two ears of corn ... grow upon a spot of ground where only one grew before, would deserve better of mankind ... than the whole race of politicians put together."* — Jonathan Swift

The Land attraction is on the west side of Future World, between Journey Into Imagination and The Living Seas. The Land consists of three parts, Listen to the Land, Kitchen Kabaret and the Harvest Theater: Symbiosis. Together, the attractions explore the history and importance of agriculture, food, nutrition, and man's interaction with the environment.

The Land pavilion also offers a full-service restaurant — The Land Grille Room, a fast-food restaurant and a small shop called Broccoli & Co. All the attractions accommodate people using wheelchairs. However, people using the three-wheeled, electric convenience carts are handicapped. At the Listen to the Land boat ride, people using the carts must transfer into a conventional wheelchair before getting into one of the boats.

Once in The Land pavilion, note the elevator to the left of the Land Grille Room taking people down to the attractions on the lower level. In all cases, ask an attendant for assistance. In our experience, attendants usually spot people using wheelchairs and offer help. This courteous attitude is one of the nicer aspects of visiting the EPCOT Center. The Disney hosts and hostesses invariably treat physically disabled visitors politely. They make everyone feel welcome.

Listen To The Land: This 14-minute ride is not a boat ride in the strictest sense. The boats are more like barges and they move along a track in a narrow, water-filled canal no more than 12 inches deep. The passengers see the evolution of farming methods through history. People using wheelchairs can roll on to these boats and enjoy the trip with everyone. Those using three-wheeled carts must transfer from them into a conventional wheelchair or one of the seats in the boats. The ride is a calm one. It should not present problems for disabled people, even those remaining in their chairs.

The trip takes you through three environments, a rain forest, prairie, and desert. These represent the way much of the Earth looked before human habitation. Then it moves through a scene of an early American farm. There is another area where they harvest fish and shrimp in carefully controlled environments called Aquacells. Finally, the boats move into a greenhouse with crops being grown, fertilized, and watered in innovative ways.

The plants in the three ecological environments are artificial.

Disney uses a type of plastic in imitating the real thing. They molded and copied tree trunks and branches. Then Disney attached thousands of fire-retardant, polyethylene leaves. They simulate grass using glass fibers and rubber mats. They provide moisture in the rain forest with a special drip system. Everything is artificial but realistic.

In contrast, the plants in the greenhouse at the end of the trip are real. Disney experiments with different growing techniques in the greenhouse. They have examples of hydroponics — plants growing in water. They have plants growing in the air, their roots fed nutrients sprayed on with water. Disney claims they grow and harvest most of the fruits and vegetables served in the restaurants of the EPCOT Center. The crops are impressively healthy-looking. Listen to the Land is a pleasurable and educational experience for all.

If you have a particular interest in agriculture, we recommend taking the Harvest Tour. This is a free, 45-minute tour of the greenhouse. The Disney agricultural staff serve as guides. Because of the leisurely pace of the tour, they encourage your questions. The tours occur on a daily basis, between 9:30 a.m. and 4:30 p.m. They require reservations. These must be made in person, on the day of the tour, at the Kitchen Kabaret Revue on the lower level of the pavilion.

Kitchen Kabaret Revue: This is a light-hearted, educational show. People using wheelchairs can comfortably and conveniently remain in them while watching. Disney uses their AudioAnimatronic talents in creating characters like Bonnie Appetit, the Kitchen Krackpots band, Mr. Dairy Goods and the Cereal Sisters. They sing and tell jokes while defining the basic food groups and the importance of good nutrition.

Imagine the Boogie Woogie Bak'ry Boy, the Colander Combo, Fiesta Fruit, and Mr. Hamm teaching their audience about food. Our favorite joke from Mr. Eggz is: "Why was Chicken Little so upset when his mom fell asleep in a hot tub? His brother was born hard-boiled." We also liked Mr. Broccoli and his punk-rocker haircut. Yes, it's silly, but children love it while it serves as an educational tool. The author, however, thinks more like Mark Twain who said,

> *"The only way to keep your health is to eat what you don't want, drink what you don't like, and do what you'd rather not."*

Symbiosis: They show this 19-minute film about the environment in an accessible theater. People using wheelchairs can remain in them if they wish. The film is short. As usual, the attendants direct people using wheelchairs to a designated seating area.

The movie is excellent. It presents a balanced view of the relationship between people and their environment. It demonstrates the inevitable conflict between the need to exploit the Earth's resources, and the importance of protecting the planet that sustains us. The film shows some abuses of the land and pollution in streams and lakes. It also shows some positive things. The clean-ups of the Thames River in England and the Willamette River in Oregon are examples. The film illustrates the use of modern forest-management methods from Sweden, Germany, and the Pacific Northwest as examples of how they grow and harvest trees without damaging the environment.

About 30 countries hosted the film crews. There are some spectacular scenes. The photography, the 70mm film, and the important environmental theme lead us to recommend this accessible experience to everyone. It is an example of why the EPCOT Center is an ideal place for physically disabled people. We are not handicapped while viewing this film; we have an equal opportunity to benefit from it.

> *"Nature, to be commanded, must be obeyed."*
> —— Francis Bacon

The Living Seas
The Disney engineers designed this exhibit to increase our awareness and understanding of the oceans. The Living Seas consists of a theater, numerous exhibits, Sea Base Alpha, and an aquarium.

Few people have the opportunity of seeing the underwater world in all its diversity and color. Disabled people in particular, are unlikely to have that opportunity. Rather than limiting us to our imaginations, the EPCOT Center's Living Seas exhibit allows us to see the ocean and its life forms in a large sea water aquarium. Nearly all of the attractions are accessible to people using wheelchairs. We recommend visiting The Living Seas.

There is an initial, three-minute ride that is inaccessible to people using wheelchairs. The Disney attendants would not let the author try it. They said he was not missing much, because the view of the aquarium from a wheelchair accessible area was better. We believe this is true.

Immediately inside the entrance, a collection of exhibits depicts the earliest attempts at subsea exploration. Undoubtedly, long ago, people wondered what lay beneath the ocean's surface. Surely the creatures fishermen pulled from their nets were mysterious, as well as tasty. The exhibits include copies of Leonardo da Vinci's ideas for underwater breathing apparatus and photos of John Lethbridge's diving barrel. Mankind has a short history of underwater exploration. It remains one of Earth's last frontiers.

Farther along, inside The Living Seas pavilion, there is a two-minute presentation showing more of our history of ocean research. You see early ships, diving bells, submarines and aqualungs. Unlike the fishes, we must take our oxygen with us when venturing beneath the waves. The aqualung makes it possible.

The author has never tried scuba diving as a paraplegic. However, one of his favorite activities is swimming. When he is out of his wheelchair, moving around is difficult, to say the least. In the water — he is free. The water supports his body and he swims well.

Farther along, you see a seven-minute film illustrating the importance of the world's oceans as a source of food, minerals, and energy. The oceans are as important as the land. It's equally as important that we avoid polluting them.

If a person is using a wheelchair, an attendant usually notices them as they approach the entrance to the Caribbean Coral Reef Ride. It is likely they will relate the same story they told the author. The ride is not accessible to people using wheelchairs. The attendants point the way to an elevator. These "hydrolators" create the sense of moving down, under the water, down to Sea Base Alpha. Disney designed this with the look and feel of an underwater research station.

Sea Base Alpha occupies two levels, connected by escalators for ambulatory people and elevators for people using wheelchairs. The author once witnessed a young man in a wheelchair go up and down an escalator, but we do not recommend it. Sea Base Alpha contains six modules, each devoted to a specific ocean research subject.

One module examines different forms of ocean life and how they adapt to their environment. It describes the use of camouflage, symbiosis, and bioluminescence. There are morays, bonehead sharks, and barracuda swimming around a coral reef in a 6,000 gallon tank. Another exhibit examines dolphins, porpoises, and sea lions.

At another station, an AudioAnimatronic submersible named Jason describes the history of the use of robots in undersea exploration. There are a variety of interactive video screens around the Sea Base. The screens allow the curious and patient to expand their knowledge of oceanography.

There is a two-story, diver lock-out chamber, allowing you to witness divers entering and exiting the surrounding aquarium. This is almost like watching someone in outer space. Astronauts do some of their training underwater because the floatation approximates the weightlessness of space. Children find these exhibits specially fascinating and stimulating.

The highlight of The Living Seas is the huge sea water aquarium surrounding Sea Base Alpha. It is 200 feet in diameter and 27 feet deep. It contains 5.7 million gallons of water. Inside, they reproduce a Caribbean coral reef. There are over 200 varieties of sea creatures floating, swimming, or crawling around in this huge fish bowl. People using wheelchairs have a view as good as anyone. They can roll up to one of the 18 feet high and 8 inch thick acrylic windows. You could spend hours studying the beautiful sea life. Disney designed the aquarium with the guests on the inside. The author wondered who was the student and who the subject.

The sea life includes sea bass, parrot fish, barracuda, puffers, angelfish, butterflyfish, and sharks. The author's favorites are the diamond rays. They seem to gracefully fly through the water, spreading and serenely flapping their wings. It is very relaxing. Finally, you might notice human divers in the aquarium. Often they are conducting experiments. Wireless radios allow them to speak to viewers and explain their work. They allow people to stay here as long as they like. Plan on at least an hour.

If you find the oceans particularly interesting and seafood appetizing, you might try the Coral Reef Restaurant. It serves fresh seafood, and while eating, you watch the activity in the aquarium through 18 foot high windows, identical to those in Sea Base Alpha. They arranged the tables in tiers, so everyone has a view of the aquarium. One of the levels is accessible to people using wheelchairs. The Coral Reef requires reservations, so make your plans early.

> *"If the human race wishes to have a prolonged and indefinite period of material prosperity, they have only got to behave in a peaceful and helpful way toward one another, and science will do for them all they wish and more than they can dream."* —— Winston Churchill

THE WORLD SHOWCASE

> *"My country is the world. My countrymen are all mankind.* —— William Lloyd Garrison

The World Showcase forms the southern half of the EPCOT Center and Future World the northern half. The exhibits in Future World emphasize the achievements of science and technology. The World Showcase is like a world's fair. Despite their differences, both areas possess the magical Disney touch.

The World Showcase exhibits the culture, history, architecture, and food of twelve different countries. Each country is on display in a separate pavilion. The pavilions encircle the World Showcase Lagoon along a broad walkway. In clockwise order, they are Mexico, Norway, China, Germany, Italy, The United States of America, Japan, Morocco, France, The United Kingdom, and Canada.

Disney captures and condenses the most notable characteristics of each country. Disney researched each country and enlisted the cooperation and contributions of each host country's government.

The buildings represent the architectural style of each country. In some cases, there are replicas of well-known structures such as the Eiffel Tower. The shops offer products made in each country. The restaurants serve characteristic food. The entertainment is authentic. Disney searches for and employs people from each country to work in their respective pavilions. Disney refers to their employees as "cast members" and they dress the part, their costumes reflecting their national origins. Disney generalizes and simplifies these things, but the total effect is informative and entertaining.

Access: Physically disabled people find the World Showcase wonderfully accessible. The walkway around the World Showcase Lagoon is usually 50 to 100 feet wide and made from smooth concrete. There are only a few slight hills and curbs, notably in the United Kingdom's pavilion. Where there are curbs, Disney places conveniently located ramps or curb cut-outs. Pushing a wheelchair around is a pleasant experience, as pleasant as it can be.

The restaurants and shops are accessible. The bathrooms have stalls wide enough to accept a wheelchair. The boats on the World Showcase Lagoon accept people using wheelchairs. There are only a few notable exceptions to the ease of access for people using wheelchairs. You must stand and walk to enjoy a ride called the Maelstrom in the Norwegian pavilion. The double-decker buses traveling around the Lagoon are inaccessible to many physically disabled people. Finally, some of the fast-food restaurants have crowd-control guide rails that are inconvenient for people using wheelchairs.

There are a few other considerations physically disabled people should note. It is almost a mile and a half around the World Showcase Lagoon and it can be hot in the summer. Anyone experienced pushing a wheelchair, or walking that far with a physical disability, knows this presents a challenge. The crowds of people test everybody's patience. A wheelchair is quite wide and difficult to maneuver through a crowd. Often, walking people overlook someone in a wheelchair and stop, blocking their progress. The author has crashed into more than a few people. There is no harm done, other than a little embarrassment — for both parties. He is in trouble if they ever require drivers licenses to operate wheelchairs.

We think learning about the world is important. We think everybody benefits from foreign travel, but we know this is not always practical or possible. The EPCOT Center offers a solution — The World Showcase. It is possible, in one day, to visit twelve countries. More importantly, everyone can. There are few handicaps for physically disabled people in this part of Walt Disney World.

Mexico

When moving around the World Showcase in a clockwise direction, Mexico is the first country. America's southern neighbor has a rich and diverse culture we think everyone will enjoy.

A stylized Mexican Indian pyramid and tropical vegetation identify the Mexico pavilion. Depending on a person's appetite, the Cantina de San Angel might be the first thing they notice. It is across from the pyramid and on the water's edge of the World Showcase Lagoon. This fast-food style restaurant offers beef-filled soft flour tortillas, tostadas con pollo, and churros — a fried pastry covered with cinnamon and sugar. A ramp leads to the wheelchair-accessible counter service and eating area. Many touristas find a cold Dos Equis Mexican beer irresistible on a hot afternoon.

A ramp on the right side of the pyramid leads to the exhibits in the Mexico pavilion. The main area is a re-creation of a small village plaza. Surrounding the plaza are buildings with balconies and tile roofs reflecting Mexico's Spanish influence. Around a central fountain are stands selling Mexican handicrafts and shops offering a variety of items from Mexico. These include brightly colored paper flowers, pinatas, sombreros, wooden bowls and trays, baskets, and pottery.

Artesanias Mexicanas: This shop has items made from beautiful stone, such as ashtrays, bookends, and chess sets.

La Familia Fashions: This shop carries Mexican-style clothing for women and children. They also have the kinds of silver and turquoise jewelry often found in Mexico.

El Ranchito Del Norte: They primarily feature gifts and souvenirs from northern Mexico.

Lively music plays an important role in Mexican culture. If you're lucky, you might encounter a Mariachi band in the plaza or on the street.

A frequently overlooked attraction in the Mexico pavilion is an exhibit called the "Reign of Glory." This exhibit of Pre-Columbian artifacts (pre-discovery by Christopher Columbus) is one of the best of its kind in the World Showcase. It is accessible to people using wheelchairs.

The highlight of the Mexico exhibit is El Rio Del Tiempo: The River Of Time. It involves a nine-minute boat ride. Disney modified some of the boats so people using wheelchairs can roll on and enjoy the trip along with everyone else. Ride attendants direct disabled guests to the exit area where boarding is easiest. Once again, visitors using the motorized carts must transfer from them into a conventional wheelchair or one of the seats in the boats.
The boat ride is similar to the one in the It's a Small World

ride in the Magic Kingdom. The boats pass scenes representing different eras of Mexican history. The original inhabitants of Mexico, the Mayan, Toltec, and Aztec Indians, had civilizations as rich and complex as the more familiar ancient Egyptians. The exhibits contain scenes of Pre-Columbian, Spanish-Colonial, and modern Mexico, and feature the familiar Disney AudioAnimatronic characters. You see a Mayan high priest, dancers in colorful costumes, and vendors in a crowded marketplace.

The largest crowds occur during the mid-day at the Mexico pavilion. You should time your visit accordingly.

There is a full-service restaurant in the Mexico pavilion named the San Angel Inn. We describe this under the section titled Dining In The EPCOT Center.

Norway

The Norway pavilion boasts one of the best rides in the World Showcase. It is also the least accessible for people with physical disabilities. They call the ride the Maelstrom. The ride attendant told the author he must transfer from his wheelchair into one of the boats. When he said he would like to try, they asked if he could walk. He said no. They politely explained that people must be able to walk in case the ride shut down and an emergency evacuation became necessary. The author suggested that someone could carry him. They said, "sorry, we can't do that, no offense, it's just company policy."

Actually, many people using wheelchairs can stand and walk short distances. If they can "maneuver down stairs in an evacuation situation," they can go on the ride. Visitors board replicas of Viking longboats for a fantasy ride. The 16-passenger boats take them on a ride through time in Norwegian history. The ride begins in a tenth-Century village as they ready the boats for sea. Soon, riders find themselves in a forest where mythical trolls force the boats to go backward. Then the boats turn and go through a maelstrom, into a beautiful fjord. Eventually, they make it into the North Sea and get caught in a storm before reaching the safety of a village. Following the ride, visitors see a five-minute film about Norway in a theater. To our knowledge, this is only accessible to people with the ability to negotiate the boat ride.

It is worth seeing the passive exhibits that make up the Norway pavilion. The displays include a courtyard surrounded by traditional Norwegian buildings. There is a replica of a 14th-century castle copied from one preserved in Oslo's harbor, a wooden church, and cottages with red-tiled roofs. There are shops in the castle accessible to people who must use wheelchairs. They offer a variety of Norwegian handicrafts, wood carvings, and glass and metal art work.

There is a popular fast-food spot in the Norway pavilion. The Kringla Bakeri og Kafe is a pleasant place for a cup of coffee and a sample of many varieties of Norwegian pastry. A full-service restaurant is the Akershus. We describe them in detail in the section on Dining In The EPCOT Center.

China

> "If a man takes no thought about what is distant, he will find sorrow near at hand." —— Confucius

In the real world, China lies on the other side of the globe. At the EPCOT Center it sits on the east side of the World Showcase, between Norway and Germany.

The Chinese exhibit features a temple, manicured gardens, reflecting ponds, a 19-minute film, a display of art and artifacts, two restaurants, and a shopping area. They play traditional Chinese music in the background. The combination of sights and sounds create a feeling of serenity, and provide a relaxing place to spend and hour or two.

The Chinese pavilion represents the People's Republic of China. The Republic is home to more than 800 million people. It has more people than any country in the world and approximately four times the population of the United States. Despite its size, most Americans know little about China and its people.

Hot and cold characterizes America's relationship with China. We were allies while fighting the Japanese during World War II. A Communist government took control in 1949, and in the Cold War years, in Korea and Vietnam, we clashed. Today, in both countries, people desire the removal of the remaining distrust. Certainly, vast cultural differences feed our inability to coexist. The Chinese pavilion in the EPCOT Center helps bridge the gap. It shows parts of China few of us will ever see. The Chinese exhibit is completely accessible. Disney offers everyone a view of China.

The Temple of Heaven marks the Chinese pavilion. This is a half-sized reproduction of the same building in Beijing (Peking). Originally built in 1420 during the Ming Dynasty, the Chinese restored it in 1896 after lightning damaged it. In the EPCOT Center, Disney recreates the Hall of Prayer for Good Harvest. The Chinese worship the land; even today, the majority of its people are farmers. Circling the main room are twelve columns representing the twelve months of the year and the years making the full cycle of the Chinese calendar. Four columns near the center of the hall symbolize the four seasons. The vines around the columns are for long life, and the square beam represents the earth.

One of the pleasures of the EPCOT Center is speaking with the attendants. They usually come from the countries represented by the pavilions they work in. Invariably, they are friendly and eager to talk about their homelands. In the Chinese pavilion, the author spoke with a young man from Beijing while waiting for the film. The young man explained the meaning of the temple. He also volunteered the fact that the film about China is 15 years old and much has changed in China since. It was obvious to the author that this Chinese man wished it would change more.

Talking with the young people staffing the pavilions is a valuable experience. They offer insight into the character of their countries that is not always obvious in the exhibits. They learn something from talking with a physically disabled person. Who knows, they might develop a positive awareness of people with physical disabilities that might not exist in their countries. We can all contribute something to make the world a better place.

The author always feels a little sad when comparing his opportunities in America with disabled people in other countries. In many places he would not be alive, much less up and racing around in a wheelchair. Let's communicate with other people and improve things. We really are in this ball game, on this spaceship earth, together.

They show a 19-minute film, *Wonders of China: Land of Beauty, Land of Time*. You enter the theater after passing through the Hall of Prayer for Good Harvest. Normally people must stand while viewing the CircleVision 360 film. An attendant usually spots someone using a wheelchair and directs them to the best viewing area. Sitting in a wheelchair is not a handicap during the movie. The screen is high enough to see it over the standing visitors. It circles all the way around the theater so the view is excellent for everyone.

The film is a Disney marvel. It shows Beijing's Forbidden City, the 2,400-year-old Great Wall of China, and the cities of Suzhou, Shanghai, and Hangzhou. There are many memorable Chinese people, like the tough-looking Mongols, or the disciplined people of Hangzhou in their morning exercise routine. The diversity of the Chinese landscape is awesome in its beauty, from the snow covered mountains, to fields of wheat, and palm-fringed beaches. The Disney photographers shot much of the film from the air, always with the cooperation of the Chinese. The film is as good as anything in the EPCOT Center and we recommend making it a priority.

Whispering Willows: This is an exhibit of Chinese art and artifacts that Disney changes every six months. It is near the exit of the theater.

Yang Feng Shangdian Shopping Gallery: Here, visitors find a variety of Chinese products like silk robes, prints, colorful paper umbrellas, fans, and small items useful as inexpensive gifts and souvenirs.

There are two restaurants in the Chinese pavilion. A fast-food restaurant and a full-service restaurant named Nine Dragons. We describe these in more detail in the section on Dining In The EPCOT Center.

Germany

You find the German pavilion on the southeastern shore of the World Showcase Lagoon, between the Chinese and Italian pavilions. The German exhibit consists of a central plaza surrounded by shops and a full-service restaurant at the rear.

They call the central plaza St. Georgsplatz. A statue of St. George slaying a dragon dominates the center of the cobblestone plaza. The buildings around St. Georgsplatz idealize rather than copy those typically seen in German villages. The cobblestone surfaces of the plaza make rolling in a wheelchair a bit bumpy but not impassable or uncomfortable. The author knows from experience that real cobblestones are a very unpleasant experience when bouncing around in a wheelchair. All the shops are accessible to people using wheelchairs. Physically disabled people find the German pavilion and its attractions completely accessible.

You see the following shops when moving around St. Georgsplatz in a counterclockwise direction:

Der Bucherwurm: This is a two-story building similar to a merchant's hall in the southern German town of Freiburg. The store offers books and printed pictures of characteristic German scenes. It also displays numerous souvenir items such as ashtrays, vases, and spoons carrying scenes of German cities. Disney artists went to considerable pains to guarantee the authenticity of this building. They took photographs of the statues of German emperors on the front of the original building in Freiburg and reproduced them in the EPCOT Center.

Volkskunst: This little shop specializes in clocks and other items from the German countryside. Among these is an incredible array of beer steins ranging in size from tiny to ones holding more than you ever would, or could drink. There are wood carvings, Tyrolean Scarves, and nutcrackers. Of course there are cuckoo clocks, one of which is almost five feet high — just the thing for your living room.

Der Teddybar: This is a shop displaying toys B.P. (before plastic). These mechanized toys are akin to cuckoo clocks. They are imaginative and cute. They range from stuffed lambs to dolls in traditional German dresses. They have a collection of LGB-brand model trains. They offer many kinds of wooden toys and building blocks. If you have small children on a gift list and want something authentic and unique, this is the shop.

Weinkeller: This is a wine shop offering nearly 250 types of German wine. They feature daily wine tastings, making it a pleasant place to stop and learn something about German wine. One of the notable features of German wines is that most are white and many are sweet. Apparently, the types of grapes used in white wine grow better in the German climate than their red cousins. Sampling wine is a tough job, but someone has to do it. And everyone has equal access.

In the Weinkeller, they sell a variety of glass and crystal wine glasses and beer mugs. The shop is quaintly reminiscent of one a person might expect in a German village. The wooden cabinets have carvings of grapes and grape vines. Disney is so conscious of accuracy that they changed the original color of the grapes from purple to green, reflecting the color of the grapes used in making white German wine.

Sussigkeiten: If cursed with an uncontrollable sweet tooth, this is a good shop to avoid. There are tempting chocolate cookies, butter cookies, and almond biscuits filled with caramel. Children love the alphabet cookies and animal crackers. A box of Lebkuchen makes a thoughtful gift. These are a type of crisp and spicy cookie prepared in Germany during the Christmas season.

Italy

Compared to the real thing, the Italian pavilion is disappointing. Italy ranges from snow-capped mountains to rugged, rocky shores, sunny beaches, and the warm Mediterranean Sea. The ruins of ancient civilizations are everywhere. Its food and wine eclipse the Americanized versions of spaghetti and meatballs or pizza and cheap red wine. However, Disney's representation of Italy is accessible to physically disabled people, and the real Italy is beyond the reach of many, disabled or not.

There are no rides or film attractions in the Italian pavilion, yet a visit is enjoyable. The buildings and sculptures are detailed and realistic. The shops offer genuine and beautiful Italian products. The food is good and the street shows are hilarious. The Italian pavilion is easily worth an hour or two when visiting the EPCOT Center.

A 105-foot bell tower stands guard over the entrance to the Italian pavilion. Disney artists and engineers copied it from the one in St. Mark's Square in Venice. Two massive columns flank the bell tower. One supports a statue of St. Mark the Evangelist and the other carries a statue of a lion. The lion is St. Mark's partner and the legendary guardian of Venice. Entering the pavilion, the building on the left is a detailed reproduction of Doge's Palace, built during the 14th Century in Venice. The rest of the structures in the Italian exhibit copy architectural styles commonly seen in Italy.

Along the shore of the World Showcase Lagoon, Disney created a Venetian-style island. The island is complete with gondolas (the water taxis of Venice) tied to their characteristic barber-pole moorings.

One of the nicer things about the EPCOT Center is the comical street shows. This is especially true for physically disabled people because they often have the best seats in the house. While others are standing, they have their own chairs. The Italian pavilion features a group called Il Commedia di Bologna. They act out 15-minute shows like "The Great Impasta." The intent is clear; they are not totally serious. The talented performers sometimes draft viewers into the act and produce laughs for everyone.

Italians make an art of everything. The four shops in the Italian pavilion are no exception.

Delizie Italiane: This is a cheerful open-air market, located on the western side of the plaza. They sell a variety of sweets and snacks.

La Bottega Italiana: Italy produces some of the highest-quality leather goods in the world and this shop displays a few samples, like purses and belts. It also offers Italian-made items like scarves, perfume, and assorted sportswear.

La Gemma Elegante: Towards the back of the Italian pavilion, another little shop specializes in jewelry. They dazzle shoppers with gold and silver chains and earrings. Other popular items are pendants made of Venetian glass, delicate brooches, and coral necklaces.

Il Bel Cristallo: Italian craftsmen mastered the art of glass-making long ago. They have not lost their touch. This little shop sits just off the walk-way, near the adjacent German pavilion. It features items like Venetian glass paperweights, bowls, and candlesticks. Visitors can find porcelain figurines and incredibly delicate glass flowers.

The full-service restaurant in the Italian pavilion is L'Originale Alfredo di Roma Ristorante. We describe it in the section on Dining In The EPCOT Center.

The American Adventure

> *"America is much more than a geographical fact. It is a political and moral fact — the first community in which men set out in principle to institutionalize freedom, responsible government, and human equality."*
> —— Adlai Stevenson

Everyone should visit the American pavilion in the EPCOT Center and learn more about the United States of America, how the country formed, and what it accomplished. Personal freedom is America's foundation. It is fitting that America has a civil rights law specifically for disabled people. The Americans With Disabilities Act (ADA) became effective in July, 1990. We hope Thomas Jefferson would be proud. He wrote as he believed, in the Declaration of Independence, that "all men are created equal." It is pleasing to report that The American Adventure pavilion and its attractions, are accessible for physically disabled people. This is personal freedom at its best.

The building housing the American Adventure graces the southern shore of the World Showcase Lagoon. It lies between the Italian and Japanese pavilions. The American pavilion is a reproduction of Independence Hall in Philadelphia. The attractions include a 30-minute theater show, an informal singing performance by "The Voices of Liberty," a shop, and a fast-food restaurant.

At the entrance, an attendant directs disabled people in to a large, domed room for a preliminary show. When the show ends, they move off to one side of the room, to an elevator, where an attendant takes them into the theater.

When enough people to fill the theater enter the central room, "The Voices of Liberty" begin the show. The young male and female singers dress in early American costumes and perform a variety of traditional songs. The author enjoyed the show, except for the ending. Their last song was the *Star Spangled Banner*. Appropriately, the sitting audience stood for the American national anthem. The problem was, they were now standing in front of the author, blocking his view of the singers. The obstructed view left him out of the emotional finale. There is little that people using wheelchairs can do in this situation because people sit or stand wherever they wish in the viewing area. If seeing the entire show is important to disabled people, they might try sitting in front of the other viewers. Otherwise, they should prepare for a little disappointment and move toward the elevator for the main show.

The elevator only holds four people sitting in wheelchairs. There was a group of about eight people using wheelchairs when the author visited, so the trip to the theater was slow. Fortunately, everyone was in the theater and positioned in a viewing area before the show began.

The main show is *The American Adventure,* a highlight of the EPCOT Center. It features 35 AudioAnimatronic characters and detailed, movable sets. Disney uses an advanced digital sound system and a wide (72 feet), rear-projection screen for the video portion of the program.

The show traces the history of America, from the Pilgrims landing at Plymouth Rock to the present. The Audio-Animatronic hosts are two beloved American figures, Ben Franklin and Mark Twain. They discuss important events in American history, like the Boston Tea Party, and George Washington at Valley Forge. Other AudioAnimatronic cast members include Thomas Jefferson; Chief Joseph, the great Indian leader; Susan B. Anthony, an early advocate of women's rights; and many others.

Thirty minutes is too short a time to tell the complete, 200-year history of the United States, so they limit the show to the most notable people and events. They do this with typical Disney attention to detail and authenticity. Many of the animated characters recite their own written or spoken words. Where possible, Disney duplicates their actual voices. The voices of Will Rogers and FDR (President Franklin Roosevelt) are their own, taken from recordings. The props used are authentic copies, including the microphone and radio used by FDR.

The stage is a masterpiece of technology. There are ten movable sets beneath the theater. They automatically roll into position and appear at the right moment. Visitors should look at the 12 statues flanking the stage, the "Spirits of America." They are Freedom, Heritage, Pioneering, Knowledge, Self-Reliance, Adventure, Individualism, Innovation, Tomorrow, Independence, Compassion, and Discovery.

The Philadelphia Symphony Orchestra plays the recorded music used in the show. The theme song *Golden Dreams,* is particularly memorable. You can ask an attendant for information about buying a recorded copy.

The American Adventure Show is busiest during mid-day. If the park is crowded, you can try racing to it early in the morning or wait until evening. Some people consider the show the best in The EPCOT Center.

Heritage Manor Gifts: In this shop, you can find a variety of pre-1940, American gifts. A few examples are glassware, porcelain, toys, and hand-made wooden and fabric items.

The one restaurant in the American Adventure pavilion is the fast-food, Liberty Inn. We describe it in the section Dining in the Epcot Center.

Japan

The Japanese pavilion lies between The American Adventure and the Moroccan pavilion. The primary attractions in the Japanese exhibits relate to architecture, art, and shopping. There are no shows or rides. There is a Japanese restaurant requiring reservations. We describe it in detail in the section on Dining in the EPCOT Center. The Japanese pavilion is accessible to all physically disabled people.

The atmosphere in the Japanese pavilion is usually peaceful and quiet. The exception occurs when a musical group called "Genroku Hanamai" plays their drums. Their music is stimulating and unusual. It's a street show, so people using wheelchairs should make a point of finding a spot in front of the crowd. We advise checking the show times with a host or in the daily schedule of events.

Disney takes great care in landscaping the EPCOT Center. The Japanese attribute a religious value to their gardening. They use rocks to represent the stability of the earth. The water in their ponds symbolizes the sea as the source of life. They associate evergreen trees with eternal life — logical when you think about it.

The Disney gardeners used non-Japanese plants because most Japanese plants dislike the Florida climate. The only plants native to Japan are the maples, notable for their small leaves. The "monkey puzzle" trees are another exception.

Monkeys have difficulty feeding on these trees because of their sharp, protruding thorns. It seems monkeys have handicaps too.

The buildings in the Japanese pavilion are authentic copies. The tall, blue-roofed pagoda duplicates the 8th Century Horyuji Temple. The torii gate on the shore of the World Showcase Lagoon has its inspiration in the Itsukushima shrine in Hiroshima Bay.

Bijutsu-Kan Gallery: This is an art gallery with exhibits that change on a regular basis. An example is "Echoes Through Time — Japanese Women and the Arts."

Mitsukoshi Department Store: The store offers traditional kimonos — the graceful, floral dresses traditionally worn by Japanese women. They have a variety of vases, bowls, and similar items. There are dozens of dolls on display. These have special meaning to the Japanese on Girls' Day, a national holiday. The shop offers fascinating masks used as part of Japan's New Year's celebrations. When the Japanese make a New Year's resolution, they color in one of the eyes. Then they place the mask in a prominent place where the eye watches them, reminding them of their resolutions.

Morocco

The country of Morocco lies on the northwest tip of Africa. It is a land of contrasts. Jet airplanes fly over farmers using tools unchanged since Biblical times. Its cities have skyscrapers next to ancient minarets and fortress walls. The shores of the Mediterranean slope up to the snow-capped Atlas Mountains. It is a land of mystique and romance. The city of Casablanca, the same as that in the Humphrey Bogart movie, sits on the Atlantic shore. At one point, Spain is only eight miles away, across the Strait of Gibraltar.

In the EPCOT Center, visitors find the Moroccan pavilion between those of Japan and France. It is a pleasant place to visit, even though there are no films or rides. It is accessible by wheelchair and presents no barriers to disabled people.

The Moroccan pavilion is notable for its beautiful architecture, shops, artwork, and one restaurant. Disney imported nine tons of handmade tile for the pavilion. Insuring authenticity, they brought 19 craftsmen from Morocco to aid in construction.

The tower at the entrance is a copy of the Koutoubia Minaret in Marrakech. The reddish colored fortress walls and narrow alleys give the feel of a typical North African town. The shops displaying Moroccan handicrafts mimic the bazaars found all over North Africa. The men working in the shops wear traditional striped robes and the curious, cylindrical hats they call a "fez."

A bazaar is a Middle Eastern market. The word and the markets originated in ancient Persia and spread throughout the Islamic world. They consist of dozens of small shops opening to a maze of narrow streets or alleys. The Persian bazaars sell almost anything. The merchants don't fix prices or label items. Everything is negotiable and bargaining is an art form. This might be the reason westerners have such problems with the Moslem world. They have been wheeling and dealing longer than we have, and they play by different rules.

The bazaar in the Moroccan pavilion differs from real bazaars in a number of ways. The shops are clean and lack some of the pleasant (and not so pleasant) smells of a Persian bazaar. There are no chickens and goats wandering around, and they don't encourage bickering over prices. Otherwise, there are many similarities.

Casablanca Carpets: This shop offers hand-woven Berber and Rabat carpets and prayer rugs. Besides serving as floor coverings, they make beautiful wall-hangings with their bright colors and geometric designs.

Jewels of the Sahara: Shoppers can pick up authentic Berber silver and gold jewelry. Beads made from onyx, amber, stones, and pieces of glass, are popular and inexpensive.

Tangier Traders: They sell leather goods, like belts, sandals, purses, wallets, and a variety of Moroccan clothing, including the traditional hats known as a fez.

The Brass Bazaar: As the name implies, they sell brass pots, bowls, trays, pitchers, and planters.

Marketplace in the Medina: They offer handmade baskets, straw hats, and lampshades. Bamboo furniture is another popular item.

Fashions From Fes: This store has traditional Moroccan women's clothing and accessories.

Morocco in Medina Arts: Shoppers can find Moroccan arts and crafts in this shop.

Berber Oasis: This is a tent at the entrance to the pavilion offering more brass items, baskets, and leather goods.

Gallery of Arts and History: This is a small museum that displays examples of Moroccan art, artifacts, and clothing, with regularly changing exhibits. For people seriously attracted to Morocco, there is even a Moroccan National Tourist Office. They offer help in planning and booking a trip and continually present a slide show of Morocco.

Marrakesh is the full-service restaurant in the Moroccan pavilion. We describe it in detail in the section on Dining In The EPCOT Center.

France

The French pavilion is in the southwestern part of the EPCOT Center, between the exhibits of Morocco and The United Kingdom. The French pavilion has the look and feel of Paris, arguably one of the more beautiful and romantic cities in the world. Graceful bridges span the River Seine as it flows through Paris. They recreate this setting in the EPCOT Center with an extension of the World Showcase Lagoon and a bridge connecting the pavilions of the United Kingdom and France.

One of many memorable aspects of Paris is its sidewalk cafes. They seem to be everywhere. Wandering the streets of the city, the cafes attract like a magnet. The mass of chairs and small round tables, sometimes covered by an awning, look cozy and comfortable. There are old men reading newspapers, sipping cognac, and smoking cigarettes, apparently without a care in the world. Young couples, whispering while holding hands over glasses of wine, remind visitors why Paris is for lovers.

We encourage everyone to stop for a while at the sidewalk cafe in the EPCOT Center, the Au Petit Cafe. It is along the promenade, in front of the French Pavilion. It is a perfect place for disabled people to exit the fast lane and have a relaxing cup of espresso, a glass of French wine, and some quiet intimacy.

Disney created the buildings to look similar to those in France. They even made the roofs from copper or slabs of slate. What would Paris be without the Eiffel Tower? Disney hasn't forgotten. If you look closely, you see the graceful tower above the buildings and trees.

Wandering through the French pavilion, and wandering is the best way of seeing and feeling any new place, visitors might encounter some street musicians. Stop for a while and be entertained. Speak with the costumed hosts and hostesses. Listen carefully to their heavily French-accented English. All of them come to the EPCOT Center from France and have the trademark Disney friendliness and enthusiasm.

Just as there is more to Italy than Venice, there is more to France than Paris. Nature blessed France with a diversity of landscapes. These range from sea-swept shores to snow-covered mountains. Mont Blanc in the French Alps is the highest mountain in western Europe. Fertile fields make France a major wheat producer. Her vineyards provide grapes for some of the finest wines in the world. A person can ski at a resort like Chamonix or, just hours away, swim in the Mediterranean Sea.

Centrally located on the European continent, many cultures met in France and influenced her people. The Greeks,

Romans, Norsemen, and Celts all played a role. The French take pride in their individuality and their art. They initiated revolutions and spread their culture throughout the world. Fortunately, the French pavilion offers a look at France beyond the buildings and streets of Paris.

The Palais Du Cinema is a small theater showing an 18-minute film bringing the diversity of France to life. Visitors see a country estate with rich fields, trees, vineyards, and a village with its flower markets. Viewers soar over Alpine glaciers and a fishing harbor swarming with seagulls. They see Paris and the Eiffel Tower, the Palace of Versailles, and much more.

The soundtrack of the film enhances the visual beauty. The music comes from classical orchestral pieces written by French composers. Imagine listening to Debussy's *Afternoon of a Faun* while floating over the fertile fields of France.

The EPCOT Center has the best theaters the author has seen anywhere. The Palais Du Cinema is no exception. They show the film on a screen made in five sections; each is 21 feet high and 27 feet wide, forming more than half a circle around the audience. We recommend that everyone see these movies. Gratefully, all are accessible to disabled people, whether they must remain in their wheelchairs or not.

The French pavilion boasts some of the nicest shops in the EPCOT Center.

The Plume Et Palette: The store specializes in artwork and crystal. The decorative theme is Art Nouveau, popular in France during the early 20th Century. The wooden display cases are beautiful in themselves. One has purple, lavender, and yellow stained glass; another has delicate red and green painted roses. The cases display small collectibles and tapestries. As beautiful as this shop is, it is not perfect.

The second level of the Plume et Palette is not accessible to disabled people in wheelchairs. Perhaps this handicap is a minor issue. However, people who love French oil paintings and prints, and have $300 to $3,000 to spend, might feel otherwise.

La Signature: The store is beautifully decorated with silk-like wallpaper, a chandelier, and velvet curtains. It offers French perfumes, fragrant bath products, and a variety of French clothing.

The Galerie Des Halles: This store tempts shoppers with French chocolates, cookies, other sweets, and souvenirs.

Tout Pour Le Gourmet: The store displays the tools of another French tradition. The French have a passion for their food and cooking. In this shop, people can see and purchase unusual and sophisticated kitchen equipment, herbs, preserves, and other specialty foods.

La Maison Du Vin: The French pavilion could not be complete without a wine shop. Some of the wine costs a few dollars per bottle, but a rare vintage can set a person back as much as $300. To sample without going bankrupt, there are daily wine tastings. They charge a bit for the wine, but they let you keep the glasses. If you decide to buy some wine and don't want to carry it around all day, the shop delivers the purchases to the Package Pick-up. You then collect the gifts as you leave the EPCOT Center. The same technique works with any items bought in the EPCOT Center.

Including the outdoor cafe, there are three full-service restaurants in the French pavilion. Besides Au Petit Cafe, there is the Bistro de Paris and Chefs de France. We describe these in detail in the section Dining In The EPCOT Center.

United Kingdom

> *"This royal throne of kings, this scepter'd isle,*
> *This earth of majesty, this seat of Mars,*
> *This other Eden, demi-paradise,*
> *This happy breed of men, this little world,*
> *This precious stone set in a silver sea*
> *This blessed plot, this earth, this realm, this England"....* — William Shakespeare

However unwillingly, the United Kingdom gave birth to the United States. The United States began life as 13 British colonies. The colonists rebelled and declared independence in 1776. They fought a war and became a separate country. The ancestors of many Americans are from the United Kingdom. We can trace our language, legal system, and cultural values back to the British Isles. Despite our common heritage, many Americans know little about the United Kingdom. They can continue their education by visiting the pavilion of the United Kingdom in the EPCOT Center.

The pavilion is more accessible to physically disabled people than the United Kingdom itself. Only the upper level of the Lords and Ladies shop is unreachable by people using a wheelchair. Elsewhere, they can wheel around on the cobblestone streets, go up the ramps cut in the curbs, into the shops, and into the restaurant and pub. Visitors can sit along the street, enjoy one of the comedy acts, and even participate in them.

The United Kingdom consists of England, Scotland, Wales, and Northern Ireland. The islands possess relatively few natural resources and their inhabitants endure a harsh climate. Britain reached out to her neighbors and spread her influence around the world.

Great Britain is the eighth largest island in the world and it contains England, Scotland and Wales. Each country maintains a unique identity, despite the fact that Wales joined England about 700 years ago and Scotland in 1707.

England occupies most of the island. It is the most industrialized and has the largest cities. Over seven million people live in London. The cities contrast with a beautiful countryside ranging from quiet moors, green valleys, lakes and rivers, to the famous white cliffs of Dover. A map of England overflows with recognizable names, like Hastings, Canterbury, Stonehenge, Stratford-upon-Avon, and Plymouth.

Scotland differs from England as Texas differs from New York. Scotland's rugged coasts and rocky land contrast with the gentler England. Its capital is Edinburgh and its largest city is Glasgow. The men of the Scottish Highlands sometimes wear a knee length dress called a kilt made from colorful plaids. These distinctive, patterned tartans identify the various Scottish clans.

Scotland claims a distinctive musical instrument called the bagpipes. This is a flexible bag filled with air and played with a double-reed melody pipe, and up to four drone pipes. Bagpipes sometimes sound disharmonious, but they can produce hauntingly beautiful music. We can't forget Scotland as the birthplace for the sport of golf. Scotland is also famous for its smoky flavored Scotch Whiskey. This is a distinctive liquor distilled from malted barley dried over a peat fire. We wonder if the Scots invented whiskey to alleviate the frustrations of golf, or invented golf to avoid drinking whiskey.

In Wales, nearly a fourth of the people still speak the native language. This is Welsh, a Celtic language preserved in the mountainous countryside. The Welsh people's love of singing and love of their soil is proverbial. So is their fierce independence and dislike of the English. Some old wounds heal slowly.

We all know about the deep wounds in Northern Ireland. Northern Ireland is a part of the United Kingdom even though it occupies the northeastern part of the island of Ireland. Its population is less than two million and its capital is Belfast.

Of course there is more to a country that its physical beauty or architecture and food. Just as there is more to a person than their outward appearance, a country has the character of its people.

The British people are notable for being calm in the face of adversity. "Keep a stiff upper lip," is a common phrase. They are a proud, determined people and have the history to prove it. They don't quit easily.

> *"We were not fairly beaten, my lord. No Englishman is ever fairly beaten."* — George Bernard Shaw

The pavilion for The United Kingdom in the EPCOT center does not have a movie like France, China, or Canada. Still, by visiting the pavilion, you see, hear, taste, and smell many characteristics of The United Kingdom.

You can walk or roll through a setting reproducing a square in London. You can wander through a scene that could be along a canal in the English countryside. The streets in the pavilion resemble many British villages. Disney attends to every detail.

Looking closely, you see the High Street building leaning a bit. Disney made the chimneys look used and they have thatched roofs, made of plastic bristles for fire prevention. You might notice a couple of the bright red phone booths that were so common all over Great Britain. The architectural styles range from Victorian, to Tudor and Georgian.

Without a film or a ride, the highlight of the United Kingdom's pavilion is its shops.

The Toy Soldier: This store offers wooden boats, colouring books, and dolls. The dolls are sophisticated and designed for collectors. The outside of the shop has its inspiration in the Scottish Abbotsford Manor. The Scottish poet and novelist, Sir Walter Scott, lived and died there in 1832.

Lords and Ladies: This shop is adjacent to The Toy Soldier. Outside, it looks like it is from a movie about King Arthur. It sports colorful banners and a huge fireplace with a pair of swords above it. They sell pottery, dart boards, perfumes, beer mugs, chess sets, musical tapes, and records. The upper level of Lords and Ladies is inaccessible to anyone unable to climb stairs.

Pringle of Scotland: They offer a nice selection of wool sweaters. People from around the world recognize Scotland for its quality wool products. Although not suited for Florida's summer climate, they make nice gifts for people living in or visiting cooler habitats. They also sell woolen hats, socks, scarves, ties, mittens, and, for the brave, Scottish kilts.

The Queen's Table: The English produce high quality china. The Queen's Table offers a variety of items from the Royal Doulton China Company. The shop is beautiful.

Disney decorated its Adams Room with complex moldings, a crystal chandelier, and painted it in cream and pale blue colors, matching the carpet. The Adams Room displays a collection of collectors' statuettes. Prices range from $5 to (gasp) $12,500. They sell less expensive items like the Royal Doulton's well-known Bunnykins cups and bowls for children. The Toby mugs are interesting; they look like the faces of famous people.

The lovely Britannia Square is in the back of the pavilion. It is difficult duplicating London's climate and vegetation in Florida, but Disney made a jolly good effort. The statue in the center of the Square is none other than William Shakespeare. The crests on the building's upper windows are a subtle touch. They identify the United Kingdom's major universities, Oxford, Cambridge, Eton, and Edinburgh.

The Magic of Wales: This shop sells pottery, jewelry, souvenirs, and an assortment of handmade items from Wales.

The Tea Caddy: What would the United Kingdom be without its tea? We have no idea how the preference for tea over coffee originated, but the British love their tea. This shop, resembling Shakespeare's Stratford-upon-Avon cottage, sells England's favorite beverage. Twinings Tea Company sponsors it and offers many types of tea, loose in the traditional fashion and in bags. Shoppers can buy teapots or biscuits and candies. The British make an event of their afternoon tea. It is as much a British characteristic as a siesta is in Mexico.

For a beer on a hot Florida afternoon, or evening (or morning?), try the Rose & Crown Pub. They serve the beer cold in deference to American taste. "Real beer drinkers" know the British tradition of drinking their beer at room temperature. The British love their tradition almost as much as their beer. Raymond Postgate said it well,

> *"Deploring change is the unchangeable habit of all Englishmen."*

We describe the Rose & Crown Pub & Dining Room in more detail in the section on Dining In The EPCOT Center.

Canada

With the dissolution of the Soviet Union, Canada is the largest country on Earth. From the Atlantic to the Pacific Oceans and from the Arctic Ocean to its southern border with the United States, Canada covers 3,851,791 square miles. The People's Republic of China is second in size, with 3,705,390 square miles. The two countries are almost the same size, but China has about one billion people where Canada has less than 23 million.

Regardless of their small population, and fortunately for us, Canada has a pavilion in the World Showcase. It features buildings, shops, a restaurant, and a film presentation the equal to any in the EPCOT Center.

Canada is diverse in every way. First thinly populated by native North American Indians, it became a French Colony. French trappers and explorers gave way to the British redcoats on the Plains of Abraham in Quebec. Following the American Revolution, the British retreated to Canada. Today, Canada is an independent nation but still bound to the British Crown as part of the Commonwealth. Elizabeth II reigns as Queen of Canada, but does not rule. The French influence remains. French and English serve as Canada's two "official" languages.

Sometimes Canada seems like an enigma. As Kenneth Boulding said,

> *"Canada has no cultural unity, no linguistic unity, no religious unity, no economic unity, no geographic unity. All it has is unity."*

Canada shows how the people of a large, culturally diverse country, can get along. The countries of the former Soviet Union could benefit from her example.

Wild, towering mountains guard Canada's Pacific shores. Clouds off the Pacific Ocean drench their western slopes, producing lush forests. The mountains shield the interior valleys, leaving them nearly as dry as a desert. The rolling prairies of the mid-continent make Canada one of the world's major granaries, while her oil and gas wells export fuel.

To the east, the land south of Hudson's Bay is heavily forested, producing almost a third of the world's newsprint. The taming of some of her powerful rivers makes Canada third in the world in the production of hydroelectric power. The area contains countless lakes, blessing Canada with more than one-seventh of the world's fresh water. Farther east, in the Great Lakes-St. Lawrence River region, lie rolling hills, fertile fields, and orchards.

The Atlantic provinces contain an extension of the Appalachian mountains of the United States. Farms lie in the valleys, but the forests and the harvest of the sea provide most of the region's bounty. Frozen northern Canada can be bleak and barren. However, it provides a home for abundant wildlife, while its subsurface yields a wealth of minerals and energy.

Eighty-five percent of Canada's people live less than 200 miles from the United States. Modern highways and railroads solidly tie Canada together. The airplane links the remainder of this far-reaching and rich land. The United States is fortunate to have such a friendly, wealthy neighbor. Canada even forgave us for flying her flag upside down in a 1992 World Series baseball game. We are fortunate Disney included Canada in its World Showcase. Visitors agree when they see the film, *O Canada!*

The Canadian pavilion is on the northwestern side of the World Showcase Lagoon, between Journey Into Imagination and The United Kingdom's exhibit. Canada shows her beauty and culture in a condensed version. Disney created a Canadian Rocky Mountain scene, complete with a clear stream falling over a waterfall into a serene little canyon. They included an immaculate garden similar to one in Victoria, British Columbia.

The main building in the exhibit is the Hotel du Canada. It reflects Canada's French heritage by copying the Chateau Laurier in Ottawa, Ontario. Disney architects used a motion picture technique called "forced perspective" in making the building seem larger than it really is. The front is larger than the back, and the bottom wider than the top. They did the same thing with the mountain. It tricks the mind and pleases the eye.

The highlight of Canada's pavilion is a 17-minute film called *O Canada*! The theater is accessible to people using wheelchairs. So is all of the Canadian pavilion. You find the entrance to the theater on the right side of the pavilion, through the Victoria Gardens and past the Le Cellier restaurant. The theater is actually inside the mountain. Disabled visitors should ask an attendant for help getting in. It's very easy. Normally, you stand along rows of wooden rails. Of course people using wheelchairs are sitting, but everyone has an equally good view.

They created and present the film in CircleVision 360. The result is spectacular. Tall screens surround everyone in the circular theater. Even if you sit, you can see over other people. It is like riding in a bubble-topped helicopter; by just turning your head, you see what is in front, behind and to the sides.

CircleVision 360 uses a 600-pound contraption with nine separate 35mm cameras. The cameras record images in all directions. When they replay the synchronized film, the scenery comes alive. Visitors to Disney World see another example of this achievement in American Journeys, in the Magic Kingdom.

In 17 minutes, the film shows the best of Canada's coastlines, mountains, and prairies. The Royal Canadian Mounted Police, in their crimson tunics, with lances, banners, and splendid black horses, put on a parade. They open the show by appearing to come out of the screen, surrounding and welcoming guests to Canada.

The movie takes its guests from Old World Montreal to the sailing ships and sea-faring history of the east coast. In one scene, Canadian geese almost explode out of the screen. If people are not already wide-eyed, they will be. The film shows eagles, ducks, bobcats, bears, wolves, deer, buffalo, and herds of reindeer. It reveals the cowboy heritage of Canada in the Calgary Stampede. Canada has some of the world's best skiing as visitors see in a scene from British Columbia's Bugaboos. They don't use chairlifts here. Helicopters carry the adventurous high into the mountains, for a ski down through the untracked, sparkling powder.

The film *O Canada!* takes its viewers to places few people ever experience. This is especially true for physically disabled people. We encourage everyone to see this film and everyone can.

The Canadian pavilion also has some shops.

Northwest Mercantile: This is on the left as visitors enter the area. The shop illustrates the frontier character of Canada. It offers piles of sheepskins imitating the furs that played an important role in Canadian history. It carries shirts like a lumberjack might wear and items commonly found in a store on the edge of the Canadian wilderness. They built the shop with logs. They decorated it with masks, statues, and paintings used by the Indians of eastern Canada. There are some serious items and a lot of silly things like toy tomahawks and coonskin hats.

La Boutique Des Provinces: This shop offers items with a French Canadian flair. The shops are nice but the jewel of the Canadian pavilion is the film *O Canad*a!

A cafeteria-style restaurant named Le Cellier, is in the lower level of the Hotel du Canada. To get there, either walking or rolling, you follow a path through the Victoria Gardens. The path is clearly marked and lies on the right side of the Canadian pavilion. We describe the restaurant in more detail in the following section, Dining In The EPCOT Center.

FIREWORKS AND LIVE SHOWS IN THE EPCOT CENTER

"Laughter has no foreign accent" — Paul B. Lowney

The major handicap facing physically disabled people anywhere is access. Fortunately for us, there are a number of activities with equal access for everyone. These are poorly publicized, perhaps because non-disabled people take them for granted. Every day Disney conducts two incredible fireworks displays and tens of live shows. Anyone can see the fireworks and many of the shows take place in the streets. People using wheelchairs often have the best, if not the only seats in the house. We recommend anticipating and planning for these shows. You can find information about the shows at the desk in the Earth Station and from the World-Key Information Service. Disabled people, especially those using wheelchairs, should find a viewing spot 10 or more minutes before the shows begin. They should be polite, but assertive, and not let anyone stand in front of them and block their views.

Surprise in the Skies: Calling this a fireworks display does it an injustice. Every afternoon, around 3:00 p.m., nearly all the people in the EPCOT Center gather around the World Showcase Lagoon and hear an announcement that a special show is beginning. Rockets erupt from islands and platforms in the Lagoon; trailing colored smoke, they explode in showers of colored sparkles. Their thunderous reports echo around the EPCOT Center. Just as suddenly, viewers hear rousing symphonic music and see huge, inflatable Disney cartoon characters rise like magic around the World Showcase Lagoon. The fireworks continue in cadence with the music. Then the aerial dancers appear.

About ten speedboats race around the Lagoon towing strings of brightly colored kites. Each boat pulls a dozen-or-so kites with long red streamers. Somehow, amazingly, everything is choreographed — the fireworks, the music, the boats, and the kites. Lines of six kites respond in unison. They rise gracefully and abruptly dart and dive as they follow the boats around the Lagoon. The kites look like the Air Force Thunderbird aerial acrobats or a drill team of colorful birds. The show produces a sense of wonder and excitement that reverberates through the crowd in time with their appreciative "oohs and ahhs...." Everyone should see this show; fortunately, everyone can.

Illuminations: Every night the curtain comes down over

the EPCOT Center with a brilliant flourish and a bang, actually many bangs. Beginning about 10:00 p.m., or whenever the park closes, Disney puts on a fireworks display involving laser light beams playing over fountains of water in the World Showcase Lagoon, colored smoke, and the dazzle of hundreds of exploding fireworks. They accent the scene with music from speakers surrounding the Lagoon and brilliant lights outlining each country's pavilion. It's a memorable ending for any visit to the EPCOT Center.

Note that when the show ends, everyone, and this can mean as many as 40,000 people, is trying to leave. Imagine leaving a packed football stadium and you have some idea what the crowds are like. We recommend disabled people anticipate this mass exodus and linger a while, let the crowd pass, and enjoy the evening. Illuminations is one of the highlights of the EPCOT Center and everyone enjoys it. Make a point of seeing it at least once during your visit to Walt Disney World.

Street Shows: The World Showcase hosts an assortment of shows. These occur in an impromptu fashion on the streets and adjacent to the different country's pavilions. There may be people playing bagpipes near the Canadian pavilion, a Mariachi band in Mexico, musicians in Italy, or medieval comedians around the United Kingdom's pavilion. All of the acts are fun. Keep your eyes and ears open for the activity. Normally it is easy finding your way to the front of the crowd. In the author's experience, the crowds were relatively small and the other people polite in allowing him a view from his wheelchair. He witnessed dozens and dozens of people sitting in wheelchairs and smiling and laughing along with everyone else.

The Future World Brass Band: This is a group of young men playing trumpets, french horns, trombones, and one character doing an incredible solo performance on a set of drums. The author found it amazing how they could play and strut around with such enthusiasm on a daily basis. Make a point of looking for them around Spaceship Earth, or between Communicore West and the Land pavilion in Future World. Positioning yourself for a good view is easy. The author was almost too close, with one young man coming out and playing a rousing trumpet solo, no more than ten feet in front of where he was sitting in his wheelchair. The performances occur on the concrete walkways, so there are no problems with access for disabled people.

Disney Cartoon Characters: These have become a fixture in the EPCOT Center the same as in the Magic Kingdom. They really are lovable. The people inside the costumes are enthusiastic and clever. The characters elicit such cute responses from children it is easy sitting and watching and smiling. Some of the characters make an appearance each morning around 9:00 a.m. at the Stargate Restaurant in Future World. They also appear at various times at the Showcase Plaza and the Odyssey Restaurant. Especially if you are with children, make a point of finding these characters. They brighten your day.

The American Gardens Stage: This is a large outdoor theater between the American pavilion and the World Showcase Lagoon. Disney brings professional entertainers from around the world for special performances. These include singing, dancing, authentic costumes, and sometimes visits by Disney's cartoon characters. You can call ahead for information on the shows or find out at the Earth Station in Future World. They also display the show times on signs in front of the theater.

DINING IN THE EPCOT CENTER: A WORLD OF CHOICES

We are enthusiastic about the dining opportunities in the EPCOT Center for disabled people and their friends. We want to share some of that enthusiasm. Dining has a different meaning for everyone. Visitors have a world of choices in the EPCOT Center and virtually all the restaurants are accessible to disabled people. Everyone can find a type of food and dining experience fitting their tastes, budgets, and schedules. In our discussion of the options, we are descriptive rather than judgmental. We provide the information people need for making their own decisions about dining in the EPCOT Center.

Some people make dining the focus of their visits to the EPCOT Center. Sometimes they favor a particular restaurant. Perhaps they love Moroccan food, and can't find it anywhere else in Central Florida. Other people simply buy a box of popcorn or an ice cream cone and wander around enjoying the scenery.

The author's sister enjoys the latter approach. She says: "it's relaxing after a stressful day at work. I don't have to rush around or even go in any of the attractions." She has an annual pass and visits the EPCOT Center at least once each month. Sometimes she goes for a musical performance, sometimes for a nice dining experience, and often just to walk around and get away from it all.

One thing is constant about dining in Walt Disney World. We refer to this as the "Disney touch." Disney does everything possible to make dining a pleasurable experience. They decorate each restaurant with authentic detail. The waiters and waitresses are friendly and polite. They prepare and serve quality food. Only a true gourmet might criticize the cuisine.

On dining, Lucius Beebe says:

> "A gourmet can tell from the flavor whether a woodcock's leg is the one on which the bird is accustomed to roost."

We are not gourmet critics and could and would not pretend. However, everyone can learn from the Italian or French and make dining an event instead of a necessary routine. Disabled people encounter a few problems, but in our opinion, they are minor.

Making an event out of dining includes learning about food and wine. Each country, or culture, has something unique about its food and these characteristics develop over thousands of years. The same is true about wine and beer. The more a person knows, the more they enjoy. The EPCOT Center offers everyone the opportunity to learn about and sample the cuisine from twelve different countries.

The atmosphere of a restaurant is equally important. The restaurants in the EPCOT Center are clean and orderly. Some are even romantic. Disney decorates them tastefully and the service is friendly and efficient. Best of all, physically disabled visitors can enjoy everything about the restaurants, along with everyone else.

We divide the EPCOT Center in two parts, Future World and The World Showcase. In each area we break the dining opportunities into three categories, fast-food, full-service and one cafeteria-style restaurant. Beginning at Spaceship Earth, we describe the restaurants in clockwise order; first around Future World and then around the World Showcase.

Future World: Fast-Food Restaurants
COMMUNICORE EAST
Stargate: This is a fast-food, counter-service restaurant, located in the CommuniCore East building. If the weather is cooperative, it is a nice place to sit and eat on the outside terrace. The breakfast menu is the most notable feature of the Stargate restaurant. They offer cold cereals, Danish pastries, fresh fruit, blueberry muffins, cheese omelets, scrambled eggs, and fried potatoes. At lunch and dinner time, they serve pizza, hamburgers, steak sandwiches, fruit salads, chef's salads, and fruit pies. The restaurant remains open until the EPCOT Center closes.

WONDERS OF LIFE
Pure & Simple: Like its name and location suggest, they offer a selection of "health food." They sell things like frozen yogurt, yogurt shakes, oat bran waffles, and muffins.

FUTURE WORLD/WORLD SHOWCASE
The Odyssey Restaurant: This is located at the intersection of Future World and The World Showcase. It is in the southeast part of Future World, between The World of Motion attraction and the Mexico pavilion. This is another counter service restaurant and it has the usual problems for physically disabled people. In addition to the problems of crowded waiting lines and the necessity of carrying food on a tray, the dining area has tables on several levels. This makes eating here difficult for people using wheelchairs.

There is only one good way of handling a situation like this. Visitors should find an accessible table first and have the person using a wheelchair wait. Then a friend or companion can wait in line, order the food, pick it up at the counter, and carry it back to the table. This is not much fun. A wait of 30 minutes or more can separate them while one orders, and the other guards the table. The Odyssey Restaurant offers typical American fast-food. This includes hamburgers and french fries, hot dogs, chicken or tuna salads, and the usual soft drinks.

The Odyssey Restaurant complex offers more than dining. There is a First Aid Station staffed by registered nurses. Visitors should familiarize themselves with this service or at least be aware of its existence. The First Aid Station frequently handles minor emergencies, ranging from cut fingers, to sprained ankles and allergic reactions. If a particular problem exceeds their abilities, the nurses know how and where to get help.

For people with small children, The Odyssey Restaurant complex has a Baby Services Center. Baby Services has everything needed for changing diapers and preparing feeding formulas. They even have comfortable chairs and private locations for nursing mothers. Not discriminating based on gender, the Baby Services Center welcomes men caring for babies. It also serves as the command center for matching lost children with their parents.

LAND PAVILION

Farmers Market: The Land Pavilion is on the west side of Future World in the EPCOT Center. In addition to its main attraction, it has a unique fast-food restaurant. Once again, it involves counter service and the associated problems for physically disabled people. The entrance to the pavilion is on the upper level, while the Farmers Market is on the lower level. People using wheelchairs can get to the lower level on an elevator located to the left of The Land Grille Room, a full-service restaurant.

The Farmers Market has nine stands. Each is different. As a group, they offer something for everyone.

The Beverage House sells chocolate, vanilla, and strawberry milk shakes, or chocolate milk, buttermilk, and hot chocolate. In addition to soft drinks, they offer vegetable juice, peach nectar, papaya juice, and orange juice.

The Potato Store sells baked potatoes topped with a variety of treats. The toppings include a beef and wine sauce, sour cream, cheddar cheese, and bacon bits.

The Ice Cream Stand offers ice cream cones and cups of creamy, soft-serve ice cream.

Sandwich Stand presents the Disney Handwich and other sandwiches.

Picnic Fare sells an array of cheeses, smoked sausage, and fresh fruits.

The Cheese Shop sells fruit and cheese plates, quiche, and more exotic items like fettucine with chicken and a vegetable lasagna.

The Barbecue Store delivers barbecued beef and barbecued chicken-breast sandwiches. They also have half-chickens, baked beans, and cornbread muffins.

The Bakery is the place for breakfast, or anytime for people with a sweet-tooth. They have bagels with cream cheese, cinnamon rolls, and a variety of Danish pastries and muffins. After breakfast, or around 11:00 a.m., they bring out the pies, cheesecake, chocolate cake, brownies, date-nut bread, cheese bread, and addictive chocolate-chip cookies.

The Soup and Salad Stand sells some nice soups, including a New England fish chowder. The salads include seafood, fruit, chicken, or pasta.

COMMUNICORE WEST
Sunrise Terrace: This is an Italian-style fast-food shop in the CommuniCore West building. They serve Italian-American favorites like pizza, pasta, and an antipasto salad. Guests order and accept their food over a counter. They receive

their meals on trays and take them to a table. Counter service presents problems for people using wheelchairs.

Moving through a crowd in a wheelchair is difficult. It is like driving a huge truck through a busy parking lot. Counter service requires that people using wheelchairs balance a tray and its contents on their laps. The balancing act is not easy while pushing a wheelchair. Reaching across a counter while sitting in a wheelchair is difficult, especially for disabled people with limited use of their hands and arms. For these reasons and more, many disabled people avoid eating in restaurants with counter service.

Disabled people have several options. If they have companions accompanying them, they can ask them for help ordering, picking up, and carrying their food to a table. Sometimes strangers or restaurant employees carry the trays, but this still requires the waiting lines. Finally, disabled people can avoid the counter service restaurants and find one with table service.

Future World: Full-Service Restaurants
LAND PAVILION

The Land Grille Room: This is located in The Land pavilion, on the western side of Future World. Disabled people can easily get to and in the restaurant, but once in, there are a couple of problems. Visitors should go through the main entrance of the pavilion and proceed straight ahead to the restaurant. The dining area has several levels with steps between them. Fortunately, one of the levels is accessible to people using wheelchairs. The restaurant continually revolves, offering diners a changing view of the exhibits in the Land pavilion.

A potential problem for physically disabled people involves the seating booths around the tables. Normally, people simply slide into them and sit around a table. This presents a handicap for someone using a wheelchair and unable to transfer from it into the seats. A possible solution is rolling the wheelchair up to and under the table from the front. This way, there is no need to transfer from the wheelchair.

Every seating area in any restaurant has potential problems for physically disabled people. People using wheelchairs may have trouble getting their legs under a table because it is too low. Sometimes they can swing the footrests of their wheelchairs aside and place their feet on the floor. This lowers their legs a bit, enabling them to roll under the table. Everyone should realize the difficulty of eating from a wheelchair while sitting away from a table. Every person's situation is unique and sometimes experimenting is the only way of making things work.

The Land Grille Room offers a unique service at lunch time. Diners can order a sample-size portion of one item and a larger portion of another. It's a nice way of spreading the risk of trying something new. At dinner, they offer Maine lobster, stir-fried shrimp, and vegetables served with pasta. Meat lovers have their choice of prime ribs, steak, or Oriental-style chicken. The lunch menu is the same as that at dinner, but with the addition of sandwiches like one made with turkey, ham, lettuce, and tomato served on toasted cheese bread. They have a children's menu with smaller portions. Recently, they added a breakfast menu.

One of the nicer features of The Land Grille Room is the fact the restaurant slowly revolves. As it turns, diners have a view of the thunderstorm, desert sandstorm, and rain forest displays of The Land pavilion. Disney designed the restaurant and the "Listen to the Land" boat ride so they share the same views. The result is a unique and pleasurable dining experience.

They recommend reservations for lunch and dinner. So do we. This is a popular restaurant. Visitors with confirmation tickets can bypass waiting lines at the entrance to The Land pavilion. They offer this privilege to people arriving with their reservations within a half-hour of their seating times.

LIVING SEAS
Coral Reef Restaurant: Sometimes people visit the EPCOT Center just to dine in a quality restaurant and in a pleasant atmosphere. They may have a multi-day pass or an annual pass and can avoid paying the daily entrance fee. In this

case, the Coral Reef Restaurant in the Living Seas pavilion is a favorite.

It's popular because it's close to the entrance to the EPCOT Center. Even then, getting there requires a bit of a hike or a roll. You must go past Spaceship Earth, through CommuniCore West, around and back to the Living Seas pavilion. However, it's faster than going to one of the restaurants in the World Showcase. Like most restaurants in the EPCOT Center, The Coral Reef Restaurant accommodates physically disabled people and one of its levels allows access for people using wheelchairs.

The unique aspect of the Coral Reef Restaurant is the aquarium. Diners sit at tables in front of huge windows revealing the world of an under water coral reef. Everyone enjoys watching the fish. The aquarium is like a constantly changing, ever entertaining, work of art. Appropriately, the menu features seafood.

They serve a variety of fish and shellfish. They offer baked clams, oysters on the half shell, and swordfish with a Thai curry and lobster sauce. Mediterranean-style shrimp with tomatoes, leeks, and onions sounds delicious. Maine lobster stuffed with crab is always a favorite. If eating seafood while fish stare through a window makes anyone feel guilty, they can order a steak or a hamburger. The Coral Reef, like The Land Grille Room, is a popular restaurant. They require reservations. Make them early.

World Showcase: Fast-Food Restaurants

There are nine fast-food restaurants and snack stands located around the World Showcase. All are accessible to physically disabled people. Note that we didn't say convenient, just accessible. We describe them in clockwise order, beginning with the one in front of the Mexican pavilion.

MEXICO

Cantina de San Angel: This fast-food restaurant in the World Showcase is one of the best. The location is perfect. It sits on the shore of the World Showcase Lagoon, across the promenade from the Mexico pavilion. There is a magnetism to its shaded patio overlooking the water. On a hot summer afternoon, just the thought of the shade is appealing; add a cold beer and it's irresistible.

In addition to the Dos Equis beer, they sell tortillas filled with shredded beef, tostadas con pollo, or tortillas with chicken and refried beans. Tortillas are a type of thin, flat, round bread that is fundamental to Mexican cooking. They offer something for people with a taste for sweets. It is a treat called churros, a lightly fried pastry, rolled in sugar and cinnamon and served hot.

NORWAY
Kringla Bakeri og Kafe: The bakery is located in the Norway pavilion. It's like a fast bakery, if there is such a thing. It is a nice place for a quick breakfast, lunch, or snack. People using wheelchairs can go through the lines, select, pick up, and pay for their food. It isn't easy, but it is possible.

There are brass rails set up to control the flow of people. These are waist-high to a standing adult and about shoulder-high to a person sitting in a wheelchair. The lanes formed by the rails are wide enough for a wheelchair, but barely. Making a right angle turn while pushing a wheelchair between the rails is difficult. We think this would be extremely difficult for someone using an electric wheelchair. This is a common problem in the fast-food eateries of the EPCOT Center. There are a couple of solutions.

The easiest solution is having a walking companion order, pick-up, pay for, and bring the food back to a table. This gets the job done, but it is less than satisfactory. Having someone order food for a person eliminates some of their freedom and pleasure of choice. We think part of the fun is looking at the variety of food and having the opportunity of asking questions. This is not a minor issue. Physically disabled people get very tired of being handicapped by unnecessary barriers. Worst of all, they can become dependent and lose the will needed in trying new things. We always encourage physically disabled people to do as much as they possibly can. In the EPCOT Center, they can do a lot.

A favorite treat in the bakery is kringles. These are sweet, candied pretzels, served in Norway on special occasions. Every day is special in the EPCOT Center. Vaflers are waffles topped with jam and powdered sugar. Kransekake is a pastry ring topped with almonds. Then there are smorbrods — open-faced sandwiches topped with smoked salmon, roast beef, or ham.

Some of the experiences in the World Showcase are like being in another country. If a person sees something they like, they can point to it and ask what it is. The reply can come in fractured English and sound strange, but that is part of the enjoyment. Of course they would die laughing if we tried speaking Norwegian. That too, is all right. They smile, we smile, and everyone laughs. Speaking with people from a foreign country is fun and educational. Waiting at a table for your companion to bring something for you is not fun or educational. It is a handicap, but there is nothing to gain by dwelling on bad experiences. A clever man says it perfectly:

> "We should be careful to get out of an experience only the wisdom that is in it — and stop there; lest we be like the cat that sits down on a hot stove-lid. She will never sit down on a hot stove-lid again — and that is well; but also she will never sit down on a cold one anymore." — Mark Twain

There is a pleasant outdoor seating area attached to the bakery and it also sells Ringnes Beer, brewed in Norway. It seems a bit odd for a bakery to sell beer, but the author never heard anyone complain.

CHINA
Lotus Blossom Cafe: This fast-food shop is located in the China pavilion. They offer sweet-and-sour pork, egg rolls, and soup. They serve the food over a counter and have an outdoor, covered dining area.

The Refreshment Outpost: This fast-food restaurant sits on the promenade, between China and Germany. It is a place for a cold soft drink or a snack of cookies, ice cream, or popcorn.

GERMANY

Sommerfest: In the German pavilion, if you want a quick lunch in a nice place, the Sommerfest is just the thing. They have an outdoor eating area and offer traditional German fare. This includes bratwurst sandwiches, pretzels, apple strudel, and Black Forest chocolate cake. Bratwurst is a type of sausage served on a bun, with toppings like mustard, catsup, onions, or sauerkraut. A bratwurst sandwich is similar to a hot dog, but tastier. They also sell wine and Beck's beer, brewed in Germany.

AMERICAN ADVENTURE

The Liberty Inn: You can find this restaurant in the American Adventure pavilion It has a covered, outdoor eating area and is a nice place for a quick meal. They sell hamburgers, hot dogs, and french fries. The menu includes chili, which is a kind of spicy, beef and bean, tomato-based stew. They add apple pie and chocolate chip cookies for dessert.

JAPAN

The Yakitori House: The Japanese have their own solution for hungry people on the move. This restaurant is in the Japanese garden area on the left side of the pavilion. They offer a dish called Guydon which is a stew-like mixture of beef, soy sauce, spices, and sake — a Japanese wine made from rice. Of course, they serve it with rice. They also offer yakitori — a type of roasted chicken. In the American fashion, they make up some of this Japanese food into sandwiches. They complete the menu with Japanese sweets and a variety of drinks.

In their search for fast-food, visitors must skip the Moroccan pavilion and move to a shop in the French pavilion.

FRANCE

The Boulangerie Patisserie: This is a bakery and pastry shop. They sell French selections such as delicate croissants, eclairs, fruit tarts, and chocolate mousse. The bakery is a nice place for an informal breakfast or a snack at anytime.

CANADA

The Refreshment Port: This stand is located on the north side of the Canadian pavilion. It is a snack stand selling the usual soft drinks, ice cream, and cookies.

World Showcase: Cafeteria Service
CANADA
Le Cellier: The cafeteria is in the middle of the EPCOT Center and easily found. They don't require reservations and they have a greater selection of food than the fast-food restaurants.

Le Cellier restaurant is in the lower level of the Hotel du Canada. To find it, people should follow the path through the Victoria Gardens on the north side of the Canadian pavilion. There is often a waiting line during the lunch hours, but it moves quickly. This is one of the advantages of cafeteria service; it satisfies a lot of people in a short time.

The menu reflects the diversity of Canada. They offer something called tourtiere from Quebec. It is a pork and potato-filled pastry shell, or pie. They have cheddar cheese and fruit plates, roast prime ribs, chicken, a meatball stew, and fresh salmon. As a dessert they present a Canadian maple-syrup pie and trifle — a British delicacy made with cake, custard, and strawberries topped with whipped cream and sherry.

Le Cellier has a larger dinner menu. They add dishes like beef and maple dumpling stew, poached salmon with crabmeat in a light cream sauce, and a lightly sauteed turkey breast. They serve a Canadian beer called Labatt's. It's a fine place for lunch or dinner, especially if you have not made reservations at one of the full-service restaurants. The only negative aspect of Le Cellier is the nature of the cafeteria service itself. People with physical disabilities often find the full-service restaurants a better choice.

World Showcase: Full-Service Restaurants
There are eleven full-service restaurants in nine pavilions around the World Showcase Lagoon. We define a full-service restaurant as one in which hostesses seat guests at a table. Then waiters or waitresses present menus, take

orders, and serve the food. This type of service offers obvious advantages to people with physical disabilities. There are a couple of disadvantages.

First, full-service can mean slow service. Second, they are more expensive than the alternatives. In the EPCOT Center everyone has the option — convenience or economy.

We stated before, and we say again, for most disabled people, we recommend full-service restaurants. Physically disabled people struggle doing the simplest daily activities many people take for granted. It is a welcome change of pace to get out of the heat and crowds. They find it a pleasure, having polite and friendly waiters and waitresses take their orders and serve their food. We advocate planning ahead, possibly spending a bit more money, and making the time. It adds to the success and enjoyment of everybody's visit to the EPCOT Center.

We describe the full-service restaurants in clockwise order around the World Showcase, beginning with Mexico.

MEXICO
The San Angel Inn: The restaurant is related to one with the same name in Mexico City. You find it toward the rear of the plaza in the Mexican pavilion and it is open for lunch and dinner. At the entrance, a hostess or host directs you to a ramp leading to the dining area. The decor highlights Mexico, and people using wheelchairs find the access excellent.

They offer more sophisticated and subtle Mexican food than the usual tortillas, tacos, and burritos. For example, one item on the menu is queso fundido. It contains melted cheese with Mexican pork sausage and either corn or flour tortillas. There is pollo en pipian, chicken in a pumpkin seed sauce. Mole poblano is chicken with a Spanish-inspired chocolate sauce. They have a Mexican-styled poached fish cooked with wine, onions, tomatoes, and peppers.

The desserts are equally tempting. They offer thin, pancake-like items filled with milk caramel and ice cream covered with caramel sauce. They serve Dos Equis beer, lemon-flavored water, or margaritas. The latter is a drink made with tequila and lemon or lime juice. They serve margaritas ice cold in a glass with a salted rim. Drinking margaritas is very easy, sometimes too easy.

NORWAY
Akershus: This is located in the Norway pavilion. The focal point of the restaurant is the Royal Norwegian Buffet, called a koldtbord. This literally means "the cold table." It seems a misnomer because they serve both hot and cold foods. They offer a variety of seafood and meats, salads, breads, and cheeses. The menu includes cocktails and Norwegian Ringnes beer. Dessert items also reflect Norwegian tastes.

CHINA
Nine Dragons: This full-service restaurant is located in the Chinese pavilion. China is a huge, diverse country. There is no single style of Chinese cooking. Instead, people refer to the provinces associated with the particular style. Diners encounter names like Mandarin, Cantonese, Hunan, Szechuan, and Kiangche.

The main courses include dishes like Cantonese-style braised duck, and Kang Bao, which is chicken stir-fried with peanuts and hot dried peppers. Another item consists of sliced bits of steak stir-fried with Chinese broccoli. Appetizers are an important part of Chinese meals. There is a selection of items like pickled cabbage, fried dumplings, and hot and sour soup.

They offer a variety of Chinese tea, beer, and wine to complement the food. The dessert menu includes unusual items, like red-bean ice cream and toffee apples. They also offer more conventional Chinese pastries. The Nine Dragons is open for lunch and dinner and it requires reservations.

GERMANY
Biergarten: This full-service restaurant has a completely different atmosphere than the Nine Dragons restaurant in China. You can choose a restaurant based on your taste and

mood. This is a large part of the fun and the enjoyment of the EPCOT Center — there are many choices.

Visitors can find the Biergarten at the rear of St. Georgsplatz, the central plaza in the German pavilion. The restaurant is large and even though set in different levels, it is accessible to people using wheelchairs. The trick is not being intimidated. Disabled people and their companions should be assertive about asking for help and joining in the fun. Disney modeled the restaurant after a German beer hall. Guests find themselves sitting at a long table along with many other people. The happy atmosphere might be a product of the beer flowing from 33-ounce steins. It is a like Munich's Octoberfest, every day.

The dinner shows add to the enjoyable atmosphere. These feature yodelers, dancers, and musicians dressed in traditional German costumes. The men wear their lederhosen, the leather shorts from the Bavarian Alps. The musicians play accordions, cowbells, a musical saw, and a harp-like stringed instrument. The performers often trick guests into joining them on the stage for the fun.

The food in the Biergarten goes with the beer. It is as hearty as the German people. This is not the place for delicate appetites. They offer smoked pork loin, roast chicken, and a German favorite known as sauerbraten — a type of spicy, marinated beef. They serve a variety of "wursts", or sausages, with names like bratwurst, bauernwurst, bierwurst, and jaegerwurst. German potato salad and potato dumplings accompany the sausages. Guests should bring an empty stomach or a hollow leg to the Biergarten. Finally, a sense of humor is almost a necessity.

There is no major show during the lunch hours, but a few "street entertainers" keep up the lively pace. This is a popular spot. We recommend making reservations.

ITALY
L'Originale Alfredo di Roma Ristorante: It is difficult imagining a greater contrast than that between a German beer hall and an elegant Italian restaurant. They are neighbors in

the EPCOT Center. This restaurant gains its inspiration from a world-famous restaurant in Rome with the same name.

Alfredo's specialty is a dish called Fettucine Alfredo. Fettucine is a wide, flat pasta noodle. They cook and mix the noodles with a sauce made from butter and Parmesan cheese. The dish sounds simple, but making it properly is difficult; the timing is critical. The butter and cheese must be exactly the right temperature and then mixed with the pasta quickly and thoroughly. It's an art. Of course the Italians have practiced the art of cooking for thousands of years.

Freshly made pasta accompanies tomatoes, beef, and other sauces in a variety of Italian dishes. Pesto sauce contains basil, garlic, and Parmesan cheese. Carbonara sauce mixes egg, bacon, cream, and Pecorino cheese. Italian dishes include foods such as chicken, eggplant, seafood, sausage, and veal. There is more to Italian food than spaghetti and meatballs or pizza. Alfredo's food is authentically Italian and some of the nicest in the EPCOT Center.

As you might guess, the Italian talent for cooking extends to their desserts. It is hard resisting ricotta cheesecake or spumoni ice cream. The restaurant is accessible to people using wheelchairs. Reservations are necessary and they are open for lunch and dinner. The only problem is finding an appetite large enough to do justice to the food.

The American pavilion doesn't have a full-service restaurant.

JAPAN
Mitsukoshi: This is the name of the restaurant complex in the Japanese pavilion and a company with the same name operates it. You find it on the west side and second level of the Japanese pavilion. There is an elevator on the first level, to the left of the entrance to the Mitsukoshi Department Store. People using wheelchairs have access to the second level by using the elevator.

The Teppanyaki Dining Rooms are similar to a chain of Japanese restaurants in America. Patrons sit around tables containing large, dish-shaped grills known as woks. The chefs double as entertainers. They chop vegetables, meat, and fish with the speed of a machine gun. They twirl the knives and forks and somehow miss losing a finger. They toss the food into a wok and stir-fry it to the delight of their audience. The entertainment, food, and camaraderie with fellow guests make the affair more than a matter of filling your stomach.

This type of experience is sometimes difficult for physically disabled people. In this situation the phrase "where there is a will, there is a way," seems appropriate. The problem involves access to the tables. It might require a bit of maneuvering and negotiating, but we think people using wheelchairs can get to and under the tables and participate in the meal along with everyone else.

They refer to one corner of the dining area as Tempura Kiku. It specializes in batter-dipped and deep-fried chicken, beef, seafood, and vegetables. The Japanese refer to this style of cooking and food as tempura. The morsels of food are deep-fried on metal skewers and are crispy and tasty. Some physically disabled people might have difficulty handling the food, but with the cooperation of a companion, the experience is rewarding.

Both of the dining areas on the second level of the Japanese pavilion accommodate people using wheelchairs. They serve lunch and dinner and recommend reservations.

MOROCCO

Marrakesh: This is a full-service restaurant accessible for people using wheelchairs. They are open for lunch and dinner and they accept reservations.

Like the other restaurants, the waiters dress in native costumes. In this case they wear long robes called djellaba. The menu lists traditional Moroccan food and it is characteristic of the food found in North Africa. It includes roast lamb or chicken and an interesting side dish called couscous. It seems every country has a unique staple food. Japan and China have rice, the Italians have pasta, Mexico has tortillas, and the Moroccans have couscous. North Africans prepare couscous from crushed and steamed wheat. It looks a little like cooked rice and usually accompanies their other foods.

Marrakesh also offers something called bastila. They make it with layers of thin pastry and strips of chicken, almonds, and flavor it with saffron and cinnamon. One of the nicer features of the restaurant is their offer of sampler plates. This allows you to sample a bit of everything. When trying new food, we find it is advantageous to spread the risk and order a little of everything.

If the food isn't enough stimulation, there are belly dancers and Moroccan musicians. They accent the decor with imported Moroccan tiles, using native craftsmen in their design and construction. This authenticity is a part of what we refer to as the "Disney touch."

FRANCE

Some people claim French people are obsessive about their food and wine. Whether or not that is true, visitors to the EPCOT Center are fortunate, because Disney invited some French chefs to operate three restaurants in the French pavilion.

Chefs de France: This full-service restaurant offers traditional French dishes but with a slight departure from the rich foods normally associated with France. The cooking style is known as nouvelle cuisine. They use less cream and butter in their sauces and serve smaller meals.

For example, a dinner might include appetizers of potato, leek and onion, Lyon-style soup; a salmon souffle, flavored with tarragon and topped with a white butter sauce; or oysters and spinach, served with a champagne sauce. Typical entrees include grouper with lobster sauce, roast duck in wine sauce with prunes, veal with a mushroom sauce, or chicken with a tangy vinegar brown sauce. If this is nouvelle cuisine, it is fine with us.

The lunch menu offers quiche, a variety of French cheeses, pates, and a croissant filled with ham and cheese. There are hot dishes like sausage baked in pastry, and a fish, shrimp, and crab casserole. They serve a rich beef, onion, and wine stew at lunch and dinner.

Eating in France is not complete without sampling their pastries and finishing off with a cup of rich, strong coffee. The French refer to this as cafe filtre and the Italians call it espresso.

They enhance the pleasure of dining in the Chefs de France with linen table cloths and a decor accented with brass and etched glass. A wine list comes with the menu at lunch and dinner. They require reservations. As a note of caution, this may be one of the more expensive restaurants in the EPCOT Center.

Au Petit Cafe: This is an outdoor, full-service restaurant. You find it in front of and on the left side of the French pavilion. It also serves as an excellent place for a relaxing break in the action.

The sidewalk cafe is covered and protected from the elements. It is easy for someone using a wheelchair to roll into and sit at one of the tables. The waiters dress elegantly in black jackets. They speak English with a French accent and serve their guests as politely as they would on the streets of Paris — maybe more so.

The Au Petit Cafe is a popular spot and they don't accept reservations. Waiting lines are common during the lunch hour, so we recommend planning a visit during mid-morning or afternoon.

Bistro de Paris: This is the third of the full-service restaurants in the French pavilion. It is on the second floor, above the Chefs de France. The restaurant is not accessible to people who can not stand and walk up and down a flight of stairs.

They reward stair-climbers with a menu offering dishes like steamed fillet of grouper, chicken breast in puff pastry, and braised beef. They also have a children's menu. The decor imitates a bistro in 1920's Paris. There are brass light fixtures, mirrors, colored leaded glass, and simple wooden chairs.

Realistically, if this was the only restaurant in town, the author might have found someone to lift him up the stairs. Sometimes waiters in a restaurant do this for him. Other times, he enlists the help of his companions, and strangers sometimes lend a hand. However, the electric wheelchairs people use when they don't have the arm strength for pushing their own chairs, are almost impossible to drag up a flight of stairs. They are large and weigh hundreds of pounds. Unfortunately, people using the electric wheelchairs are handicapped more often than people using the lighter manual chairs.

UNITED KINGDOM

Rose & Crown Pub & Dining Room: The British are not noted for their culinary skills, but everyone enjoys this restaurant. It is the last of the full-service restaurants found in our journey around the World Showcase Lagoon.

You find the Rose & Crown on the water's edge in front of the United Kingdom pavilion. The restaurant, the pub, and the outdoor terrace are accessible to people using wheelchairs. Everyone can enjoy the Rose & Crown.

The lunch menu contains traditional "pub grub" like fish and chips, steak and kidney pie, chicken and leek pie, and roast lamb. They have hot roast beef served with gravy and mashed potatoes, a vegetable plate accompanied with Stilton cheese and a walnut dressing. The dinner menu adds roast prime ribs with horseradish sauce. A British favorite is what they call mixed grill — broiled pork loin, beef tenderloin, and veal kidney.

Appetizers include a dish called Scotch eggs. This consists of hard-boiled eggs covered with sausage meat. They fry it, chill it, and serve it with a mustard sauce. If anyone has room for dessert, they offer a sherry trifle. This is a layered treat of custard, strawberries, whipped cream and sherry.

Disney put a lot of effort into decorating the Rose & Crown. The exterior includes different architectural styles. It looks like London's Cheshire Cheese Pub, or one encountered in rural England. The interior design is polished wood and etched glass accented with brass. It gives a sense of warmth and friendliness — increasing in proportion to the amount of beer consumed.

Any pub worthy of the name must serve beer. The Rose & Crown offers Bass India Pale ale from England, Tennent's lager from Scotland, and Guinness stout and Harp lager from Ireland. The British have a few habits that Americans find odd. They drink their beer warm and sometimes mix it. A black and tan is half Guinness stout and half Bass ale.

The pub section offers food like fruit and cheese plates, meat pies, and Scotch eggs. The pub is popular and they don't take reservations; so you might try making your visit during the late afternoon or early evening. In America, we refer to this as "happy hour." We think everyone will feel the same after a visit to the Rose & Crown, regardless of their physical ability.

CHAPTER 5

DISNEY-MGM STUDIOS

"An ounce of image is worth a pound of performance"
——Laurence J. Peter

INTRODUCTION AND OTHER THINGS YOU SHOULD KNOW
What Is Disney-MGM Studios And How Big Is It?

Disney began and thrived for years by producing movies and cartoons for children. About six years ago, they entered the adult movie and television business. Their new production company achieved immediate success at the box office. Disney rarely misses an opportunity to build on success, so their next step was obvious.

First, they acquired the rights to the MGM (Metro-Goldwyn-Mayer) name, titles, costumes, music, sets, and film library. Then, combining Disney and MGM, they built a television and movie theme park in Walt Disney World. They based the design of the Disney-MGM Studios Theme Park on Hollywood of the 1930s and 1940s, its golden years. The two-part attraction incorporates over 60 years of movie-making history.

Physically disabled people enjoy the Disney-MGM Studios as much as The Magic Kingdom or the EPCOT Center. Only one of the attractions in the Disney-MGM Studios presents a problem for people using wheelchairs and incapable of transferring into another seat. The Star Tours feature requires that people sit in theater-type seats. The seats move quite violently during the show and demand significant hand and arm strength from the participants. The seats and action in Star Tours are similar to those in the Body Wars ride in the EPCOT Center. Later, we describe the attraction in detail, and offer advice on who can and who cannot experience Star Tours.

They built the $300 million, Disney-MGM Studios Theme Park on a 110-acre site southwest of the EPCOT Center and opened it in 1989. Each of the three theme parks at Walt Disney World has a landmark structure. The Magic Kingdom has the Cinderella Castle, the EPCOT Center has the geosphere Spaceship Earth, and the Disney-MGM Studios has the "Earffel Tower."

In their infancy, in the 1920's and 1930's, the Hollywood movie studios were like small towns. Each studio had its own water supply in a distinctive tower. They created the same effect in Walt Disney World, but with a twist. They topped the 13-story water tower standing over the Disney-MGM Studios with a Mousketeer-style hat. The ears of the mouse are everywhere.

The Disney-MGM Studios consist of two areas. The first is an Open-Access Movie Theme Park. This means you can move from one attraction to another, freely, and at your own pace. It includes displays, rides, and shows. The Park traces the history of the movie industry. A variety of shops and restaurants complement the main attractions. The second area covers about one-half of the Disney-MGM Studios Theme Park. Everyone can participate in the Backstage Studio Tours and see what goes on behind the scenes. They control access in the backstage area because it doubles as a working, movie and television, production facility. It contains three sound stages, back-lot street scenes, wardrobe shops, administrative offices, and animation studios. Physically disabled people, including those using wheelchairs, can tour the backstage areas along with everyone else.

Getting To The Disney-MGM Studios

There are many hotels and motels in and around Walt Disney World. This creates many possible routes to the Disney-MGM Studios. For simplicity, we assume most people are traveling by automobile from either the Orlando area, to the northeast, or from Tampa and St. Petersburg in the southwest. The main highway connecting these areas is Interstate 4, or I-4.

If you are driving from the Orlando area, get off at the I-4 exit marked: Caribbean Beach Resort, Walt Disney World Village, and the Disney-MGM Studios Theme Park. People coming from the Tampa area can get off I-4 one exit earlier. They can take US Highway 192 west and proceed directly to the Disney-MGM Studios. This is the same route to the Magic Kingdom. Either way, there are two choices. If you miss an exit, there is no need for panic. Keep going to the next exit and take it from there.

Follow the signs to the Disney-MGM Studios 7,500-space parking lot. You must stop at the Auto Plaza and show your

DISNEY-MGM STUDIOS THEME PARK

- Wheelchair/Stroller Rental
- First Aid
- Accessible Rest Rooms

Map not to scale

1. Hollywood Boulevard
2. Indiana Jones Epic Stunt Spectacular
3. Backlot Annex
4. Star Tours
5. Superstar Television/The Monster Sound Show
6. The Great Movie Ride
7. Chinese Theatre
8. Echo Lake
9. Animation Tour
10. Production Center

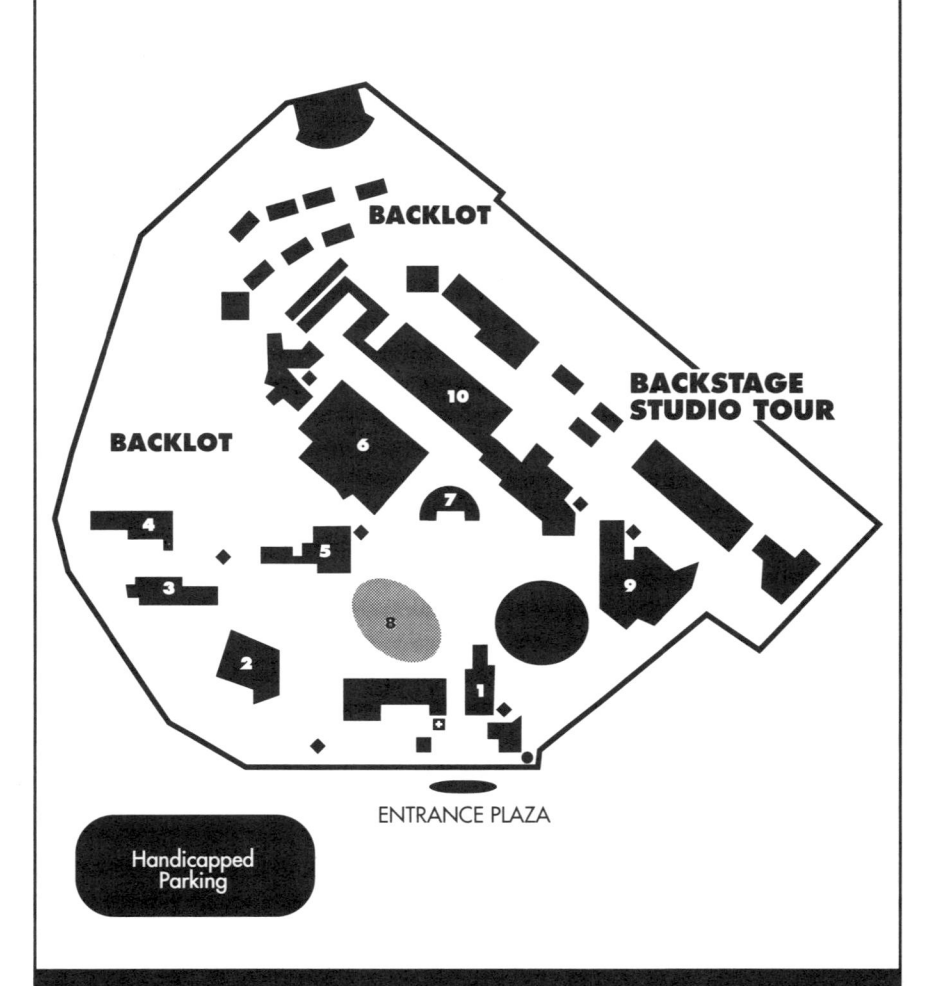

BACKLOT

BACKSTAGE STUDIO TOUR

BACKLOT

ENTRANCE PLAZA

Handicapped Parking

pass, or pay the daily parking fee of $4. Parking is free for people with Annual Passports and guests at any of the Walt Disney World resorts. Ask for directions to the handicapped parking area. The attendants give you a sign with the handicapped symbol to place on your dash. Continue to the parking area directly in front of the Entrance Plaza and ticket booths. Visitors without the handicapped parking sign, park farther away and take a motor tram to the entrance.

The entrance is only about 100 yards from the handicapped parking area. Here, you must either show your admission pass or buy a one day ticket.

Wheelchair Rental
Physically disabled people traveling without their own wheelchairs have the option of renting one. There is a limited number of rental wheelchairs at Oscar's Super Service Station. This is just inside the entrance, to your right, and across from the Guest Services Center. If you have babies or small children, you can rent strollers at Oscar's Super Service Station. Children under five years old benefit from riding in a stroller. Children and parents get less tired when using a stroller. The strollers also provide a place to carry and hang purses, backpacks, and souvenirs collected along the way.

Locker Rentals
We recommend traveling with as little accessory gear as possible. However, if you have things like baby-care supplies, rain gear, or bulky cameras, you don't have to carry them all day. You can store your excess baggage in a rental locker. They cost 50 cents per use. You can find them next to Oscar's Super Service Station. If you parked close to the entrance, in the handicapped area, it is almost as easy returning to your vehicle as using the rental lockers.

MOVIE THEME PARK
Hollywood Boulevard
Once you enter the Disney-MGM Studios, proceed straight ahead to Hollywood Boulevard. You can bypass all of the guest services if you have done your homework. Time is money. Planning ahead pays.

If you only have one day at the Disney-MGM Studios, cruise down Hollywood Boulevard as quickly as possible. If you have more time, slow down, and enjoy some of the shops, the scenery, and restaurants. Hollywood Boulevard looks like what the Disney designers imagined it was in the 1930's and 1940's. It is a romantic vision. They accent the architecture with neon signs and chrome art deco displays. Background music from roving street bands, or recorded from popular movies, adds to the ambiance.

They further the fantasy with costumed characters roaming the streets, sometimes asking for an autograph, as if you were someone important — if you don't think you are, pretend. You may encounter someone selling maps to the homes of the movie stars, or an occasional television reporter searching for the latest gossip. We recommend leaving your inhibitions behind when entering Walt Disney World. Relax and have fun.

Next, we describe the shops along Hollywood Boulevard. You can find details about its restaurants in the section, Dining at the Disney-MGM Studios.

EAST SIDE HOLLYWOOD BOULEVARD SHOPS
The east side of the street is on your left as you enter the park.

Movieland Memorabilia: This is a haven for souvenir hunters. There are toys, hats, books, sunglasses, key chains, and other small items, most sporting a Disney theme.

Crossroads of the World: This is a small shop in the center of the entrance plaza. On top of it, you can see Mickey Mouse standing guard over his empire. The shop sells many items such as sunglasses, film, rain gear, and assorted souvenirs.

Sid Cahuenga's One-of-a-Kind: The name of this shop fits its merchandise. It offers antiques and Hollywood curios. There are autographed photos, old movie magazines, and posters. People might not buy much in these shops, but half the fun is just looking.

Mickey's of Hollywood, Pluto's Toy Palace, Disney & Co.:
These are three connected shops. They offer the most popular Disney souvenirs, like T-shirts, sweatshirts, hats, toys, dolls, watches, jackets, socks, wallets, tote bags, and books. Some people wear clothes with Disney logos as fashion statements. It's like saying, "Hey, I'm a relaxed and fun-loving person, I've been to Walt Disney World. I'm cool."

Keystone Clothiers: This shop is for people with healthy wallets or credit cards. How about a jacket with flashing electric lights for only $200? You could look like Elton John. Maybe you prefer a pair of earrings, one of Mickey Mouse and one of Minnie. We don't have any idea who you would look like then. The author wanted the umbrella that opens into a Mickey Mouse hat, complete with ears. The only problem was he couldn't figure out how to carry it and push his wheelchair at the same time. All right, so he is a little goofy.

Lakeside News: Now this is serious. The shop has a great selection of comic books. They also sell a variety of movie magazines and other souvenirs.

Sights & Sounds: This shop offers potential. Visitors can record their own music videos. Who knows, you may have undiscovered talent? We think the world needs a Michael Jackson in a wheelchair. Go for it; this is Hollywood.

WEST SIDE HOLLYWOOD BOULEVARD SHOPS
As you enter the park, the west is on the right hand side of the street.

Oscar's Classic Car Souvenirs & Super Service Station:
The first thing people notice about Oscar's is the 1947 Buick parked in front of the station. The shop offers souvenirs with an automotive theme. They sell mugs, models of automobiles, and key chains. Sorry about the car, it's not for sale. This is the place for renting strollers for children, wheelchairs for people who have difficulty walking, and lockers for pack-rats.

The Darkroom: The art deco doorway of this shop takes you through the lens of a camera. They offer rental cameras. The

Kodak disk cameras are free for a day. All you need is a $50 deposit and the price of the disks. They rent 35mm cameras at $5 per day with a $145 deposit. The shop has VHS video cameras for $40 a day. These require a $400 deposit and a driver's license, or $1200 without the license. The Darkroom offers a discount on the video cameras if you rent for more than one day. If you do your part and return the cameras, Disney returns your deposit. The shop sells other types of film and cameras. We recommend bringing your own.

Cover Story: Farther into the Darkroom, they offer something a little unique. They will photograph your face and put it on the cover of one of several popular magazines, such as *Life, Cosmopolitan, Sports Illustrated, Muscle,* or *Time.* They provide a few costumes and accessories. We think someone using a wheelchair would be appropriate on the cover of *Sports Illustrated.* Especially after touring all three parks!

Celebrity 5 & 10: Disney modeled this shop after a Woolworth's store of the 1940's. They sell a variety of souvenirs reminiscent of the Hollywood that was. They carry costume jewelry, picture frames, shirts, jackets, aprons, and teddy bears. Not all of it is Disney-related and people can live without most of it, but shopping doesn't necessarily mean buying.

Sweet Success: Disney knows many of us are sweet addicts and they supply the goodies.

La Cinema Storage: The shop sells movie-related merchandise, but most importantly, they offer visitors a screen test. They film you and sell you a tape. You can take it home and tell your friends you almost made it in Hollywood. Who will know the truth?

The Great Movie Ride

This attraction is in a full-sized reproduction of Hollywood's famous Grauman's Chinese Theater. You see it in front of you and across the square, at the end of Hollywood Boulevard. We think it is one of the highlights of the Disney-MGM Studios. Try making it the first attraction you visit because it is popular, and there might be a line of people waiting to enter. Best of all, physically disabled people find it one of the most easily accessible rides at Disney World. We hope the author's experience serves as the rule rather than the exception. It was hot and sunny the day he visited. He was a bit discouraged upon seeing a long line of people waiting to get in, and he wasn't in the mood to sit and cook in the sun. He wasn't there more than two minutes and, as if reading his mind, one of the Disney ride attendants spotted him and politely asked if he wanted to come inside. He gratefully accepted the invitation.

Once inside, an attendant directed him to the room where visitors get on the ride, and explained how he could roll his wheelchair into one of the ride vehicles. The operation went very smoothly. It's a true, tourist assembly line. The ride attendants keep people moving as quickly and efficiently as possible. The ride vehicles are about twenty feet long and seat three or four people abreast and in rows. An attendant lowered a gently sloping ramp and the author pushed his chair aboard and locked his brakes. The ride attendants know what they're doing. They make sure the wheels of the chairs are locked or the brakes on. They don't want anyone rolling around and getting hurt during the ride. If anything, the author had a better view than the other passengers because he was sitting higher in his wheelchair than they were in their seats. It was quite comfortable.

The vehicles began moving and went through an old-fashioned theater marquee and into the first of many movie sets. Don't be mistaken, these are not passive exhibits. They contain the scenery you expect, but add Disney's sophisticated, AudioAnimatronic characters.

The author is not particularly nostalgic about movies, but he enjoyed seeing Gene Kelly in his famous scene from *Singin' in the Rain*. The next scene included Mary Poppins with her magic umbrella and Bert, the chimney sweep.

Farther along you witness a gun battle between gangsters in a scene from the movie, *Public Enemy*. Look closely and you recognize James Cagney. A moment later you're in the midst of a bank robbery from a western movie. You see the most famous cowboy of all, John Wayne, on horseback, surveying the scene. The action heats up when the robbers blow the safe and flames shoot from a building. It's so real you feel the heat, just enough for a thrill with no actual danger.

Then you quickly move light years ahead, into the spaceship Nostromo, from the movie *Alien*. You see Officer Ripley on guard while a slimy monster threatens you from overhead. It's all great fun. Rental videos will never be the same. It is worth noting that this scene, and a couple of others, takes place in a darkened room and may be frightening for some people. The scenes change quickly so any fear is momentary.

Next you see Harrison Ford in a scene from *Raiders of the Lost Ark*. A bit later they treat you to Tarzan's famous cry as he swings through the jungle on a vine, while his mate, Jane, rides an elephant. His other companion, Cheetah, appropriately screams and bounces around.

Anyone familiar with the movie *Casablanca*, remembers the next image. Who can forget the scene on the runway in front of the plane, as Humphrey Bogart and Ingrid Bergman courageously bid each other farewell? The next scene is happier, but no less famous. There's Dorothy, Toto, the Tin Man, the Cowardly Lion, and the Scarecrow, following the Yellow Brick Road from *The Wizard of Oz*. As the ride ends, you see a series of clips from other famous films.

When the ride was over, the author felt ready for an instant replay. It was that good. The ride was 25 minutes of pure, cool, pleasurable entertainment. The ride represents the best of what Disney offers at the Disney-MGM Studios and it's perfect for physically disabled people. If they use a wheelchair, they can get on the ride and enjoy it along with everyone else. This includes standard manual wheelchairs, electric wheelchairs, and the electric-powered convenience carts. There are no abrupt or jarring movements, and we doubt any of the scenes are scary enough to harm anyone.

Superstar Television

This attraction is a live theater presentation. It's unique in that it involves participants from the audience. First, the attendants usher you into a waiting area where you gather in front of a stage. When the pre-show area fills, a Disney cast member appears on stage and explains what happens next.

No, they didn't choose the author and he was thankful for it. Even after all these years of using a wheelchair, he still feels self-conscious — but maybe he was always that way. The point is, even though physically disabled people can easily get in and view the show, we question whether they would fit into the pre-arranged acts. However, we don't make that judgment for anyone. If you are up for it, mention your interest to one of the attendants. Anything is possible, that's our motto.

The host or hostess on the stage explains they're looking for volunteers to appear in a series of live television shows. They choose ten or twelve people from the audience and direct everyone else into a large, 1000-seat theater. If you use a wheelchair, they steer you into a seating area at the rear of the theater. This is for convenience and the author didn't feel any sense of discrimination. The stage is at a distance, that's true, but the view is good and everyone can see the television monitors overhead.

The volunteer actors continue backstage for costuming and quick acting lessons while everyone is being seated. In a few minutes the show begins. There are several sets and the scenes unfold one act at a time. As they film the action, backstage technicians splice it into film footage from familiar television shows. They combine the antics of the volunteer actors and actresses with well-known comedians and project the resulting images into the over-head TV monitors. Everyone in the audience has a good view of the result. These merged scenes are the highlight of the attraction.

One scene has a female guest playing the role of Ethel Mertz, opposite Lucille Ball's Lucy Ricardo, in a memorable scene from the TV show, *I Love Lucy*. Many people are too young to remember this program, but it doesn't matter — the humor is timeless.

Another scene has amateur actors in a scene from the TV soap opera, *General Hospital*. They play two of the three people involved in a love triangle. In the act the author saw, the amateurs took their roles seriously. As planned, and to the delight of the audience, they muffed some of their lines.

Several young people appear in the opening scene from *Gilligan's Island* and three more people dress as the "Vonzells," to sing *Da Doo Run Run* on the *Ed Sullivan Show*. As we said, if you have the courage to star in this type of frivolity, we encourage you.

Our favorite scene is one from the TV show, *Cheers*. Four lucky visitors have the opportunity of trading verbal jabs with Woody, Norm, and Cliff. In another episode, a young man hits a home run in Shea Stadium and afterward, Howard Cosell interviews him. Finally, there are scenes from *The Tonight Show*, *The Three Stooges*, and *The Golden Girls*.

The live performances take 30 minutes and the complete attraction requires about 45 minutes. We liked this attraction immensely. We think everyone enjoys the show. Its accessibility for disabled people is an important bonus.

Monster Sound Show

The name of this attraction is misleading, since it suggests something frightening. In reality, it's good for a few laughs, much like the previous show, SuperStar Television. It's in the same building, on the south side of Echo Lake. The 15-minute show occurs in a smaller, 270-seat theater and involves the participation of a few members of the audience.

The theater is completely accessible for disabled people using wheelchairs, including electric ones. The designated seating area for people using wheelchairs is in the back of the theater, but the view is good. As in the SuperStar Television attraction, we doubt they will select anyone in a wheelchair to come onto the stage and take part in the show. However, if someone really wants to participate and thinks they can, they should ask one of the attendants. The acts are enjoyable, whether a person is part of them or sitting and watching with everyone else.

The show begins outside, as you wait to get into the theater. David Letterman introduces the forth-coming show in a short video presentation and warns with his typical sense of humor, "If you break anything, security guards in mouse suits will beat you senseless."

After they seat everyone, a host appears on stage and introduces the show. He asks for, and selects, a few members of the audience to help in creating the sound effects for the coming event. While the volunteers are getting ready, the audience watches a short comedy "monster show" starring Martin Short and Chevy Chase. It contains the usual scary sounds of thunder, rain, squeaky doors, and crashing chandeliers.

The amateur sound technicians are now on stage and watch the film a second time while being prompted into duplicating the sound effects. The volunteers know they are being watched by the audience and do their best. Of course the audience is laughing and the volunteers are nervous, so the results are less than perfect. Finally, they play the original film back and dub in the amateur sound effects. You guessed it, the thunder doesn't match the storm, or the chandelier falls when the door should be creaking. The result is fun, and it leaves you with a greater appreciation for the sound effects in movies.

Indiana Jones Epic Stunt Spectacular

This attraction IS spectacular. It's one of our favorites. The show takes place in a huge, covered, 2,000-seat, out-door theater. Access is easy for people using wheelchairs. However, once again, an attendant directed the author to the last row, at the rear of the theater. For people able to leave their wheelchairs and negotiate some stairs, we suggest moving closer to the stage. It was at least 150 feet from where the author sat to the stage, sort of like outfield seats at a baseball game. Even though he was far away, the seats in front of him sloped down toward the stage, providing a good view of the action.

It takes most people, except the author, about 15 minutes to find seats. Then the show takes another 30 minutes. We recommend arriving at least 20 minutes before the show begins. Initially, a host appears on a stage as big as a football field. He gives a brief review of the role played by stunt people in the movie industry. Professional stunt people appear and demonstrate a few dangerous-looking routines.

The show director, Glenn Randall, has some impressive credentials. He was the stunt coordinator for action-packed movies like, *Raiders of the Lost Ark, Indiana Jones and the Temple of Doom, Poltergeist, E.T., Firestarter,* and *Jewel of the Nile.*

After preparing the audience, the show begins with a scene from *The Raiders of the Lost Ark.* A Harrison Ford look-alike narrowly escapes being crushed by a huge, stone ball. Escaping steam and flame is real, but controlled — we hope. When the action ends, the Disney staff dismantles and moves the set. The audience sees the stone ball is a fake, because the stunt man pushes it back up the slope.

The next act takes place in a Cairo marketplace. A few extras from the audience participate with the professionals. You see the classic scene where the bad guys are coming after Harrison Ford to chop him to pieces with swords, and he calmly pulls out his pistol. Go ahead Mohammed, make my day. The action continues across the roof-tops at a fast pace. Harrison Ford's female companion keeps pace in an impressive display of athletic ability. It is easy understanding why it costs so much money making an adventure movie. Movie-goers have high expectations and these acts show how it's done.

The climactic scene shows Harrison Ford and his lady battling the evil Nazis at a desert airport. There are explosions, flames, fist fights, and a gun battle. The effect is like watching a football game in the stadium instead of at home on TV. The author left feeling he received good value for his money.

The Indiana Jones Epic Stunt Spectacular is one of the more popular attractions at the Disney-MGM Studios. If your visit coincides with the busy season, we suggest you attend the first performance in the morning. Usually, at around 9:15 a.m, you can roll right in to the theater. If it's busy, and you arrive later, prepare for a wait of 30 minutes or more.

Star Tours

The Star Tours attraction is not really a "ride," but it is a trip. If you enjoy a jolt of adrenaline, Star Tours provides it. You can find it in the southeast corner of the Disney-MGM Studios, across from the Monster Sound show. The Star Tours experience takes only five minutes, but it's so addictive it may have you coming back for more. Star Tours is not for everyone, but the author found it accessible and exciting — perhaps his favorite attraction at the Disney-MGM Studios.

Disney got their inspiration for Star Tours from George Lucas' *Star Wars* movies. Guests board a space ship called a StarSpeeder. This is a sophisticated flight simulator, the same as the military and civilian airlines use for training their pilots. Disney synchronizes the movement of the simulator with a spectacular film. For five wide-eyed, teeth-clenching minutes, you feel as if you really are in a Star Wars spaceship. It might even satisfy Tom Cruise's "need for speed."

Always the masters of detail and illusion, Disney sets the scene by moving guests through a waiting area and into an inter-terrestrial travel agency. The Star Wars robots R2D2 and C3PO greet you as you enter. They tell their passengers they are about to begin a pleasant trip to the Moon of Endor and ask them to fasten their seat belts. The pilot proves to be a rookie "droid," or robot, and the spaceship is out of control from the beginning. The pilot dodges giant ice crystals and avoids the lasers fired by enemy fighters. Somehow, he manages a safe landing. After you get your heart out of your throat and exit the ride, you might feel the urge to do it again. This attraction was so exciting that the authors wife was sure it was the best ride she's been on and she is a roller coaster fanatic.

We agree, but it isn't for everyone.

Regarding accessibility, Star Tours is an example of why this book and our experiences are valuable. The Disney *Disabled Guests Guide Book* says,

> "This attraction is accessible to guests who can, with assistance, leave their wheelchairs and enter a seat in the StarSpeeder."

What if you don't have "assistance?" We already explained why the Disney ride attendants won't lift anyone who can't stand and walk by themselves. If you don't have someone in your party capable of lifting you from your wheelchair, you might believe you cannot experience Star Tours. This is not necessarily true.

The Star Tours attraction involves moving into a 40-person theater and sitting in another chair. Contrary to common perceptions, not all disabled people are "confined to a wheelchair." Many people using wheelchairs transfer from them into an automobile and drive it with hand controls. If a disabled person can get into a car, alone or with the help of a companion, they can get into the movie theater-type seats in Star Tours. Note: the procedure involved in getting into these seats is identical to that required in the Body Wars attraction in the EPCOT Center.

Many non-disabled people use the term "confined to their wheelchairs" when referring to disabled people. This is wrong. The author remembers a curious little girl approaching him in a store and asking, "Why are you sitting in that chair?" He said, "Well — because I can't walk." Innocently, she replied, "Why?" He said, "Because my legs don't work." The little girl's next question revealed a lot about non-disabled people's impressions of those using wheelchairs. She asked, "How can you sleep in that chair?" Many people using wheelchairs can lift and transfer themselves into beds, automobiles and other chairs, just like the one in the Star Tours attraction. That is exactly what the author did and he knows other disabled visitors can do the same.

Near the entrance Disney has signs stating passengers must not have heart conditions, back problems, or other physical limitations. However, someone reading that statement could be mislead and frightened away from the ride. We are not encouraging reckless behavior. People should carefully consider their own or their disabled companion's situation. Does a spinal cord injury and its resultant paralysis constitute a "back problem?" Well, yes, but in the author's case, he figures that after 14 years, his damaged vertebrae are stable. What do they mean by "other physical limitations?" The statement is unclear. We encourage you to read our description of the ride and decide for yourself if Star Tours fits your circumstance.

The ride is rough. When you get into a Star Tours seat, you secure a seat belt across your lap. A shoulder harness as pilots or race car drivers wear may be appropriate for some disabled people. During the five-minute ride, everyone holds on to the chair's arm rests with their hands and arms and all of their strength. The seats move up and down and unpredictably jerk and jolt the passengers. The physical sensations, combined with the video images on the screen, make the adrenaline flow. It's very exciting, but we can't recommend it for all disabled people.

For example, even if a quadriplegic had someone lift them into one of the ride's seats, they are not strong enough to hold themselves upright while being jolted and tossed around. The same advice applies to anyone without substantial strength in their hands and arms.

If a woman is pregnant and feels "handicapped," she should probably not try Star Tours. Disney advises against blind people taking their leader dogs into the attraction. The author's adult sister maintains she would never go on the ride because of her susceptibility to motion sickness. We think hearing impaired people might enjoy the experience as much as anyone because the audio portion of the attraction plays a minor role.

After all that, what's so special about a five minute ride? Well, what is so special about skiing down a mountain, barely in control, at forty miles per hour? It's thrilling. It's exciting and it scares the heck out of you. Somehow people keep doing it. It is more fun than spending years using a wheelchair and never exceeding a few miles per hour. A disabled person enjoys a good thrill as much as anyone. Maybe we even need it, to keep from becoming terminally bored.

Jim Henson's Muppet*Vision 3-D
The Muppets are a favorite of children. However, this 3-D movie delights everyone with its innovative special effects. The theater is directly south of the Star Tours attraction.

The theater is large, cool, comfortable, and accessible to all disabled people, including those using wheelchairs. Disney designed the theater for MuppetVision with their usual attention to detail. The show extends the use of the 3-D technology employed in Michael Jackson's *Captain Eo* movie, as seen at the Journey Into Imagination Pavilion in the EPCOT Center. The MuppetVision show originates in the Muppet Labs run by Dr. Bunson Honeydew, his assistant Beaker, and Waldo, the "Spirit of 3-D."

Disney compliments the 3-D movie effects with live Muppet characters, fiber optic visual displays, simulated fireworks, and cute detail decorating the walls of the theater. The show stimulates more than our visual and auditory senses; added special effects play with our perception of smell and touch.

Honey, I Shrunk The Kids Movie Set Adventure Playground

This is an elaborate playground for children younger than twelve years. It's opposite the MuppetVision theater on New York Street. The design of the play area relates to the movie's theme of children being reduced in size. The playground stimulates children's imaginations by letting them cavort among giant lawn sprinklers, 20-foot-high blades of grass, and giant ants. They can scramble through tunnels and climb on rope ladders and giant Lego toys. A favorite activity is crawling into a huge film canister and sliding back out on an over-sized roll of film. The playground is safe and most children love it, but there are a few problems.

First, they haven't designed the playground for physically disabled children, although they may enjoy seeing some of the props if their parents explain what is happening. Second, the playground only accommodates 240 people and many of these are supervising adults. Since there is no time limit imposed on visitors to the playground, waiting lines develop. Finally, the playground is poorly ventilated and becomes uncomfortably warm during the summer months.

If you're traveling with rambunctious, non-disabled children, everyone might benefit if you allow them some time in the playground. They can burn a little energy and you can relax. If you or your party do not fit this description, we recommend detouring around the Honey, I Shrunk The Kids Movies Set Adventure.

Teenage Mutant Ninja Turtles

Cowabunga, dude! That's Ninja Turtle talk for, "Go for it, guy." Or at least that's what the author thinks they mean. Several times daily, Leonardo, Raphael, Michelangelo, and Donatello appear and put on an energetic show at the end of New York Street. These adult-sized characters sing, dance, and sign autographs. Why anyone wants the autograph of a teenage, mutant turtle, exceeds the author's comprehension. Nevertheless, children willingly stand in line for the opportunity.

The show takes place outside, on a replica of a loading dock in New York City. After their performance, the turtles wander around and interact with the crowd. Even if you're not into Teenage Mutant Ninja Turtles, the show is professional and quite amusing. Disabled people and those using wheelchairs can participate as well as anyone. If the turtles appeal to you, and the park is crowded, we recommend inquiring about the show times. Five or ten minutes before the show begins, position yourself in front of the stage for the best view. The author enjoyed the act, even if he didn't understand it — probably a generation gap.

New York Street Back Lot

A short time ago this area was only available to visitors riding the tram on the Backstage Tour. Pedestrians and people rolling around in wheelchairs find this area past the end of New York Street, beyond the area where the Teenage Mutant Ninja Turtles perform. The park managers probably opened this area to relieve some of the congestion in other parts of the Disney-MGM Studios. Although not a primary attraction, it's a pleasant place for some exercise while marveling at the detail and precision Disney puts into a movie set. The scenery resembles an ordinary residential street from suburban America. As pleasant as the area is, we rank it at the bottom of our list of attractions. Try seeing the other attractions first. If you have extra time, and on your second or third visit, it's a fine place for a stroll or a roll.

STUDIO ANIMATION TOUR

> *"Animation is not the art of drawings-that-move, but the art of movements that are drawn."*
> —— Norman McLaren

The working animation studios lie in the northwestern corner of the Disney-MGM Studios. If you're at the end of Hollywood Boulevard and looking at the Chinese Theater and its Great Movie ride, the entrance to the Animation Tour is to your right. The entire attraction is accessible to physically disabled people, including those using wheelchairs. It's popular and waiting lines develop. Again, please take our advice and make your plans before you arrive at the Disney-MGM Studios. Ask yourself the questions, "How much time do we have?" "How crowded will the park be?" Finally, ask, "What can we see and what is most important to us?" In other words, prioritize your options.

After moving through the lobby with its collection of 13 Oscars awarded to Disney animators and its drawings of Disney characters, you enter the Disney Animation Theater. You see a film narrated by the straight man, Walter Cronkite, while Robin Williams provides the comedy. Robin Williams is amusing while Walter Cronkite patiently explains how Disney creates their famous cartoons. Few of us think about the artistic talent and hard work done behind the scenes. The author recalls an argument between himself and his younger brother, while both were boys. He burst his brother's bubble by insisting that cartoon characters were not real, but merely drawings. The Animation Tour shows how Disney creates that illusion.

Following the eight-minute film, you begin a leisurely walking tour through the animation studios. The author had no trouble keeping pace while pushing his wheelchair. We think other disabled people will find it just as easy. The narration by Walter Cronkite and Robin Williams continues on overhead TV monitors.

You move along a winding hallway, and if it's during working hours, see the Disney artists and technicians at work. They make this possible with large windows. The author wondered if the workers felt self-conscious about being scrutinized by thousands of onlookers every day. We imagine they go through an adjustment period before becoming comfortable. We hope they feel flattered.

First you see the story room, where they put together the scripts for the cartoons or movies. Then you view the drawing tables where the artists transform the ideas into characters and to the "clean up" area, where they transform the drawings into polished artwork. The next step involves adding background and effects. They photograph the drawings and transfer the images to plastic cells; then they send them down the line for the finishing touches of ink and painted-on colors. Finally, they photograph the completed cells, link, and edit them. If this sounds laborious, consider that it takes 34,650 drawings and detail from 300 background scenes to produce one 24-minute film. The animation team in the Disney-MGM Studious consists of 71 people and they work in shifts, seven days per week. Now that sounds like job security!

The walking and rolling part of the Animation Tour isn't as structured as some of the other attractions. So if the processes fascinate you, feel free to linger. When you complete the tour through the working facilities, you enter the Disney Classics Theater. Here they treat you to a sampling of the Disney magic, with scenes from their famous animated movies and cartoons. As a side-light, working as an animator or artist is one of the jobs many physically disabled people could perform without being handicapped. Watching these people at work is inspirational and another reason disabled people need to get out and see the world.

In November 1992, Disney began showing their 31st animated movie spectacular. Again, in *Aladdin: Arabian Flights*, the Disney animators exhibit their talent for bringing inanimate objects and animals to life with lovable personalities. This time they use an unruly magic carpet, a fun-loving monkey, and a cocky parrot named Iago. Will Finn, the chief animator for the film, says,

> "A great animation character is really a synthesis of three things: the voice, the writing from the story department, and the animator."

Robin Williams provides the voice for the genie, *Full House's* Scott Weinger is Aladdin, and the actress Linda Larkin speaks the role of Princess Jasmine. The Animation Tour at the Disney-MGM Studios shows how they create the magic.

Backstage Studio Tour

Two-thirds of the Disney-MGM Studios is a working production facility. They create and film TV commercials, game shows, and parts of full-feature motion pictures. Disney extracts the maximum from everything they do. In this case, they allow you the opportunity of touring the backstage area. They transform a working environment into an entertaining and educational experience. This is American ingenuity at its best.

The entrance to the Backstage Studio Tour lies to the right of the Chinese Theater. First you pass through an elaborate gate and into an area where two lines are usually forming. The one on the left leads to the Backstage Studio Tour and the one on the right to the Animation Tour.

The Backstage Studio Tour consists of two parts. One involves riding in a motorized tram. This is a kind of train pulled by a small vehicle. Riders sit in open cars and listen to the narration while watching the activity around them. The second part of the attraction is a walking tour of the remaining facilities. The complete tour takes approximately two hours and it is accessible to physically disabled people, including those using wheelchairs.

As you reach the entrance, an attendant will probably approach if a person's disability is obvious. If they don't, we recommend that you seek them out. They inquire about your interests and politely offer guidance. People using manual and electric wheelchairs can roll aboard the trams and remain sitting in their chairs throughout the tour. Guests using the larger motorized carts, must transfer out of them and into a standard wheelchair — if one is available. The walking part of the tour is also possible for people using wheelchairs. If anyone chooses to bypass that portion of the tour, they can remain on the tram and return to the entrance.

The entertainment begins while you wait in line. Overhead TV monitors show a brief history of the Walt Disney Studios, narrated by Carol Burnett and Tom Selleck. A few familiar faces, such as Mel Brooks, Clint Eastwood, and Eddie Murphy, appear and lend a little humor to the scene. It may take 30 minutes, or more, before you get on the ride. Take this into account in your planning.

As a warning, the tram takes you through an attraction called Catastrophe Canyon, and people sitting on the left side will probably get wet. If you're afraid of water or melt when doused, like the Wicked Witch of the West, sit on the right side where you're less likely to get wet.

First, the tram goes through buildings where they work on television shows such as the Mickey Mouse Club. Disney refers to another as the "greens" department, where they store trees and plants until needed on the sets. Farther along you pass through the wardrobe department and see people at work on costumes. They have examples on display, such as those worn by Warren Beatty in *Dick Tracy*, Julie Andrews in *Mary Poppins*, and Michael Jackson in *Captain Eo*. Disney employs over 100 people in their wardrobe department. They produce new costumes and maintain an inventory of 2.25 million garments.

Visitors then pass through the camera, lights, and props area. This is where they store and maintain the equipment until called upon to use it in one of Disney's movies or television shows. You see carpenters and artists at work on new props and gain an appreciation for the details behind the scenes. The tram takes you into the backlot residential street area. Here you can see the fronts of hollow buildings as used in motion pictures and television shows.

The highlight of the Backstage Studio Tour is a trip through Catastrophe Canyon. Apparently Disney believes people become bored looking at static displays. This is the motion picture industry, which means action. The tour guide leads visitors on by asking, "Where in central Florida can you find an oil field, in a desert canyon prone to flash floods?" He explains they're working on a movie sequence in which a tram gets caught in one of these floods. He says, "But, don't worry, because they're not filming today." (We'll bet he sells Florida swampland is his spare time.)

Surprise, a thunderstorm begins and suddenly the oil field explodes into flames and heat, making everyone flinch and gasp. The road and the tram tilt as a tremendous flood of water flashes down the canyon. This is not a video. It's controlled reality and not dangerous; it just looks that way.

When the tour guide stops chuckling, the tram moves into New York City with its detailed building facades. The Empire State Building, the Chrysler Building, and others use a technique called forced perspective to appear life-sized. They are not just for show; Disney often uses them in various movies and film productions.

The tram ride ends at the Backstage Plaza where there are rest rooms, refreshments, and shops. Here you get off and prepare for the walking portion of the Backstage Studio Tour. Remember, people using wheelchairs can accompany the others on the walking tour, but if they prefer passing the opportunity, they can remain on the tram and return to the starting point.

Inside The Magic Special Effects And Production Tour

After surviving Catastrophe Canyon, you're ready to follow Roger Rabbit's footprints into the Loony Bin shop and the Studio Catering Company for ice cream, soft drinks, and other snacks. The Loony Bin sells souvenirs and provides a chance for the children among your group to play with some of the props used in the movie.

At the first stop on the walking or rolling tour, they select a volunteer for the honor of playing the role of "Captain Duck." The show features some of the special effects used in creating sea battles, complete with a rain storm, a miniaturized, flaming battleship, depth charges, torpedo boats, and attacking airplanes. Technicians explain how they create the mechanical effects and optical illusions, and turn them into a movie.

The next stop is in the Special Effects Workshop. They choose two children from the crowd and place them on a model of a giant bee used in the movie, *Honey, I Shrunk the Kids*. They explain how they film someone against a blue screen and then superimpose that image on any background they choose. They demonstrate this technique by filming the children and pasting them into scenes from the movie. This delights everyone, especially the children.

From there, you continue into the sound stages. The viewing area is soundproof, so you can talk without disturbing the action. The tour passes three sound stages where filming may be underway for a variety of movies or TV shows. The tour guide explains what is happening, and they show a video with Warren Beatty and other movie stars, explaining the technical and artistic details of the soundstage.

The next stop is for viewing a four-minute movie, filmed entirely in the Disney-MGM Studios. Perceptive visitors recognize the sets of New York City they saw while on the tram part of the tour. The *Lottery* stars Bette Midler as she struggles to recover her winning lottery ticket after it falls from a window. While amusing, the short film demonstrates a finished product. Finally, you will see a soundstage displaying interior sets used in the movie, while a hostess explains some of the special effects.

At the last stop, the master movie producer, George Lucas and his assistants, C3PO and R2D2, explain in a video, the art of film editing. Mel Gibson details the role of sound effects and how they incorporate them into the final film.

DINING AT THE DISNEY-MGM STUDIOS

There are three full-service restaurants, one offering cafeteria service, and eight fast-food restaurants or snack shops. The full-service restaurants require reservations and their policies are subject to change. If you have questions about reservations, call Walt Disney World Information at (407) 824-4321. Guests in any of the Walt Disney World Resorts can make reservations as much as two days in advance at 828-4000, but not on the same day. The same rule applies for people staying in the Disney Village Hotel Plaza. They need to call 824-8800.

Full-Service Restaurants

Hollywood Brown Derby: In this restaurant, Disney recreates the 1930's atmosphere of the original Brown Derby on Hollywood's Vine Street. They decorated it in teak and mahogany and added elaborate chandeliers and side lights shaped like Derby hats. The china has the Brown Derby logo and the waiters and waitresses wear formal black tie costumes. Except for the tourists in their casual clothes, it provides a semi-formal atmosphere.

The house specialty is Cobb Salad, named after the 1930's owner, Bob Cobb. It consists of finely cut salad greens, tomato, bacon, turkey, egg, blue cheese, and avocado. They prepare it at the table and serve it with a French dressing. They also offer a version containing shrimp or lobster. Another popular dish is Fettuccine Derby, with pasta, chicken, and red and green peppers in a Parmesan cheese sauce. They also serve fresh fish, veal, other chicken dishes and top it off with a Derby's dessert tray. They have a children's menu and an adult's full bar.

The Hollywood Brown Derby requires reservations. The easiest way of making reservations is by stopping at the restaurant on your way in. It may be possible to roll in without reservations during the slower hours, between approximately 3:00 and 4:00 p.m.

50's Prime Time Cafe: The decor takes you back to the 1950's, if you can remember that far. Disney trimmed the plastic laminated tables with chrome and hung a pull-down lamp over each. There are video screens all around, showing black and white film clips from 1950's TV comedy shows. The placemats have television trivia questions and they serve the food on either Fiesta Ware plates or TV dinner-style, in trays with three compartments. The waitresses play the role of Mom and threaten withholding dessert if visitors don't clean their plates.

The menu reflects the supposedly simpler times of the 1950's with a variety of All-American food. The house favorites are meat loaf served with mashed potatoes and gravy, broiled chicken and roasted potatoes, chicken pot pie, and pot roast. Of course there are hamburgers, with your choice of toppings, hot roast beef sandwiches, club sandwiches, and chicken salad. They offer soft drinks, milk shakes, ice cream sodas, and root beer floats. Finally, if and when you've finished (and cleaned your plates), Mom asks what you want for dessert. A treat called S'mores is a favorite of all children who ever attended a summer camp. It consists of graham crackers, chocolate, and toasted marshmallows. Other classic American favorites include banana splits and strawberry-rhubarb pie. Adults have a choice of beer and wine and they offer a special menu for children. The 50's Prime Time Cafe requires reservations, like the other full-service restaurants in the Disney-MGM Studios. The surest way of getting in is by making reservations in person, preferably early in the day.

Sci-Fi- Dine-In Theater: This restaurant imitates a 1950's-era, drive-in movie theater. With the usual Disney attention-to-detail, they designed the seating areas to look like cars from that time, with their big tail fins and whitewall tires. They have stars overhead in the darkened ceiling and there are vintage drive-in speakers next to each car. The waiters even cruise around on roller skates.

Everyone sits facing a large screen continuously showing a 45-minute science fiction film. It contains parts of such classics as *The Attack of the 50-foot Woman, Robot Monster,* and *Son of the Blob.* They add a few commercials advertising the treats in the fictitious concession stand, and they show some cartoons and movie previews.

They serve popcorn before the meals. The names of the main dishes fit the science fiction theme of the movie. There is the Monster Mash — a Sloppy-Joe-type sandwich made with turkey. They appropriately named their chef's salad, Tossed In Space. Ask your kids if they would like something called They Grow Among Us. It's actually a simple fruit salad. A dish made with linguini and vegetables has the title, The Red Planet, and they claim to make Meteoric Meatloaf with smoked meat. Cute.

The desert offerings include the Cheesecake That Ate New York, a banana split called the Twin Terrors, a blend of fruit cobblers known as Science Gone Mad, and strawberry shortcake named When Berries Collide. No, this isn't the children's menu. They have a special one for the little people, offering smaller portions.

Again, they require reservations at the Sci-Fi Dine-In. It's possible to make reservations up to two days in advance, but not for the same day. The easiest way for anyone making reservations is visiting the restaurant early and requesting a seating time.

The unique seating areas may pose a problem for people using wheelchairs. We suggest asking a host or hostess for assistance. The primary attraction in the Sci-Fi Dine-In is the setting and the memories it generates.

Cafeteria Service

Hollywood & Vine "Cafeteria of the Stars": The cafeteria is a Disney version of a 1950's diner and it has lots of stainless steel and pale colors. This is a walk or roll-in restaurant; it doesn't require reservations. They serve breakfast as well as lunch and dinner. Prices are slightly less than in the full-service restaurants.

The menu is varied, as it should be in a cafeteria. They refer to their breakfast special as the Hollywood Scramble, consisting of two eggs, bacon or sausage, potatoes or grits, and a biscuit. Other breakfast items are French toast, pancakes, omelets, lox and bagels, several hot and cold cereals, and fresh fruit. For smaller appetites they offer muffins, croissants, and Danish pastries. The lunch menu includes salads, and heartier fare, like baby-back ribs, roast chicken, and tortellini. At dinner-time, they add prime ribs, veal chops, and grilled pork chops with Mesquite flavoring. A variety of pies top the dessert menu. They also sell beer and wine.

We described some of the problems disabled people face when eating in a cafeteria-style restaurant. The main problem involves people using wheelchairs and trying to maneuver through a crowd and selecting, receiving, and carrying the food back to a table. The author dislikes cafeterias for those reasons. If he has no choice, he asks a companion for assistance and on the occasion when he is alone, he asks for help from one of the waiters. Ordinarily, this works well — but nothing beats independence.

Fast-Food And Snacks

None of the fast-food and snack shops require reservations. However, at busy times, eating in these places involves a wait. Try changing your normal eating patterns so you're on a different schedule than the majority of other people. It's more enjoyable seeing the attractions than waiting in line for food.

Soundstage: The set-up of this restaurant, resembles a "wrap party," similar to those movie companies put on when they complete their filming. The restaurant has three separate areas. The Pizza and Pasta Shop offers deep-dish pizza, linguini, tortellini, and a cold pasta salad. The Sandwich Shop sells a meatball sub sandwich, chicken salad, and the Soundstage Special, with salami, pepperoni, bierschinken, and jarlsberg and smoked Swiss cheese. The Soup and Salad Shop offers chef's salads, chicken salad, New England-style clam chowder, and a chicken soup containing tortellini. The peanut butter and jelly sandwiches are not just for children. Each area sells the same desserts, such as a toffee cheesecake, chocolate chip pie, and coconut cream pie.

Disney-MGM Studios Commissary: It offers chicken salad, chicken breast sandwiches, teriyaki burgers, stir-fried vegetables, and a vegetarian chili. They have a children's menu and serve lunch and dinner.

Starring Rolls Bakery: This bakery is a nice place for a quick breakfast or snack. They offer fresh rolls, muffins, croissants, and other pastries. They sell coffee, tea, and soft drinks.

Dinosaur Gertie's: This small snack stand is in a large model dinosaur on the east side of Echo Lake. Its specialty is "Ice Cream of Extinction." No, that isn't a typo. They serve ice cream bars, fruit-flavored frozen yogurt bars, ice cream sandwiches, and frozen bananas.

Backlot Express: The theme in this fast-food restaurant is that of an old-fashioned movie craft shop. There is a separate paint shop, sculpture shop, model shop, and stunt hall. The paint shop has paint splattered floors, tables, and chairs. Fortunately, the paint is dry. The prop shop features a delta wing kite, engines, bumpers, fan belts, and other automotive equipment. Artificial plants, trees, and street lamps used in movie sets decorate an outdoor eating area. They serve the food over a counter and offer broiled chicken with flour tortillas and salsa, hamburgers, hot dogs, chef's salads, and chili. For those preferring dessert, the menu includes apple pie, carrot cake, chocolate chip cheesecake, and fresh fruit. They serve beer and wine and they are open for lunch and dinner.

Min & Bill's Dockside Diner: Disney built and anchored a small ship on the shore of Echo Lake. The boat looks like a miniature tramp freighter and it contains Min and Bill's Diner. The menu includes turkey, tuna salad, and the Santa Monica Submarine Sandwich. The Cucamonga Cocktail is not a drink. It's a special dish containing shrimp and fresh vegetables. The San Pedro Pasta contains multi-colored pasta, crab, and shrimp. They serve fresh fruit with yogurt and cups or cones of soft-serve frozen yogurt. The restaurant is open for lunch and dinner.

Studio Catering Company: This fast-food restaurant is located near the end of the Backstage Studio Tour. It's located behind the Loony Bin shop and offers desserts and snacks. To dampen the adrenaline rush of Catastrophe Canyon, you might need one of the cold beers sold by the Studio Catering Company. The author obviously likes his beer.

Studio Pizza: Disney converted a studio warehouse into a pizza place, creating the atmosphere for this fast-food restaurant. Supposedly, they bake the pizzas in a wood-burning oven and grill the fish and steaks over a hardwood fire. They serve lasagna, chicken, veal chops, and pasta with different sauces. The pizzeria is popular, so they recommend visitors make reservations. Guests staying in the Walt Disney World resorts can call 828-4000 and those at the Hotel Plaza should call 828-8800. Once again, they accept reservations up to two days in advance, but not on the same day. Everyone else must stop by the restaurant and make their reservations in person and on the same day they plan on dining.

CHAPTER

6

THE REST OF THE WORLD

INTRODUCTION

There is more to the world than the Magic Kingdom, the EPCOT Center, and the Disney-MGM Studios. The three theme parks are the primary attractions, but they occupy less than two percent of the 43 square miles that is Walt Disney World. In the remaining area, Disney has two water-theme parks, River Country and Typhoon Lagoon. Pleasure Island is an impressive nighttime entertainment complex and the Walt Disney World Village contains hotel and villa-type lodging, a clubhouse, a conference center, and the Disney Village Marketplace. Discovery Island is a botanical garden and bird sanctuary. There are numerous sporting options including tennis, golf, biking, hiking, jogging, water skiing, sailing, canoeing, fishing, and swimming. The Wonders of Walt Disney World is a structured program offering children a look at the inner workings of the World.

Few visitors take advantage of these opportunities because they spend the majority of their time in the Magic Kingdom, the EPCOT Center, and the Disney-MGM Studios. The same is true for disabled people, except many of these secondary activities are inaccessible or impractical. The author would love to water ski but it's not practical in a wheelchair. The same is true for golf. Interestingly, some people play tennis and basketball while using wheelchairs. Both playing surfaces are level and smooth, making rolling easy.
However, wheelchair athletes must have very good use of their upper bodies. Whatever a person's abilities, sports provide fun and healthy exercise. We describe these attractions and activities to complete the picture of Walt Disney World and provide information for people who can participate.

PLEASURE ISLAND

Disney recognized a demand for evening entertainment that was missing in the Magic Kingdom, EPCOT Center, and Disney-MGM Studios. Filling the void, they created Pleasure Island, a six-acre island containing six nightclubs, several restaurants, a ten-screen movie theater, and shops. Pleasure Island is on the east side of Walt Disney World and near the Disney Village Marketplace. The parking lots in the Disney Village Marketplace connect with Pleasure Island across three foot bridges. There are stairways on Pleasure Island but there are also ramps. The major handicap facing people using wheelchairs is the crowd of people. If visitors are looking for a party and a few laughs, it is possible to overcome the minor inconveniences. The shops and restaurants are open from about 11:00 a.m. until midnight. The nightclubs open around 7:00 p.m. and stay open until 2:00 a.m., or later.

Admission is free during the day, but at 7:00 p.m. there is a $11.95 charge for the nightclubs, shows, and fireworks. Every night is New Year's Eve on Pleasure Island, not figuratively, but literally. Each night they put on a fireworks display with confetti, special lighting effects, and lively dancers. If you forgot your New Year's resolutions, you can try again, every night.

As might be expected, a Disney Pleasure Island is quite innocent. The age that people can drink alcoholic beverages in Florida is 21 and Disney rigidly enforces the law. They admit people over 18, but only serve drinks to those over 21. Anyone looking as young as the author's sister must have some identification proving their age.

Mannequins: This is a nightclub featuring contemporary dance music. Costumed mannequins celebrate the joy of dance. There are "Cats" from the musical, as well as scenes from *The King and I*. A turntable forms the main dance floor and they light it with an array of lights or bombard it with bubbles, confetti, or "snow."

Neon Armadillo: This club is a play on a Texas honky-tonk saloon with its live country & western music and southwestern decor.

The Adventurers Club: This place represents a private club and watering spot for world travelers. The setting is from the 1800's, the golden era of global exploration. Books and memorabilia from member's travels fill the rooms. Roaming the club and interacting with visitors are a group of eccentric characters. There is a pilot you would not want to fly with — Hathaway Brown, the resident bug expert, and prankster bartenders.

The Comedy Warehouse: This is a popular spot and features five nightly shows. The comedians involve the audience with "improvisational comedy," taking their comments and inventing a comical routine. The seating area is tiered and guests usually sit on stools. People using wheelchairs may have difficulty seeing the stage. If they do, they should contact the hosts or hostesses for assistance.

XZFR Rock and Roll Beach Club: This is a combination dining and dancing facility. They have a dance floor on the lower level, and pool tables and game rooms on the second and third floors. If disabled people have difficulty with access, they should ask for assistance.

Cage: This is a nightclub offering music videos displayed on 170 TV monitors.

West End Plaza: Here, they feature live bands and big-name groups. Each night there is an act accompanied by Pleasure Island's own dancers, The Island Explosion.

Restaurants On Pleasure Island

The two restaurants on Pleasure Island are open from 11:00 a.m. until midnight and serve lunch and dinner.

The Portobello Yacht Club: This restaurant is an elegant, Bermuda-style beach house. The restaurant contains several dining areas seating 340 guests. The decor is nautical, with model ships, sailing trophies, pennants, navigational charts, and photos. The Italian cuisine makes The Portobello Yacht Club one of the favorite restaurants in Walt Disney World. They offer grilled meat, fish, and small pizzas. Pasta dishes include spaghetti al Portobello, and pasta with shrimp, scallops, clams, mussels, and calimari — a seafood feast. The deserts are tempting, with a glazed custard or a layer cake with chocolate toffee filling topped with warm caramel sauce. They have a children's menu and do not accept reservations.

The Fireworks Factory: This is the other restaurant on Pleasure Island. Stretching believability, the 377 seat restaurant is supposedly a former fireworks factory. The atmosphere is casual but no longer explosive. Guests sit on benches at tables set with colorful tablecloths. The restaurant serves barbecued baby-back and Texas beef ribs. They have other southern specialties like catfish, barbecued shrimp, and spicy-hot chicken wings. Regular entrees include barbecued chicken, filet mignon, Kansas City strip steaks, and pork chops. Deserts range from chocolate cake to that all-time favorite — key lime pie. Again, there are children's menus and they do not accept reservations.

Sweet Surrender: This is one of the two snack shops on Pleasure Island. They offer frozen yogurt and ice cream and serve the different flavors in cups or cones.

D-Zertz: This is the other snack shop. They have pastries, chocolates, candy, coffee, and cappuccino. The snack shops are usually open from 10:00 a.m. until 2:00 a.m.

Shops on Pleasure Island

The eleven shops on Pleasure Island operate from 10:00 a.m. until midnight. They offer an interesting array of souvenirs, gifts, and trivia.

Jessica's: This shop pays tribute to the Jessica Rabbit character in the Disney movie, *Who Framed Roger Rabbit*.

Avigator's Supply: The trademark character is a winged alligator. You will find this strange critter on T-shirts, sweatshirts, and other items. Aviation is the theme, and they sell flyer's jackets and accessories.

Changing Attitudes: This store offers merchandise that is black or white. We wish everything was this simple.

Party Headquarters: This shop has hats, horns, and gadgets for creating your own party.

Front Page: Here, you can have your photo taken and become famous on the cover of your favorite magazine.

Hammer & Fire: This shop features colorful titanium jewelry, pottery, and other popular gift items.

The Mouse House: They offer another opportunity for buying the World's favorite mouse T-shirts, sweatshirts, toys, and dozens of other Disney trophies.

Suspended Animation: They have posters, prints, and other examples of Disney's art in this shop.

Yesteryears: This shop features examples of older Disney art and souvenirs.

Superstar Studios: This shop lets you make your own music video. Pick a song you like, mouth the words, rock and roll a bit, and have the audio and video combined. Send a copy to Hollywood and save a copy for your mother. It will confirm her worst fears.

Propeller Heads: This shop is for video game fanatics, and not just the young ones.

TYPHOON LAGOON

The newest Disney water-theme park covers 56 acres. It is on the east side of Walt Disney World, near the intersection of highways I-4 and S.R. 535. A one-day ticket for adults costs $20, and children three through nine pay about $16. Most people should plan on spending an entire day in the park to get their money's worth. There are plenty of activities for even the most energetic people. However, beware of the strong Florida sunshine. Even while swimming, wearing a T-shirt is a smart idea. Disney offers a one-year pass at about $80.

NOTE: People with the Five-Day Super Pass can visit Typhoon Lagoon free, for up to seven days from when they first use the pass.

A typhoon lagoon is not exactly the best of places for someone using a wheelchair. Wheelchairs float miserably and roll across sandy beaches almost as poorly. The author is comfortable swimming in a pool, but not one with four-foot waves. We considered leaving a description of Typhoon Lagoon out of our guide book because we think few physically disabled people can enjoy it. However, the author knows paraplegics who scuba dive and paddle kayaks. He even read a story and saw a photo of a quadriplegic parachuting (after his injury). So who knows, disabled people do some amazing things.

Typhoon Lagoon sounds fun, interesting, and imaginative. The scenario is that of a tropical village after suffering a triple calamity. First, a typhoon floods the village, then an earthquake shakes it. Finally, the local volcano erupts. Apparently the gods were not happy. Visitors see trees toppled, boats beached, and debris deposited everywhere. Somehow the residents survived and created a happy, watery playground for visitors to Walt Disney World.

The highlight of the attraction is a lagoon the size of two football fields. A monstrous mechanism creates four-and-a-half-foot waves. There are two speed slides sending 30 mile-per-hour human torpedoes through a cave and two storm slides. There was a time when the author would have liked this. The central feature in the area is Mt. Mayday. At its peak, a shrimp boat lies stranded. It should never have left its home port of Safen Sound, Florida. Every five to ten minutes, a 50-foot geyser erupts from her smokestack, and sends a cooling spray of water over visitors.

There are volleyball nets along the beach and hammocks strung between trees. Thatched huts provide protection from the occasional thunderstorm. Lifeguards are always on duty, with nine around the lagoon and more in the slide areas. The whole idea is staying wet and cool. Typhoon Lagoon is popular during the hot Florida summer. Disabled people could visit and watch others having fun, but we'd rather be in Philadelphia — or the EPCOT Center.

Typhoon Lagoon covers two-and-a-half acres and contains 2.75 million gallons of water. White sand beaches surround the lagoon and four-foot, man-made waves roll across it every 90 seconds. There are areas where the water is calm for tired or timid bodysurfers. Castaway Creek is a 2,100-foot long, gently flowing river. Visitors sit in free tubes and float along the 15-foot-wide, 3-foot deep stream. Periodically, cooling water sprays them as they float by caves and shady grottoes. The total float trip takes about 35 minutes. With a little help from their friends, disabled people might ride in one of these tubes. Check with the ride attendants for approval before lifting any disabled people into a tube.

The Humunga Kowabunga
This attraction consists of the two speed slides. These 214-foot chutes propel sliders up to 30 miles per hour through a series of caves. Supposedly, the 51-foot drop is over quickly. We can imagine. We do not recommend this ride for physically disabled people. Any disability is too much disability .

Shark Reef
This attraction might be fun and possible for some physically disabled people. If you think dancing with wolves or swimming with sharks sounds like fun, you can actually swim with the sharks in this 362,000-gallon sea water tank. You can borrow snorkeling gear and go under water with "small, passive" nurse and bonnethead sharks. Snorkelers (and sharks) swim around an artificial coral reef and near a capsized and sunken tanker ship. Guests must shower before entering the water. Apparently they don't want the sharks getting food poisoning. Actually, we are sure it is safe. Disabled people must decide for themselves if they want to swim with the fish.

Other Water Attractions
There are three more water slides, **Jib Jammer, Rudder Buster,** and **Stern Burner**. These are a bit more tame than the Humunga Kowabunga, with sliders only reaching 20 miles per hour. The slides are 300-feet long and wind in, out, and around artificial rock formations. Again, some disabled people might try these slides if they can stand, walk, and have nerves of steel.

There are three white water raft trips in the Typhoon Lagoon area. Each trip takes riders in oversized inner tubes through caves and waterfalls in a wet and rocky landscape. **Mayday Falls** involves a 460-foot slide. The ride begins quickly, slows in a quiet pool, and continues. **Keelhall Falls** takes riders on a spiraling 400-foot journey. Like the others, the speed rarely exceeds ten miles per hour. Groups of up to four people can sit in extra-large tubes at **Gangplank Falls** for a 300-foot ride. If disabled people can stand and walk, they might enjoy these rides. Ask the ride attendants for information and permission.

Ketchakiddie Creek caters to the younger and shorter crowd. Children must be under four feet tall and accompanied by an adult. They float down slides, past boats, fountains, waterfalls, and seals and whales. There's a gentle set of rapids and other wet entertainment for children.

Typhoon Lagoon has two restaurants. The dining areas are outdoors under colored umbrellas.

Leaning Palms: This was renamed from Placid Palms after the triple catastrophe. They offer hamburgers and hotdogs, chef's salads, and snacks.

Typhoon Tilly's Galley and Grog: They sell similar food plus frozen yogurt and ice cream. There are food carts scattered around the park offering cold drinks, ice cream, and snow cones. Two picnic areas allow visitors to dine on food from home.

Typhoon Tilly's: There are changing rooms and restrooms with showers near the main entrance. The restrooms say "buoys" (boys) and "gulls" (girls). The names are cute and sure to confuse foreign visitors. Rental lockers for storing clothes and valuables are in each dressing room.

Singapore Sal's: This is a small shop offering a variety of very brightly colored beach clothing and accessories.

A first aid station is near the main entrance to the Leaning Palms restaurant.

RIVER COUNTRY

This is Disney's first water theme park and visitors find it north of the EPCOT Center and east of the Magic Kingdom Main Entrance Toll Plaza. All the rocks and boulders in the small mountain are artificial. They scattered real pebbles around and created a realistic effect. The water slides are fun for everyone — except many physically disabled people. We describe River Country for people who can visit and swim or those who might visit and watch.

River Country has several different areas. The main area is a large, walled-off portion of Bay Lake. An adjacent section is for children and has its own beach. There is a grassy area with picnic tables and a fountain for frolicking youngsters. There is also a boardwalk along the edge of the lake and through a cypress swamp. The 330,000-gallon swimming pool is heated in the winter and has a pair of water slides. It takes courage to plunge into the pool from the slide; the final drop is about seven feet.

The part of Bay Lake, known as Bay Cove, has rope swings and a ship's boom swinging people over and into the water. White Water Rapids offers a leisurely ride in inner tubes through a twisting series of chutes, pools, and into Bay Cove. However, White Water Rapids subjects tube riders to some rocking, jostling, and contact with other riders. It is not a good place for many disabled people.

River Country costs adults about $13 per day and children three through nine, pay around $10. Combination River Country and Discovery Island tickets are approximately $16 for adults and $12 for children. Holders of a Five-Day Super Pass get in free to River Country. River Country's summer hours are 9:00 a.m. to 8:00 p.m. It has shorter hours the rest of the year and closes entirely during January. Children under ten years old must have adult supervision and everyone must have swimming ability. We do not recommend it for the majority of physically disabled people.

River Country is popular and it can be crowded in the summer. One trick involves visiting later in the day, around 4:00 p.m. Many visitors leave by then, the rates are reduced, the air is still warm, and the park stays open until 8:00 p.m. There are men's and women's dressing rooms, with rental lockers for storing clothing and valuables. Small towels cost $.50. Of course, you must bring your own swimming suit.

There's a small fast food stand, Pop's Place, selling hamburgers, hot dogs, assorted snacks, and cold drinks. People can bring their own food and drink, except for alcoholic beverages. There are shaded areas and tables for eating.

There are several ways of getting to River Country. There are buses from the Transportation and Ticket Center, near where people board the Monorail for the trip to the Magic Kingdom. Boats take people from the entrance to the Magic Kingdom to River Country. People driving cars park in the River Country parking lot and take buses to River Country.

DISCOVERY ISLAND

One of the nicer things about Walt Disney World is its diversity. For a little seclusion, you can visit the 11-acre Discovery Island. It is in Bay Lake, east of the Magic Kingdom. There are regularly scheduled boat trips to Discovery Island from Fort Wilderness, River Country, the Magic Kingdom, and the Contemporary, Grand Floridian, and Polynesian resorts.

In *The Disabled Guests Guide Book*, Disney does not say if the motor launches to Discovery Island are accessible for people using wheelchairs. The same is true for the island. There are paths and boardwalks, but we think disabled people traveling with companions could probably manage. The author was alone when visiting this part of Walt Disney World, so he did not visit Discovery Island.

Discovery Island is basically a wildlife sanctuary. Disney sculpted the island by adding tons of sand, soil, and boulders. They imported dozens of tropical plants from around the world, including palms, bamboo, and many varieties of flowers. The plants provide realism and beauty to the setting, but the prime attractions on Discovery Island are the animals, and birds have top billing.

There are trained macaws and cockatoos, including a threesome named Moe, Larry, and Curly. You can see trumpeter swans, two species of cranes, brown pelicans, peacocks, and flamingos. The Avian Way is a one-acre aviary you can walk (and probably roll) through. It is home to the largest breeding flock of scarlet ibis in the United States. Disney preserves the wilderness feeling by discreetly hiding the enclosing netting.

Discovery Island is not only for the birds. You can see Patagonian cavies, which are large, friendly members of the guinea pig family, and lemurs, wallabies, tiny deer, marmosets, and marsh rabbits. Finally, there are reptiles, like the immense Galapagos tortoises, a few alligators, and lizards.

Discovery Island is a fine place for photographers and a nice place for a quiet picnic lunch. You can bring your own food or purchase sandwiches, snacks, soft drinks, and beer at a fast-food shop called the Thirsty Perch.

Discovery Island is open from 10:00 a.m. until 5:00 p.m. (7:00 p.m. during the summer). Admission to the island is about $8.50. This seems a bit high, but a combination ticket to River Country and Discovery Island is a relative bargain for around $15. The Five-Day Super Pass includes admission to the three major theme parks for five days; for an additional two days, you can visit Typhoon Lagoon, River Country, Discovery Island, and Pleasure Island. Remember, these tickets are only a bargain if the attractions are accessible — many are not.

WALT DISNEY WORLD VILLAGE

The Walt Disney World Village is near the intersection of Highway I-4 and S.R. 535. It is primarily a shopping complex, and contains hotel and villa-type lodging, the Walt Disney World Conference Center, the Village Clubhouse, and the Disney Village Marketplace. Some people enjoy shopping and disabled people are no different. The area is accessible for people using wheelchairs, so we offer a brief description.

The Disney Village Marketplace is the main attraction. It contains eight buildings along the shores of the Buena Vista Lagoon. The shops offer a variety of merchandise, much of it related to Disney.

Mickey's Character Shop: Here, you can find your favorite Disney characters, Mickey and Minnie, and many others. They come as soft toys, porcelain figures, and printed on T-shirts, or almost anything you can think of. The shops mainly sell gift items.

Cristal Arts: They sell cut glass from the same source as the shop in the Magic Kingdom.

The Great Southern Country Craft Co.: The Craft Co. sells leather goods, silver items, and pottery.

The Gourmet Pantry: They have many food items and although expensive, the shop is convenient.

Conched Out: This shop features souvenirs reminding you of Florida.

Board Stiff: They offer beach-type, casual clothing. There are other clothing shops like Country Address, Resort Wear Unlimited, Sir Edward's Haberdasher, and Team Mickey's Athletic Club. Finally, there is a shop called Village Spirits — there is nothing mystical about it; they sell wine, beer, and distilled liquors. We think you get the idea. There are shops providing something for everyone.

CROSSROADS OF LAKE BUENA VISTA SHOPPING CENTER

This is across from the Disney Village Hotel Plaza. It might be the most economical place for eating and shopping. There is a Gooding's Supermarket with a full-service pharmacy, clothing and shoe stores, a Disney merchandise shop, an electronics store, White's Bookstore, a dry cleaner, a store selling eyeglasses, a Sun Bank, and a post office. Some relatively inexpensive restaurants include : McDonald's, Taco Bell, T.G.I. Fridays, Perkins, Pizzeria Uno, Red Lobster, Pebbles, and Jungle Jim's.

APPENDIX

ADDITIONAL INFORMATION

The Handicapped Driver's Mobility Guide is published by the American Automobile Association; Falls Church, Virginia. 1981, 75 pages, free. Available from local AAA clubs, the guide provides information for disabled drivers on equipment and services.

Well Spouse Foundation, P.O. Box 28876; San Diego, CA 92198-0876. This is a nationwide group supporting spouses and partners of people with chronic disabilities and illnesses. Membership costs $15 per year. They offer support group and information sources.

Breaking New Ground Resource Center; Purdue University; 1146 AGEN Building; West Lafayette, IN 47907. This group is developing a resource called *A Guide for Farmers Making Career Decisions Following a Disability*. Contact Mr. Barry Delks for more information.

The American Academy of Allergy & Immunology has an asthma/allergy hotline allowing callers to locate doctors specializing in allergies and asthma. This can be helpful for travelers. Call 1-800-822-ASMA.

OTHER TRAVEL INFORMATION
Arthritis
Travel Tips for People with Arthritis is available from the Arthritis Foundation; P.O. Box 19000; Atlanta, GA 30326. (404) 872-7100.

Traveling With Oxygen
The American Lung Association offers a free brochure, *Air Travel With Oxygen*. People can obtain a copy from their local chapter of the Association or from their headquarters, P.O. Box 596-EV; New York; NY 10116-0596, or they can call (212) 315-8700.

Good, But Not Great Travel With Oxygen is the title of a book by Phil Petersen due out in January, 1993. Mr. Petersen describes his travel experiences with his wife who has chronic obstructive pulmonary disease (COPD). It should provide useful advice and resource information. For information contact Raven Publishers, Inc.; 1427 Hartford Ave.; Charlotte, NC 28209, or call (704) 523-6566.

Information For Diabetic Travelers

The American Diabetes Association offers a booklet titled *Travel and Diabetes*. It is free, printed in English or Spanish. To order, write The American Diabetes Association; 1660 Duke St.; Alexandria, VA 22314.

A quarterly newsletter, *The Diabetic Traveler*, costs $19.95 per year. Write to them at *The Diabetic Traveler*; Box 8223; Stamford, CT 06905, or call (203) 327-5832.

Information For Kidney Patients

This is a bimonthly magazine for kidney patients focusing on travel and leisure. It is titled *For Patients Only*. It includes a guide to worldwide dialysis centers and costs $17 per year. Contact them at 20335 Ventura Blvd.; Suite 400; Woodland Hills, CA 91364, or call (818) 704-5555.

The U.S. Government offers a guide to dialysis centers around the country. It is titled ***1992 National Listing of Medicare Providers Furnishing Kidney Dialysis and Transplant Services*** and costs $7.50. Contact the Superintendent of Documents; Government Printing Office; Washington, DC. 20402 or call (202) 783-3238. Request stock # 017-060-00477-1.

Travel For Hearing-Impaired People

Travel Resources for Deaf People; National Information Center on Deafness/LWD; 800 Florida Ave. NE; Washington, DC. 20002. It includes a listing of travel agencies and costs $1.00.

National Information Center On Deafness

A 1992 Directory of National Organizations of and for Deaf and Hard-of-Hearing People contains information on a variety of topics, including travel. It is free and available from the National Center on Deafness; Gallaudet University; 800 Florida Ave., NE; Washington, DC. 20002 or call (202) 651-5051 or TDD: (202) 651-5052.

National Resource Directory For Amputees

The American Amputee Foundation offers a National Resource Directory. It is free to their members and membership currently costs $25. Contact them at P.O. Box 250218; Little Rock, AR 72225, or call (501) 666-2523.

FEDERAL CONSUMER PUBLICATIONS OF INTEREST

The Government lists over 200 free or low cost publications in their Fall 1992 *Consumer Information Catalog*. Many relate to health, disabilities and travel. Of particular note are *Access Travel: Airports* (580Y). It provides information on facilities and services for disabled people at 533 airports worldwide. Another important booklet is,*The Americans with Disabilities Act: Questions and Answers* (585Y).

A new, 33-page brochure is available but not listed in the catalog. It comes from the Department of Transportation and details the Air Carriers Access Act published in March 1990 and changes resulting from The Americans With Disabilities Act (ADA). *New Horizons for the Air Traveler with a Disability* includes information on accessibility of airports and aircraft, the requirements for advance notice, attendants, medical certificates, the handling of assistive devices and more. It even includes information on how to file a complaint.

These three publications are free from S. James; Consumer Information Center-2D; P.O. Box 100; Pueblo, CO 81002. They charge a $1.00 service fee for ordering up to 25 booklets. The catalog is free.

MAGAZINES AND NEWSLETTERS FOR DISABLED PEOPLE

Accent On Living is a quarterly magazine for disabled people and rehabilitation professionals. It contains articles on housing, transportation, jobs, sports, travel and self-improvement. It was established in 1956 and has a circulation of 20,000. Write, *Accent on Living*; P.O. Box 700; Bloomington, IL 61702, or call (309) 378-2961. FAX: (309) 378-4420.

Access USA News is a monthly newspaper that reports news from all over the U.S., including travel information for disabled people. A subscription costs $10 per year. Write Road-runner Publishing, Inc.; P.O. Box 9134; Crystal Lake, IL 60014 or call (815) 363-0900, TDD: (815) 363-0922. FAX: (815) 363-0923.

Arthritis Today is a bimonthly magazine about living with arthritis and it contains the latest information on research and treatment . For information, write: Arthritis Foundation; 1314 Spring St. NW; Atlanta, GA 30309; (404) 872-7000. FAX: (404) 872-8694.

Careers & the Disabled is a career guidance magazine for disabled people. It comes out three times per year and is aimed at college students and professionals. For information, write: Equal Opportunity Publications; Suite 420; 150 Motor Pkwy.; Hauppauge, NY 1178 8-5145, or call(516) 273-0066. FAX: (516) 273-8936.

Diabetes Self-Management is a bimonthly magazine containing how-to health care articles. Contact: R.A. Rapaport Publishing, Inc.; Suite 800; 150 W. 22nd St.; New York, NY 10011-2421 or call (212) 989-0200.

Disability Now, 12 Park Crescent; London W1N 4EQ; Great Britain. Tel. 071-636-5020. This paper focuses on news and issues related to disabled people. It is published monthly by the Spastics Society (how we wish they would change that name). They cover many disabilities and have a circulation of 28,000. Their January 1992 issue included a holiday guide and contains resources and advertisements. Overseas subscriptions cost £20.

The publishers of *Exceptional Parent* magazine initiated a quarterly periodical in the spring of 1992 titled *Guide for Active Adults with Disabilities*. In their first issue, they focus on mobility, wheelchair maintenance, powered scooters and van lifts. They include sections on resources, news, books, and sports. Their intention is to "fully cover the spectrum of adult life for individuals with disabilities." The cost is $18 per year. For information, write to Exceptional Parent's Guide for Active Adults; P.O. Box 889; Boston, MA 02134 or call (617) 730-5800.

Family Travel Times is an 8-page newsletter. It is not specifically aimed at disabled travelers but, as the publisher, Dorothy Jordan comments, "not only are families traveling with handicapped children, but also with elderly parents who have reduced mobility. Besides, wheelchair access also benefits people with strollers." The newsletter includes travel news, children's programs, book reviews and reports on particular destinations. Ten issues per year cost $35, a sample copy is $1.00. You can write 45 West 18th St.; New York, NY 10011 or call (212) 206-0688.

Free Spirit is monthly newsletter that covers a variety of issues relating to people with disabilities. The yearly cost is $15. To order write P.O. Box 560186; Miami, FL 33256 or call (305) 388-2574.

Independent Living, The Health Care Magazine Serving Dealers, Rehabilitation Facilities and Their Clients, is a quarterly magazine on home health care, rehabilitation and disability issues. Contact: Equal Opportunity Publications, Inc.; Suite 420; 150 Motor Pkwy. ; Hauppauge, NY 11788-5145 or call (516) 273-0066. FAX: (516) 273-8936.

International Ventilators Network News; G.I.N.I.; 5100 Oakland Ave.; #206; St. Louis, MO 63110. This is a biannual newsletter for ventilator users and health care professionals. Their spring 1992 issue contained an article on Travel and Ventilators. Write them to subscribe or request a copy of a particular issue.

Kaleidoscope is an international magazine for disabled people. They explore disabilities through literature and the fine arts. A sample copy is $2.00. To order, write 326 Locust St.; Akron, Ohio 44302-1876.

Mainstream, Magazine of the Able-Disabled, is published ten times per year and contains articles on daily living, travel, computers, laws and other subjects relating to disabled people. Contact: Exploding Myths, Inc.; 2973 Beech St.; San Diego, CA 92102 or call (619) 234-3138.

Mobility International; 62 Union Street; London SE1 1TD; England 01-403-5688. **Mobility International USA;** P.O. Box 3551; Eugene, OR 97403 or call (503) 343-1284 (Voice and TDD). This organization formed in London in 1973 and has offices in at least 25 countries around the world. Their primary purpose is integrating disabled people into educational exchange programs around the world and promoting their participation in travel experiences. Some of their activities include: educational exchange programs, host families, international work camps, conferences, living exchanges, student internships, group exchanges, travel information and referral, and international correspondence. They publish a quarterly newsletter, *Over the Rainbow* for $10 per year. Individual membership is $20 per year.

Moss Rehabilitation Hospital, Travel Information Center; 12th Street & Tabor Road; Philadelphia, PA 19491 or call (215) 456-9600, (215) 329-5715, or TTY: (215) 329-4342. The Travel Information Center offers data on transportation, accessible lodging, cruises, restaurants, and general travel information in the U.S. and overseas. They make referrals to travel agencies, airlines, and others providing services for disabled people.

Moving Forward is is a bimonthly newsletter in its 8th year. It contains useful travel information for disabled people and a yearly subscription costs $10. To order write P.O. Box 3553; Torrance, CA 90510, or call (310) 320-8793.

Movin' On is a publication put out by Craig Hospital, a national center specializing in the care and treatment of people with spinal cord and head injuries. *Movin' On* is their newsletter for former patients, their families, and friends of the hospital. To order write Craig Hospital; 3425 Clarkson Street; Englewood, Colorado 80110-2899, or call (303) 789-8000.

The National Focus is a bimonthly paper that focuses more on issues than news, but is of interest to all disabled people. A year's subscription costs $10. To order, write Southwest Focus Communications, Inc.; P.O. Box 37485; Phoenix, AZ 85069 or call (602) 866-9206 (Voice and Fax) or TDD: (602) 375-2022.

Paraplegia News is a monthly magazine containing news and information for all people using wheelchairs. Contact: Paralyzed Veterans of America; Suite 111; 5201 N. 19th Ave.; Phoenix AZ 85015, or call (602) 246-9426.

The Paralyzed Veterans of America has a 32-page booklet titled *Wheelchair Sports and Recreation*. It includes descriptions of sports and recreation for wheelchair-using disabled people and a list of recreation organizations and equipment suppliers. A free copy is available from PVA, Sports and Recreation Dept.; 801 Eighteenth St. NW; Washington, DC. 20006 or call (800) 424-8200.

Parenting With a Disability is a newsletter for parents with disabilities and service providers. For more information, write to Looking Glass; 801 Pearlta Ave.; Berkeley, CA 94707.

Peoplenet, "Where People Meet People," is a networking news-letter for disabled single people. Contact: Peoplenet; P.O. Box 897; Levittown, NY 11756-1042, or call (516) 579-4043.

Seasons is a newsletter for disabled people. For information, write to The Christian League for the Handicapped; P.O. Box 948; Walworth, WI, 53148.

Society For The Advancement Of Travel For The Handicapped (SATH). The Society "is dedicated to the creation of barrier-free access and to the widest possible circulation of information concerning travel conditions for all disabled travelers." They were founded in 1975 and publish a monthly newsletter. They serve as a resource center on travel facilities and literature provided for disabled people by carriers, hotels, destinations, and car rental agencies. Membership in 1993 is $100 for travel companies, $45 for individuals, and $25 for students and senior citizens. Contact SATH for additional information at 347 Fifth Avenue; Suite 610; New York, NY 10016, or call (212) 447-SATH. FAX: (212) 725-8253.

Sports & Spokes, The Magazine for Wheelchair Sports and Recreation is a bimonthly magazine covering sports and recreation for people with spinal cord injury, spinabifida, amputation, and some congenital defects. Contact: Paralyzed Veterans of America; Suite 111; 5201 N. 19th Ave.; Phoenix, AZ 85015, or call (602) 246-9426. FAX: (602) 242-6862.

Travel Agendas, Travel Health and Disability Institute; 1259 El Camino Real; Suite 254; Menlo Park, CA 94026-0640. This groups goal is facilitating travel by people with disabilities. They offer many publications and a newsletter for people over 50 years old, or those with hearing, sight, and physical disabilities. They also relate to people with asthma, allergies, kidney disorders requiring dialysis, people with ostomys, and anyone interested in travel health and health care providers. Contact Judith Russell for more information.

TOUR GROUPS FOR DISABLED PEOPLE

Access Adventures/Bonaparte Travel; 300 Main St.; East Rochester, NY 14445; (716) 385-6050 or FAX: (716) 385-6053. Contact Debra Lisena-Tyo for information on wheelchair accessible package vacations. Among their many offerings is a 6-day Walt Disney World tour.

Accessible Journeys; 35 West Sellers Avenue; Ridley Park, PA 19078; (215) 521-0339 or FAX: (215) 521-6959. This organization has been escorting groups of disabled travelers since 1985. They offer a unique service of arranging companions for people needing assistance. They maintain a list of doctors, nurses, and therapists willing to accompany disabled travelers. The company provides proof of their professional status, personal profiles, and photographs. A written contract is prepared, protecting both parties. Of course this is a cost, usually the companions are paid for their room and board, transportation, and a salary.

Flying Wheels Travel, Inc.; 143 West Bridge; P.O. Box 382; Owatonna, MN 55060; (507) 451-5005, (800) 535-6790, or FAX: (507) 451-16 85. This group sponsors many wheelchair accessible tours, including one to Walt Disney World.

Multi-Travel; Dept. for the Disabled Traveler; 2 West 47th St.; New York, NY 10036; (212) 382-3370, (800) 234-7172, or FAX: (212) 3 98-9304. This group arranges unique packaged tours for disabled travelers. We recommend you contact them for more information.

New Directions; 5276 Hollister Ave.; Suite 207; Santa Barbara, CA 93111; (805) 967-2841. This non-profit group organizes vacations for people with developmental disabilities. They welcome people using wheelchairs and those requiring 1:1 care. Contact them for more information.

People and Places, Inc.; 483 Elmwood Avenue; Buffalo, NY 14222; (716) 886-6240. This non-profit organization provides vacation tours for adults with developmental disabilities. They usually limit their trips to eight people accompanied by two staff members. Travelers requiring continual care might require their own attendants. The cost for their trips include transportation, accommodations, all meals, tour, and supervision costs. Contact them for more information.

TRAVEL AGENCIES FOR DISABLED PEOPLE

Helen Hecker has compiled a *Directory of Travel Agencies for the Disabled*. It lists agencies across the United States as well many international agencies. You can order a copy by writing Twin Peaks Press; P.O. Box 129; Vancouver, WA 98666, or call (206) 694-2462, or (800) 637-2256. Price not listed.

TRAVEL COMPANIONS & PERSONAL ESCORTS

These companies link bonded or licensed assistants with disabled travelers:

Accessible Journeys; 35 Sellers Ave.; Ridley Park, PA 19078; (215) 521-0339.
Travel Buddy; P.O. Box 31146; Minneapolis, MN 55431; (612) 881-5364.
Traveling Nurse's Network; P.O. Box 129; Vancouver, WA 98666; (206) 694-2462.
MedEscort International; P.O. Box 8766; Allentown, PA 18105.

ACCESSIBLE RENTAL MOTOR HOMES

Bates Rent-A-Motor Home, Inc.; 6000 South Eastern; Suite 5C; Las Vegas, NV; (702) 736-2070 or (800) 732-2283. Bates has rentals in 100 U.S. cities and 18 foreign countries. Although they currently have only two wheelchair accessible motor homes, one in Las Vegas and another in Los Angeles; they say they will provide more as the demand warrants. The units have ramps, wide interiors, and accessible toilets. Contact Sandy Bates for more information.

Ordinary RVs are not equipped for disabled people, but many dealers modify them with accessories like wheelchair lifts, hand controls, special bathrooms, bathing facilities, and grab bars. If you name it and can afford it, they can do it. The following is a partial list of companies providing RVs and accessories for disabled people. The information is from: *Access to the World, A Travel Guide for the Handicapped*, by Louise Weiss, 1983, published by and available from, Facts on File, Inc.; 460 Park Avenue South; New York, NY 10016.

Beach-Craft Motor Homes Corp.; 52684 Dexter Drive; Elkhart, Indiana 46514-9535; (219) 264-4178. Custom-built motor homes.
Braun Corp.; 1014 South Monticello; Winamac, Indiana 46996; (219) 946-6157. Lifts for vans and motor homes.
Delux Homes; 2800 West Farmington Road; Peoria, Illinois

61604; (304) 674-6131. Mass-produced vans and motor homes.
Esquire, Inc.; Rt. #1; Box 19925-M205; Edwardsburg, Michigan 49112; (616) 641-5194. Mostly mini-motor homes.
Handi-Ramp, Inc.; P.O. Box 745; Mundelein, Illinois 60060; (312) 566-5861. Manufactures ramps.
Quality Coach; Route 309; Montgomeryville, Pennsylvania 18936; (215) 643-2211. Custom-outfitted RVs.
Ricon Corporation; 11684 Tuxford Street; Sun Valley, California 91352; (213) 768-5890. Motor homes and vans, lifts and hand controls.
R. J. Chair Lift Company, Inc.; 715 South Fifth Avenue; Maywood, Illinois 60153; (312) 344-2705. Equipped vans and motor homes.
Ted Hoyer & Company, Inc.; P.O. Box 2744; Oshkosh, Wisconsin 54903; (414) 231-7970. Lifts.
Total Mobility; 4060 Stewart Road; Eugene, Oregon 97402; (503) 686-9706. Equipped vans and motor homes.
Travel Equipment Corporation; Box 512; Goshen, Indiana 46526; (219) 533-4161. Customized vans and mini-motor homes.
Turtle Top, Inc.; P.O. Box 537; 116 W. Lafayette Street; Goshen, Indiana 46526; (219) 533-4116. Customized vans and mini-motor homes.
Winnebago Industries, Inc.; Commercial Vehicle Department; P.O. Box 152; Forest City, Iowa 50436; (515) 582-3535. Modified commercial vehicles.
Xplorer Motor Home Division; Frank Industries, Inc.; P.O. Box 130; 3950 Burnsline Road; Brown City, Michigan 48416; (313)346-2771. Customized motor homes.

The Recreation Vehicle Industry Association (RVIA) will be of further assistance. For a current listing of manufacturers and modifiers of vehicles for disabled people, write to: RVIA Publications Department; P.O. Box 204; Chantilly, Virginia 22021. They appreciate a self-addressed, stamped envelope.

Another group for disabled travelers is the **A Will-AWay RVers Association, Inc.;** 97 Wellesley Avenue; Wellesley, Massachusetts 02181; (617) 237-0305. They publish a newsletter for $10 per year and provide a variety of information on trip planning, health care and RVs.

BIBLIOGRAPHY
Guides to Walt Disney World

Birnbaum, Stephen, Editor. *Walt Disney World, the Official Guide*. 1992 Edition, 249 pages. Avon Books & Hearst Professional Magazines, Inc.

Haberfeld, Caroline, V., Editor. *Fodor's Disney World & the Orlando Area*. 1992 Edition, 146 pages. Fodor's Travel Publications, 2 01 E. 50th Street, New York, NY 10022.

Saine, Maria. *Disney World for Kids of All Ages: Plus Universal Studios, Sea World, Spaceport USA, Cypress Gardens, and much more*. 1992 Edition, 372 pages. Travel Keys, P.O. Box 160691, Sacramento, California 95816.

Sehlinger, Bob. *The Unofficial Guide to Walt Disney World and EPCOT*. 1992 Edition, 418 pages. Prentice Hall Press, 15 Columbus Circle, New York, NY 10023.

Wiley, Kim Wright. *Walt Disney World With Kids, The Unofficial Guide*. 1992 Edition, 284 pages. Prima Publishing, P.O. Box 1260KWB , Rocklin, CA 95677.

Travel Guides For Disabled People

Freedman, Jaqueline and Gersten, Susan. *Traveling...Like Everybody Else, A Practical Guide For Disabled Travelers*. 1987, 175 pages . Adama Books, 306 West 38 Street, New York, NY 10018.

Hecker, Helen, R.N. *Directory of Travel Agencies for the Disabled*. 1991, 46 pages. Twin Peaks Press, P.O. Box 129, Vancouver, Washington 98666.

Hecker, Helen, R.N. *Travel For The Disabled, A Handbook of Travel Resources and 500 Worldwide Access Guides*. 1985, 185 pages. Twin Peaks Press, P.O. Box 129, Vancouver, Washington 98666.

Watt, Jill and Calder, Ann. *Taking Care. A Self-Help Guide For Coping With An Elderly, Chronically Ill, Or Disabled Relative*. 1986, 128 pages. International Self-Counsel Press, Ltd. 306

West 25th Street, North Vancouver, British Columbia, Canada, V7N2G1.

Weiss, Louise. *Access To The World*. 1983, 221 pages. Facts On File, Inc. 460 Park Avenue South, New York, NY 10016.

Hoffman, Susan Thompson and Storck, Inez Fitzgerald, Editors. *Disability in the United States, A Portrait From National Data*. 1991, 260 pages. Springer Publishing Company, Inc. 536 Broadway, New York, NY 10012-3955.

Index

A

Accessible Lodging Questionnaire, 69
Accommodations, see Lodging
Admission, 34, 39, 83, 153, 270, 279
    credit cards, 33, 37
    annual passport, 34
    five-day superpass, 34
    four-day passport, 34
    one day ticket, 34
    Pleasure Island, 34, 270
    Typhoon Lagoon, 34, 273
    River Country, 277
Adventureland, 89-92
    Jungle Cruise, 89-90
    Pirates of the Caribbean, 90-91
    Restaurants, 133-134
        Fast-food, 133-134
    Shopping, 144-145
    Swiss Family Treehouse, 89
    Tropical Serenade (Enchanted Tiki Birds), 91-92
Adventurers Club, 270
Airline Travel, 41-48
    for Disabled travelers, 41-46
    for everyone, 47-48
Alcohol, 135, 270
All American College Marching Band, 123
American Adventure, The, 194
American Gardens Stage, 214
American Journeys, 119-120
Amputees, see Appendix, 285
Animation Tour, 255-257
Arthritis, see Appendix, 283
Automobiles, Travel, 48-50

B

Baby care, 39
    at Disney-MGM Studios, 240
    at EPCOT Center, 217
    at Magic Kingdom, 85
Backstage Magic, 163
Backstage Studio Tour, 257-259
Banjo Kings, 124
Banking services, 33
Barbers, 143
Beach Club, see Disney's Beach Club Resort
Big Thunder Mountain Railroad, 95-96
Boats, 63, 85, 155, 184, 278
    to Discovery Island, 63, 278
Body Wars, 167-170
Bus Travel, 52

C

Cafeteria Service,
    at Disney-MGM Studios, 263
    at EPCOT Center, 225
    at Magic Kingdom, 132
Campgrounds, see Fort Wilderness Campground, 62-63
Canada, 208-211
Captain EO, 177
Car Rentals, 50
Caribbean Beach Resort, 58
Carousel of Progress, 117-118
Cash, 33
Castaway Creek, 274
Children, 38-39
    Baby services, 38-39, 217, 240
    Day care, 56
    lost, 39, 85, 217
    first aid, see First Aid
    playgrounds, 253
    strollers for, 83, 141, 153, 242
    traveling with, 38-39
Cinderella Castle, 86, 137, 147
Cinderella's Golden Carousel, 105
City Hall, 85-86, 122
Climate, see Florida
Clothing, 30, 38,
Comedy Warehouse, 271
CommuniCore East and West, 161-163
Computer Central, 162
Contemporary Resort, 57
Conference Center, Walt Disney World,
    see Swan & Dolphin Hotels
Country Bear Jamboree, 93
Cranium Command, 170-171
Credit cards, 33, 37
Crossroads of Lake Buena Vista Shopping Center, 280
Crowds, 29, 125, 127, 213
Currency exchange, 33

D

Diabetics, Air Travel for, 45
Dialysis, Air Travel for, 45-46
Diamond Horseshoe Jamboree, 92

Dining, see Restaurants
Dinner theaters,
    Hoop Dee Doo Revue, 62
Directions,
    see How To Get There
Disabled People,
    Accessible lodging, 56-76
    Additional information, 283-293
    Advice for, 35-37, 41-47
    Companions/Escorts, 39-40, 291
    Magazines for, 283-290
    Newsletters for, 283-290
    Tour groups for, 290
    Travel agencies for, 291
    Travel information, 40-46, 48-54, 283
    Who is, 17
    Why handicapped, 17
Discovery Island, 278-279
DISNEY-MGM STUDIOS, 236-266
    Animation Building, 255-257
    Backstage Studio Tour, 257-259
    Dining, 261-266
        Cafeteria service, 263
        Fast-food restaurants, 264-266
        Full-service restaurants, 261-263
    Disney-MGM Studios Animation Tour, 255-257
    Great Movie Ride, The, 243-245
    Here Come the Muppets, 252-253
    Hollywood Boulevard, 240-243
        East Side Shops, 241
        West Side Shops, 242
    Honey, I Shrunk the Kids Movie Set Adventure Playground, 253-254
    Indiana Jones Epic Stunt Spectacular, 248-249
    Inside the Magic Special Effects and Production Tour, 259-260
    Jim Henson's MuppetVision 3-D, 252-253
    locker rentals, 240
    Map of, 239
    Monster Sound Show, The, 248
    New York Street Back Lot, 254
    Shopping at, see
        Hollywood Boulevard
    Star Tours, 250-252
    Studio Animation Tour, 255-257
    SuperStar Television, 245-247
    Teenage Mutant Ninja Turtles, 254
    Wheelchair rental, 240
Disney's Beach Club Resort, 61
Disney cartoon characters, 109, 214
Disney souvenirs, see Shopping,
Disney's Village Resort, 63-64
Disney's Yacht Club Resort, 61
Dixie Landings Resort, 59
Dolphin Hotel, 60
Dreamflight, 118-119
Dumbo, the Flying Elephant, 104-105

E

Earth Station, 154
Eating, see Dining
    in Disney-MGM Studios, 261-266
    in EPCOT Center, 214-234
    in Magic Kingdom, 127-139
    on Pleasure Island, 271-272
Electric Cart Rentals, see Wheelchair Rental
Electronic Forum, 163
Enchanted Tiki Birds, 91-92
Energy Exchange, 163
EPCOT CENTER, 150-235
    Dining, 214-234
        Future World fast-food restaurants, 216-219
        Future World full-service restaurants, 219-221
        World Showcase cafeteria service, 225
        World Showcase fast-food restaurants, 221-225
        World Showcase full-service restaurants, 225-234
    Earth Station, 154
    Fireworks, 211-213
    Future World, 157-183
    How To Get There, 152
    Information, 154
    Live shows, 211-214
    Locker rentals, 154
    Map of, 156
    Orientation, 155
    Shopping at, 183-211
    Street shows, 213

Wheelchair rentals, 153
WorldKey Information
  Service, 154
World Showcase, 183-211
EPCOT Computer Central, 162
EPCOT Outreach and
  Teacher's Center, 162
Expo Robotics, 162

F

Fantasy Faire, 104
Fantasyland, 102-108
  Cinderella's Golden Carousel, 105
  Dumbo, the Flying Elephant, 104
  Fantasy Faire, 104
  It's a Small World, 103-104
  Mad Tea Party, 106-107
  Magic Journeys, 102
  Mr. Toad's Wild Ride, 107-108
  Peter Pan's Flight, 102-103
  Restaurants, 137-139
    Fast-food, 138-139
    Full-service, 137-138
  Shopping, 147
  Skyway to Tomorrowland, 104
  Snow White's Adventures, 108
  20,000 Leagues Under the Sea, 106
Fast-food restaurants,
  in Disney-MGM Studios, 264-266
  in EPCOT Center, 216-219, 221-225
  in Magic Kingdom, 127-139
Film, 142, 242
Fireworks in,
  Magic Kingdom, 126
  EPCOT Center, 211-213
First aid, 36, 217, 240, 276
Fitness Fairgrounds, 166-167
Flag Retreat, 124
Florida,
  climate, 28-29
  maps, 20-22
Food, see Dining, or Restaurants
Foreign currency exchange, 33
Foreign language assistance, 154
Fort Wilderness Campground, 62-63
France, 200-203
Frontierland, 92-98
  Big Thunder Mountain
    Railroad, 95-96
  Country Bear Jamboree, 93
  Diamond Horseshoe
    Jamboree, The, 92-93
  Frontierland Shootin' Arcade, 93-94
  Restaurants, 135-136
    fast-food eating places, 135-136
    full-service restaurants, 135
  Shopping, 145-146
  Splash Mountain, 94-95
  Tom Sawyer Island and Fort
    Sam Clemens, 97-98
  Walt Disney World Railroad, 96-97
Full-service restaurants,
  in Disney-MGM Studios, 261-263
  in EPCOT Center, 219-221, 225-234
  in Magic Kingdom, 127-139
FutureCom, 161-162
Future World, 157-183
  CommuniCore East and
    West, 161-163
    Backstage Magic, 163
    Electronic Forum, 163
    Energy Exchange, 163
    EPCOT Computer Central, 162
    EPCOT Outreach and
      Teacher's Center, 162
    Expo Robotics, 162
    FutureCom,161-162
    Travelport, 163
  Earth Station, 154
  Horizons, 171-173
  Journey into Imagination, 175-177
    Image Works, The, 176
    Journey into Imagination
      Ride, 175-176
    Captain EO, 175, 177
  Land, The, 177-180
    Harvest Theater:
      Symbiosis, 180
    Kitchen Kabaret, 179
    Listen to the Land, 178
  Living Seas, The, 180-183
  Map, 156
  Orientation, 155
  Spaceship Earth, 157-161
  Universe of Energy, 164-165
  Wonders of Life, 166-171
    Body Wars, 167-170

Cranium Command, 170-171
Fitness Fairgrounds, 166-167
Making of Me, The, 166-167
World of Motion, The, 173-174
It's Fun to Be Free, 173-174
TransCenter, 174
Future World Brass Band, 213

G

Germany, 191-192
Grand Floridian Beach Resort, 57
Grand Prix Raceway, 111-112
Grandma Duck's Petting Farm, 109
Great Movie Ride, The, 243-245
Group tours, 39, 290
Guide dogs, 33, 69

H

Handicapped, why, 17
Hall of Presidents, The, 100
Harvest Theater: Symbiosis, 180
Harvest Tour, 179
Haunted Mansion, The, 100
Hearing-impaired people, 45, 284
Here Come the Muppets, 252-253
Hollywood Boulevard, 240-243
Honey, I Shrunk the Kids Movie Set Adventure Playground, 253-254
Hoop Dee Doo Revue, 62
Horizons, 171-173
Hospitals, 37
Hotels, see Lodging
How to get there,
　Disney-MGM Studios, 238
　EPCOT Center, 152
　Magic Kingdom, 82
Humunga Kowabunga, 275

I

Illuminations, 212-213
Image Works, The, 176
Indiana Jones Epic Stunt Spectacular, 248-249
Inside the Magic Special Effects and Production Tour, 259-260
International Gateway, 36
Italy, 192-194
It's a Small World, 103-104
It's Fun to Be Free, 173

J

J.P. and the Silver Stars, 124
Japan, 197-198
Jib Jammer, 275
Jim Henson's MuppetVision 3-D, 252-253
Journey into Imagination, 175-177
Jungle Cruise, 89-90

K

Ketchakiddie Creek, 276
Kids of the Kingdom, 123
Kitchen Kabaret Revue, 179

L

Land, The, 178-180
Liberty Square, 98-102
　Hall of Presidents, The, 100
　Haunted Mansion, The, 100
　Liberty Square Riverboat, 98-99
　Mike Fink Keelboats, 99
　Restaurants, 136-137
　　fast-food eating places, 137
　　full-service restaurants, 136-137
　Shopping, 146-147
Listen to the Land, 178
Live entertainment, see Street Shows
Living Seas, The, 180-183
Lockers, 83, 154, 240, 276
Lodging, 54-76
　Caribbean Beach Resort, 58
　Contemporary resort, 57
　Disney's Beach Club Resort, 61
　Disney Village Hotel Plaza, 64-68
　Disney's Village Resort, 63-64
　Disney's Yacht Club resort, 61
　Dixie Landings Resort, 59
　Fort Wilderness Campground, 62
　Grand Floridian Beach Resort, 57
　Questionnaire, 69
　Polynesian Resort, 57-58
　Port Orleans Resort, 58-59
　Walt Disney World Swan and Dolphin Convention Resort Complex, 59-60
Lodging Along Highway U.S. 192, 73-76
Lodging in the Lake Buena Vista Area, 70-72

Lodging in Walt Disney World, 56-68
Lodging Outside Walt Disney World, 68-76
Lost and found, 39, 85, 217
Lost children, 39, 85, 217
Luggage, 31, 47-48

M

Mad Tea Party, 106-107
Maelstrom, 187
Magic Journeys, 102
MAGIC KINGDOM, 78-149
    Adventureland, 89-92
    Fantasyland, 102-108
    Ferry, 85
    Fireworks, 126
    Frontierland, 92-98
    Getting to, 82
    How big, 80
    Information, 85-86
    Locker Rentals, 83
    Liberty Square, 98-102
    Live shows, 122-124
    Main Street U.S.A., 86-88
    Map of, 81
    Mickey's Starland, 108-110
    Monorail, 84
    Orientation, 86
    Parades, 124-126
    Ramps, 85
    Restaurants, 127-139
    Restrooms, 84
    Shopping, 139-149
    Special events, 126-127
    Street Shows, 122-124
    Tomorrowland, 110-121
    What to take, 82
    Wheelchair rental, 83
Main Street, U.S.A., 86-88
    City Hall, 86-86
    Main Street Cinema, 88
    Penny arcade, 88
    Restaurants, 131-133
        cafeteria, 132
        fast-food restaurants, 131-132
        full-service restaurants, 133
    Shopping, 141-144
    Walt Disney Story, The, 87-88
    Walt Disney World Railroad, 87
Making of Me, The, 166-167

Mannequins, 270
Maps,
    of Disney-MGM Studios, 239
    of EPCOT Center, 156
    of Florida, 20
    of Magic Kingdom, 81
    of Orlando, 21
    of Walt Disney World, 22
Medical needs, 36
Mentally impaired travelers, Air Travel for, 46
Mexico, 185-187
Mickey Mouse Club, 110
Mickey's Starland, 108-110
    Grandma Duck's Petting Farm, 109
    Mickey's House, 109-110
    Mickey's Starland Show, 108-109
Mike Fink Keelboats, 99
Mission to Mars, 121
Money, 31-33
Monorail, 57, 84, 152, 278
Monster Sound Show, The, 247-248
Morocco, 198-200
Motels, see Lodging
Mr. Toad's Wild Ride, 107-108
Muppets, musical stage show, see Here Come the Muppets
Muppets, 3-D movie, see Jim Henson's MuppetVision 3-D

N

New York Street Back Lot, 254
Night Life, see Pleasure Island
Norway, 187-188

O

O Canada, 209-211
Oxygen, travel with, 44-45

P

Parades,
    in The Magic Kingdom, 124-126
Parking, handicapped,
    Disney-MGM Studios, 240
    EPCOT Center, 153
    Magic Kingdom, 82
Penny Arcade, 88
Peter Pan's Flight, 102-103
Pet Care, 33

Pirates of the Caribbean, 90-91
Planning, 27-76
   climate, 28-29
   crowds, 29
   costs, 31-32, 34
   saving money, 31-32, 34
   what to bring, 30
   when to visit, 28-29
   why plan, 27-28
Pleasure Island, 269-273
   Restaurants, 271-272
   Shops, 272-273
Polynesian Resort, 57-58
Port Orleans Resort, 58-59
Prescriptions, 37

R

Rain gear, 30
Recreational vehicles, 51-52
Reservations, Lodging, 32-33
Restaurants,
   in Adventureland, 133-134
   in Disney-MGM Studios, 261-266
   in EPCOT Center, 214-234
   in Fantasyland, 137-139
   in Frontierland, 135-136
   in Future World, 214-221
   in Liberty Square, 136-137
   in Main Street, U.S.A., 131-133
   on Pleasure Island, 271-272
   in Tomorrowland, 139
   in World Showcase, 221-234
Restrooms, 36, 84
River Country, 276-278
Rudder Buster, 275

S

Sea Base Alpha, 182-183
Sea Base Concourse, 181
Senior Citizens,
   Advice for, 39-40
Shark Reef, 275
Shopping,
   in Crossroads of Lake
     Buena Vista, 280
   in Disney-MGM Studios, 240-243
   in EPCOT Center, 183-211
   in Magic Kingdom, 139-149
   on Pleasure Island, 272-273
   at Walt Disney World Village, 279-280
Sight-impaired guests, Air
   Travel for Disabled Travelers, 45
Skyway to Fantasyland, 115
Skyway to Tomorrowland, 104
Snow White's Adventures, 108
Souvenirs, see Shopping
Space Mountain, 112-114
Spaceship Earth, 157-161
Splash Mountain, 94-95
StarJets, 115-116
Star Tours, 250-252
Stern Burner, 275
Strollers, 36, 83, 153, 240
Sunscreen, 30, 38
SuperStar Television, 245-247
Swan Resort, 59-60
Swiss Family Treehouse, 89
Symbiosis, 180

T

Teenage Mutant Ninja Turtles, 254
Telecommunication devices, 37
Time, how much to visit, 24
Tickets, see Admission
Tomorrowland, 110-121
   Carousel of Progress, 117-118
   CircleVision 360 American
     Journeys, 119-121
   Dreamflight, 118-119
   Grand Prix Raceway, 111-112
   Mission to Mars, 121
   Restaurants,
     fast-food eating places, 139
   Shopping, 148
   Skyway to Fantasyland, 115
   Space Mountain, 112-115
   StarJets, 115-116
   Tomorrowland Theater, 118
   WEDway PeopleMover, 116
Tomorrowland Theater, 118
Tom Sawyer Island and
   Fort Sam Clemens, 97-98
Train travel, 53
TransCenter, 174
Transportation and Ticket Center, 33, 36, 83, 278
Travel,
   by air, 41-48
   by automobile, 48-51

by bus, 52-53
by recreational vehicle, 51-52
by train, 53
by van, 51-52
Travelport, 163
Tropical Serenade
 (Enchanted Tiki Birds), 91-92
20,000 Leagues Under
 the Sea, 106
Typhoon Lagoon, 273-276
 Admission, 273
 Castaway Creek, 274
 First aid, 276
 Humunga Kowabunga, 275
 Jib Jammer, 275
 Ketchakiddie Creek, 276
 Restaurants, 276
 Rudder Buster, 275
 Shark Reef, 275
 Stern Burner, 275

U

United Kingdom, 203-207
United States, see
 American Adventure
Universe of Energy, 164-165

V

Vans, 51-52

W

Walt Disney Story, The, 87
Walt Disney World,
 map, 22
Walt Disney World
 Conference Center, 59-60
Walt Disney World Dolphin, 60
Walt Disney World Railroad, 87
Walt Disney World Swan, 59
Walt Disney World Village, 269, 279
Water Theme Parks,
 River Country, 276-278
 Typhoon Lagoon, 273-276
Weather, see Florida climate
WEDway PeopleMover, 116
Wheelchairs, battery-operated, 43-44
Wheelchair rentals,
 in Disney-MGM Studios, 240
 in EPCOT Center, 153
 in Magic Kingdom, 83

Wonders of China, 190
Wonders of Life, 166-171
WorldKey Information Service, 154
World of Motion, 173-174
World Showcase, 183-211
 American Adventure, The, 194-197
 Canada, 208-211
 China, 188-190
 France, 200-203
 Germany, 191-192
 Italy, 192-194
 Japan, 197-198
 Live Shows, 211-212
 Mexico, 185-187
 Morocco, 198-200
 Norway, 187-188
 Restaurants, 221-234
  cafeteria, 225
  fast-food restaurants, 221-225
  full-service restaurants, 225-234
 United Kingdom, 203-207

Y

Yacht Club, see Disney's
 Yacht Club

COMMENTS AND ORDERING INFORMATION

SouthPark Publishing Group, Inc. and the author have an obligation to you, the reader. Our goal is providing accurate, useful information, and you can help. We encourage comments about this book and disabled people in general. We appreciate hearing your experiences regarding:

- Travel and accessibility
- Lodging and accessibility
- Attractions and accessibility
- Your favorite attractions
- Your favorite theme parks
- Restaurants and accessibility
- Other resources we should know about
- The helpfulness of this guide book
    - Did you purchase it before leaving on your trip?
    - Did you purchase it during your trip?

Please mail or fax your comments to:

SouthPark Publishing Group, Inc.
4041 W. Wheatland Road
Suite 156-359
Dallas, Texas 75237-9991
Fax: (214) 296-4686

Our books are available through your local bookstore or library. If you are unable to locate this book, please call (214) 296-5657 for information on ordering or FAX: (214) 296-4686.

Special Sales

Quantity discounts are available from SouthPark Publishing Group, Inc. For more information, call, fax, or write to the above address or numbers.